From Silence to Sound

From Silence to Sound is a transformative guide that explores the creative, emotional, and philosophical dimensions of music production.

Written by award-winning producer and composer Thomas Lemmer, the book invites readers to move beyond technical manuals and into the heart of artistic expression. It is designed to empower aspiring and experienced music producers—alongside music educators, audio engineers, sound designers, immersive sound designers, and composers working for sync—to unlock their creative potential by addressing both the psychological and practical aspects of making music. It covers the full journey from the initial spark of inspiration to the completion of a fully produced track, placing equal emphasis on artistic mindset and production techniques. Readers will gain a refreshed creative mindset, practical tools and exercises for staying productive, and inspiration to push artistic boundaries. The book acts as both a mentor and a companion in the studio, offering technical guidance as well as emotional and motivational support for navigating the challenges of creative work.

Bridging the technical and artistic aspects of music production, this book is a valuable resource for producers, songwriters, recording artists, audio engineers, sound designers, and music educators.

Further resources and supporting materials are available at the author's website: www.fromsilencetosound.com.

Thomas Lemmer is an award-winning German producer and composer working across ambient, electronic, and neo-classical/cinematic music. He began with classical piano training and later studied the church organ before moving into music production. A self-taught producer, he combines musicality with detailed sound design and rich sonic textures, and has produced immersive audio, including releases in Dolby Atmos. In 2025, he won the German Songwriting Award in the category Music for Motion Picture. With more than two decades in the music industry, he has collaborated with artists around the globe and worked with labels and professionals across the field.

From Silence to Sound

Unlocking Creativity in Music Production

Thomas Lemmer

Routledge
Taylor & Francis Group
LONDON AND NEW YORK

Designed cover image: Getty Images

First published 2027
by Routledge
4 Park Square, Milton Park, Abingdon, Oxon OX14 4RN

and by Routledge
605 Third Avenue, New York, NY 10158

Routledge is an imprint of the Taylor & Francis Group, an informa business

British Library Cataloguing-in-Publication Data
A catalogue record for this book is available from the British Library

Library of Congress Cataloging-in-Publication Data
Names: Lemmer, Thomas author
Title: From silence to sound : unlocking creativity in music production / Thomas Lemmer.
Description: Abingdon, Oxon ; New York, NY : Routledge, 2026. | Includes bibliographical references and index.
Identifiers: LCCN 2026014921 (print) | LCCN 2026014922 (ebook) | ISBN 9781041192091 hardback | ISBN 9781041192060 paperback | ISBN 9781003710622 ebook
Subjects: LCSH: Music--Production and direction | Sound recordings--Production and direction | Music--Psychological aspects | Creative ability | Creation (Literary, artistic, etc.)
Classification: LCC ML3790 .L456 2026 (print) | LCC ML3790 (ebook) | DDC 781.49--dc23/eng/20260504
LC record available at https://lccn.loc.gov/2026014921
LC ebook record available at https://lccn.loc.gov/2026014922

ISBN: 978-1-041-19209-1 (hbk)
ISBN: 978-1-041-19206-0 (pbk)
ISBN: 978-1-003-71062-2 (ebk)

DOI: 10.4324/9781003710622

Typeset in Galliard
by SPi Technologies India Pvt Ltd (Straive)

A range of online resources can be found at www.fromsilencetosound.com. These materials are created and maintained by the author and are not the responsibility of Taylor & Francis Group.

For my parents, with deep gratitude for all you set in motion—the first piano lessons and a home where music could take root. I know success often includes luck; mine was growing up with you.

To my children, Malea and Liam: may you keep discovering what is truly yours, and build lives that are fulfilled and happy.

Contents

About This Book

From Silence to Sound: Unlocking Creativity in Music Production

When I set out to write *From Silence to Sound*, I wanted to create the book I wish I'd had when I first began producing music. Not a dry manual, but a creative companion—something real, personal, and practical—to inspire and support others on their journey through the world of music production.

This work is built around six core sections that reflect the challenges and breakthroughs I've experienced: developing a mindset that supports creativity, expressing emotion through sound, pushing through blocks and burnout, mastering tools without losing your soul, collaborating with others, and balancing your art with a professional career. Each section draws from what I've learned over years of making music—not just as a producer but as a human being growing through sound.

From Silence to Sound is for anyone who creates music—from aspiring and independent artists to seasoned professionals looking for new inspiration or a different perspective. Whether you're producing in a bedroom studio, composing for sync, or navigating life as a full-time musician, this guide speaks to the universal need to stay creatively alive in an ever-evolving world.

By the time you finish reading, I hope you'll feel more confident in your voice and direction. You'll feel motivated to stay true to yourself, to create the art you really want to put into the world, and to approach your craft with greater clarity and emotional depth. You'll discover new perspectives on many aspects of music production: from mindset to workflow, artistic courage to energy management, storytelling with sound to finishing tracks with confidence. You'll also gain clarity on essential topics such as collaboration, legal rights, ownership, and how to protect your work—helping you make informed, empowered decisions as you move forward.

I believe this book is needed now more than ever. In a fast-moving, noisy world, creative voices can easily become overwhelmed or unsure of where they belong. With this guide, I want to offer support, encouragement, and permission to slow down, go deeper, and reconnect with the joy of creating.

Unlike many production books that focus on the technical side—like how to mix a pop song, adjust a compressor, or explain different EQ types—*From Silence to Sound* focuses on something more foundational: the emotional core of music. This book is based on lived experience, hard-earned insights from the music business, and the mindset required to navigate a creative life. It's about what ultimately draws listeners in: the emotional depth and authenticity of the music we make.

At its heart, this is a book about what drives us all—creating beautiful music that moves people, that stands the test of time, and that may one day outlive us. Whether you're feeling stuck, burned out, or simply need a spark, you'll find strategies and stories here to help you keep going and feel supported.

You'll find moments from my own journey, practical approaches you can apply immediately, and reflections on the emotional and spiritual dimensions of making music. I also explore immersive formats such as Dolby Atmos and how new technologies can enrich your creative vision when used with purpose.

Above all, *From Silence to Sound* is a call to creative freedom. To break free from perfectionism. To stop creating for approval. To make art that is honest, vulnerable, and deeply your own. Whether you're just starting out or have been producing for years, I hope this book brings you fresh tools, renewed clarity, and the energy to keep going.

Music isn't just about sound. It's about meaning. It's about connection. And it's one of the most personal things you can create.

This guide is my invitation to you—to step into the silence and make something truly unforgettable from it.

Let this book be a reminder that your creativity matters—now more than ever. Art can shift how people see the world—and that shift can lead to change. It's meaningful, it's precious, and it deserves to exist.

I create beautiful things because it makes life worth living.

That's what I wish for you: to create art that fulfills you, and that enriches the lives of those who hear it.

So let's begin.

In a world that moves fast and forgets easily, create something that lingers. Let your music be the echo of your soul.

Companion Website

Beyond the Book: Resources, Inspiration, and Updates

This book is meant to be a creative companion—not just something you read but something you return to.

To continue the conversation beyond these pages, I've created a companion website with interviews, articles, and additional material designed to spark ideas, deepen your perspective, and keep you connected to the world behind the music.

www.fromsilencetosound.com

On the companion site, you'll find:

- artist **interviews** and real-world stories from the creative process
- thoughtful **articles** and creative input related to the themes of the book
- curated recommendations to **discover music** and interesting artists (and the stories behind them)
- additional material that expands on selected topics and ideas
- occasional **updates** as the project evolves over time

If you'd like to explore the music that shaped this book—and follow my ongoing journey as an artist—you can visit my artist website.

www.thomas-lemmer.com

There you'll find:

- my albums and latest releases
- selected videos and behind-the-scenes insights
- background stories and updates from my artistic journey

You can also find me on social media—links are available on both websites. I'd love to connect.

Section 1

The Inner Artist

Mindset, Vision, and Authenticity

This section covers foundational reflections—why you create music, staying true to your artistic voice, and navigating inner struggles.

Introduction: My Journey in Music Production

Welcome to an exploration into the essence of music production, where each note and rhythm forms part of a broader emotional narrative. Born on April 15, 1977, in Marburg, Germany, and raised in Neustadt, Hessen, I was fortunate to grow up in a musically rich environment. Influenced early by my father, who played in various bands, and surrounded by musically inclined siblings, my childhood was steeped in diverse musical influences. This book is an extension of my gratitude and an opportunity to share the invaluable insights gained throughout my eclectic journey in music—spanning genres such as electronic, downtempo, ambient, and chillout, and experiences from performing in pop and Christian worship bands to undergoing rigorous classical music training.

This guide emerged from a desire to support and inspire both new and experienced artists to embrace their unique paths in the music industry. Two years ago, I realized the potential impact of my experiences when many producer friends sought advice on a range of topics from navigating music contracts to refining production techniques and overcoming personal and creative challenges. Their inquiries illuminated the need for a comprehensive resource—one that not only guides but also motivates artists to stay true to themselves, to continuously evolve, and to ultimately leave a legacy they can be proud of.

In these pages, I delve into the complexities and challenges of the music industry, drawing from a career that spans independent work and collaborations with labels, publishers, and marketing agencies. My artistic approach has been enriched through partnerships with a wide array of talented artists, which have significantly shaped my musical style and expanded my creative horizons.

Moreover, I address the emotional highs and lows of music production—a journey often characterized by intense competition and the constant pressure to produce. Here, I offer insights on maintaining mental resilience, fostering personal well-being, and navigating moments of doubt. This book serves as a

DOI: 10.4324/9781003710622-1

beacon for those feeling stuck or questioning their path, providing guidance and encouragement to persevere and thrive.

Whether you choose to read this book from cover to cover or dip into chapters that resonate with your current needs, each section is designed to stand alone, addressing specific music production topics from technical skills to emotional intelligence. The aim is to help you discover and refine your unique voice in an increasingly crowded industry.

Ultimately, this book celebrates music as a profound form of art and a medium of personal expression. It is about crafting sounds that touch people's hearts and thriving in a digital age where the music scene is more accessible yet more saturated than ever. I share my story and insights in the hope that they will inspire you to explore, create, and shine in your musical endeavors.

Embrace each sound, each note as a reflection of life's diverse melodies—a journey not just of music, but of soulful exploration.

Authenticity First: Embracing Your Unique Sound

Why Authenticity Matters

We all recognize successful artists for their distinct sound, style, or genre. Many of the artists I admire weren't chasing trends—they were trusting a personal vision. When I think of The Beatles or Queen's *Bohemian Rhapsody*, I don't think of a "market-approved" blueprint—I think of music that feels boldly itself. To me, that's the point: sometimes the work that lasts is the work that doesn't ask for permission first.

What I take from artists like these is not a formula for success, but a reminder that music feels strongest to me when it seems deeply rooted in the artist's own identity. Rather than sounding designed to satisfy expectations, their work feels personal and self-directed. From my perspective, that kind of honesty often creates a stronger emotional connection and gives an artist a clearer path for long-term growth.

Lessons From My Journey

When I began my career in the ambient and downtempo genre, I was often advised to "sound like this artist or that, and you'll be more successful." But being an artist is about expressing your own voice, not replicating someone else's. If you spend your time imitating others, you will only ever be a second-rate version of someone else. Authentic fulfillment comes from being yourself and creating something that is uniquely yours.

This doesn't mean ignoring influences—music is part of a cultural conversation. Drawing inspiration from others can enrich your work, but your mission as an artist is to uncover what makes you *you*. That means identifying your creative DNA—those themes, sounds, or approaches that feel natural and true to you—and letting them guide your work. Your goal isn't to please everyone; it's to reveal your unique vision to the world. By staying rooted in your own truth, you invite an audience who connects with you deeply and consistently.

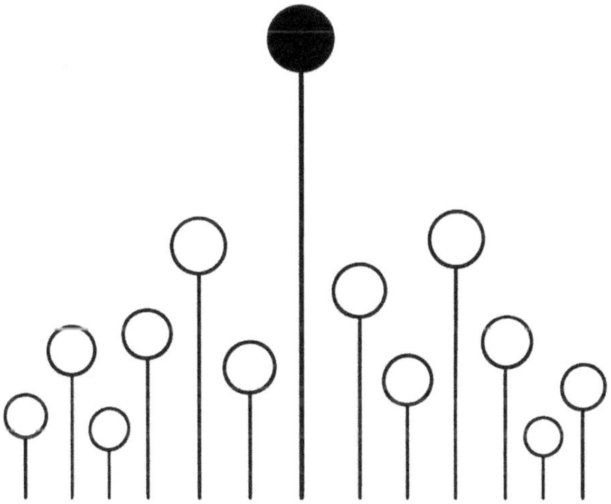

Authenticity isn't about being the loudest—it's about being the truest. And that truth inspires.

Examples of Authentic Voices

When I listen to Brian Eno, I'm drawn to how his music can feel like a space you step into—sound that behaves more like atmosphere than "song." With Bonobo, what stands out to my ears is the balance between organic detail and electronic precision: it feels warm, tactile, and still modern. Adele is a reminder to me that a direct vocal performance can carry an entire record—when the emotion is believable, the arrangement doesn't need to over-explain itself.

Coldplay is another reference point for me because, even as their production choices shift over time, there's often a consistent emotional tone underneath—a sense of uplift and sincerity that I can recognize quickly. With Billie Eilish, I hear the power of restraint: close-up vocals and minimal production that leave room for tension and intimacy. And with Ed Sheeran, I associate his writing with story-first songwriting—lyrics and phrasing that feel conversational, even when the production moves into bigger pop territory.

I'm not presenting these as universal facts but as personal examples of what authenticity *sounds like to me*: a coherent emotional center that stays present even when the surface style changes.

In my own career, authenticity has been my compass. Every album stems from my emotional landscape, not market pressure. While I love evolving and exploring new ideas, certain elements—like my piano playing, the way I voice chords, or my approach to melody—remain constants. These defining features ensure that no matter how far I explore creatively, my audience can always recognize and connect with my music.

The Career Advantage of Authenticity

I see authenticity as one of an artist's strongest long-term advantages. Trends may come and go, but I've often felt that a distinctive voice gives listeners a stronger reason to stay connected, even when the music evolves. From my perspective, people return not only for a particular style but for the sense that the work still carries the same artistic honesty.

How to Find Your Unique Sound

- **Follow your instincts**:
  Write the music you truly want to hear—this ensures an emotional bond with your work that listeners can feel. For example, if you're naturally drawn to intimate, minimal arrangements, lean into them rather than forcing yourself into dense production trends.
- **Embrace your influences**:
  Let inspiration shape you, but transform it through your own lens so it becomes yours uniquely. Study what you admire in others and reinterpret it in a way that feels natural to your style.
- **Refine, don't imitate**:
  Adopt techniques or ideas you admire, but adapt them until they reflect your style completely. For instance, if you love another artist's rhythmic approach, explore how it might work with your chord structures and melodies.
- **Stay consistent**:
  Let your sound evolve naturally while keeping signature elements—specific instruments, chord voicings, or melodic tendencies—so your audience always knows it's you. My piano, melodic phrasing, and harmonic choices are constants that tie my discography together, no matter the production style.

In the symphony of life, authenticity resonates the loudest. Play your truest notes, and the world will listen.

Action Items

- **Identify your constants**.
  Write down three musical elements that consistently appear in your work—regardless of genre, tempo, or project. These might be harmonic tendencies,

instruments, emotional moods, or compositional habits. These are clues to your creative DNA.

- **Create without an audience in mind.**
  Set aside one session where you deliberately ignore trends, platforms, and expectations. Ask only one question: *What do I genuinely want to hear right now?* Create from that place.
- **Reframe your influences.**
  Choose one artist who inspires you. Instead of copying what they do, write a short note on *why* it resonates with you emotionally. Then create a short sketch that expresses that feeling in your own musical language.
- **Notice where you force yourself.**
  Reflect on moments in your creative process where you feel tension, resistance, or self-doubt. Write a few sentences on whether this comes from external pressure rather than inner alignment.
- **Protect one signature element.**
  In your next project, consciously keep one personal constant intact—an instrument, a harmonic approach, or a melodic style—even if you experiment elsewhere. Observe how this anchors the piece.
- **Redefine success for yourself.**
  Complete this sentence in writing: *"For me, creative success means…"*
  Let the answer be honest, personal, and independent of charts, streams, or approval.

Trusting Your Vision: Why Too Much Advice Can Harm Your Art

The Temptation of Advice

When I started producing music, I was eager for feedback, hoping for constructive advice to support my vision. Many people gave me valuable input, but others suggested I should change my genre, believing another style would be more successful. These weren't experienced producers offering technical tips—they were well-intentioned but misguided opinions from consumers who thought they knew better. As an artist, when you're still finding your footing, such advice can be confusing, even dangerous to your creative vision.

It's only natural to seek feedback when we're unsure. After all, advice can be a shortcut to clarity. But it can also be a detour. If you're not careful, the wrong advice can plant seeds of doubt that derail your original intention before it has fully taken shape.

The Illusion of Popularity

It's crucial to remember that there is an audience for every type of art. Just because someone close to you can't see your vision doesn't mean it won't resonate with others. I often think of artists like Michael Jackson or The Beatles as reminders that original work doesn't arrive by consensus. To me, music is an offering: you present something honest, and only then do people discover whether it speaks to them. When we create solely by copying what already seems popular, we risk losing the part that could have made the work distinct.

This happens with the best intentions. People see success in one area and assume that you should replicate it. But following a trend isn't the same as starting one. Trends shift. What endures is work made with integrity and intention.

When I decided to produce chillout and ambient music, I hardly knew anyone in my circle who listened to that style. In fact, several friends repeatedly told me to pursue something different—simply because they didn't enjoy this genre themselves. And that's okay. Everyone has their personal taste, and ambient music is far from mainstream. But I loved it. I felt deeply connected to it.

Over the years, I've built a listener base that truly appreciates my music. Many people return to it because they find peace and solace in the sound. I've received many heartfelt messages that reassured me I was on the right path. All I did was follow my passion—and everything else gradually aligned.

Standing Your Ground: Personal Experiences

I've encountered this personally. Early in my career, people advised me to focus on pop music instead of ambient or downtempo, claiming I'd never find success in those genres. While I love pop and have produced it, my passion also lies in ambient music. Those who suggested otherwise didn't understand that, as an artist, I wasn't there to fulfill someone else's idea of success. I was there to express my own voice.

The same thing happened when I started writing this book. I initially decided to keep it a secret, knowing people's opinions could easily throw me off course. When I eventually shared the idea with someone I trusted, their first comment was discouraging—they believed the audience was too small for such a book. Instead of encouraging me or offering constructive ideas, they dismissed the project entirely. But for me, the book is already a success if it helps even a handful of people. I believe there's a market for it, and I feel I can contribute something valuable to the world.

This kind of premature judgment is harmful because it shifts focus from creation to validation. We begin to ask, "Will people like this?" instead of, "Is this meaningful to me?"

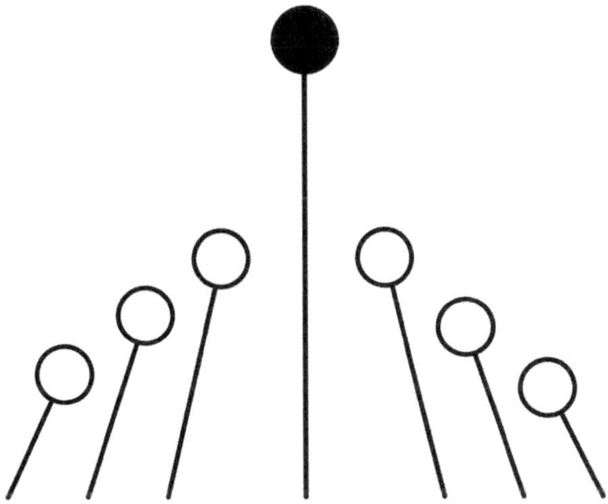

Trust your vision; it's the compass that guides you through the noise.

Good Advice vs. Distracting Opinions

Advice isn't inherently bad. The key is to understand who it comes from. Constructive criticism from a skilled mentor or someone familiar with your genre can be invaluable. It might improve your technique, broaden your perspective, or save you from common pitfalls.

Some of the most impactful feedback I've received came from professional mixing and mastering engineers. A single sentence like "your stereo image is collapsing in mono" or "the transient shaping makes this section feel too aggressive" helped me improve my work drastically. It's feedback rooted in deep understanding, not just opinion.

I remember asking a trusted mastering engineer for feedback on one of my ambient albums. Their comments helped me identify imbalances I had become blind to after weeks of listening. Their fresh perspective led to subtle adjustments that elevated the entire album's cohesiveness and emotional impact.

Over time, I've built a trusted network of professionals whose input I value highly. These are people who understand my style and creative goals. When I share my work with them, I listen carefully to every bit of feedback they offer. Then, I step back, reflect, and decide whether or how to integrate their suggestions. Sometimes I change things, sometimes I don't—but I always listen.

But advice from someone without context or knowledge can do the opposite. They might try to mold your work into something they understand or prefer—not something that reflects your vision.

You don't need to reject all input, but you do need to filter it. Ask yourself:

- Does this person understand what I'm trying to create?
- Are they offering insights or imposing tastes?
- Will this feedback help me grow, or just make me doubt myself?

If feedback feels like it's steering you away from your truth, rather than sharpening it, it's okay to let it go.

Your Voice Is the Compass

The most important thing is to stay true to yourself. Art is about expressing who you are, not meeting someone else's expectations. You don't owe the world familiarity. You owe the world your truth.

At the start, your voice may not be fully formed. That's normal. But you strengthen it not by following every suggestion, but by returning again and again to your instincts, your values, and your unique perspective.

I'm often drawn to the idea that work can feel risky precisely because it doesn't fit familiar expectations. Some music stays with me for exactly that reason: it sounds as if the artist followed the inner logic of the piece rather than trying to make every choice feel immediately safe or familiar.

When I think of Queen's *Bohemian Rhapsody*, I don't treat it as proof of a general rule, but as a personal reminder that bold creative decisions can draw their strength from refusing to conform too quickly. Whether a piece is embraced immediately or only reveals itself over time, I find that conviction often gives it a special kind of presence. Music like this encourages artists to trust a strong vision, even when the result feels unusual, excessive, or difficult to categorize at first.

Trust your vision; it's the compass that navigates through the noise toward your artistic truth.

Action Items

- **Map your sources of advice.**
  Write down the people whose opinions most influence your creative decisions. For each, note whether they understand your artistic goals—or whether they primarily reflect personal taste or trends.
- **Define your intention before asking for feedback.**
  Before sharing a work-in-progress, write one clear sentence about what you're trying to express emotionally or artistically. Use this as your reference point when receiving feedback.

- **Practice selective listening.**
  The next time you receive advice, pause before reacting. Ask yourself: *Does this sharpen my vision, or does it pull me away from it?* Allow yourself to keep what resonates—and release the rest without guilt.
- **Create in protected silence.**
  Choose one project or phase where you deliberately avoid external opinions until it feels complete to you. Notice how this affects your confidence and creative flow.
- **Separate craft from taste.**
  Reflect on recent feedback you've received. Identify which parts relate to technical craft (clarity, balance, execution) and which parts are about personal preference. Treat them differently.
- **Reaffirm your compass.**
  Write a short statement beginning with: *"I trust my vision because…"*
  Return to this whenever doubt creeps in or external noise becomes overwhelming.

The Importance of Intuition: Trusting Your Musical Instincts

In a world overflowing with tutorials, presets, feedback loops, and production advice, it's easy to lose touch with the quiet voice inside that simply *knows*. That voice is intuition. And in music, it's often your most powerful guide.

In music, intuition doesn't feel magical or random to me. It feels more like the quiet result of accumulated listening, experience, emotion, and practice. I experience it as the moment when technical understanding and feeling begin to work together in a way that becomes easier to trust over time.

Listening to the Voice Within

There's a moment in every creative process when you face a decision: Should this section be longer? Does this sound need more reverb? Should I leave this imperfection, or fix it?

In those moments, your intuition often knows the answer before your rational mind catches up. It's that subtle pull, the gut feeling, the emotional nudge that says, "*This feels right.*" And the more you trust it, the more confident and authentic your work becomes.

I've had moments when I tried to "fix" something that wasn't broken—simply because I overthought it. Later, I'd realize my first instinct was right. Learning to recognize and respect that initial feeling is a skill. It's the muscle of intuition.

When logic steps aside, music finds its soul.

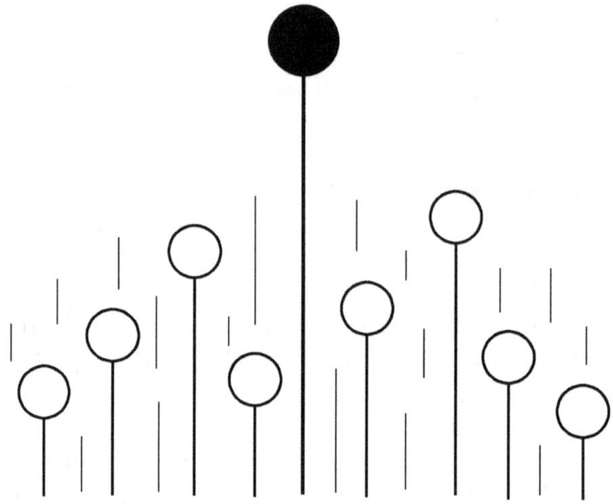

Intuition is the clear note within the noise.

Overthinking vs. Intuitive Flow

Analysis is not only important but it can also become a trap. If you overthink every move, you might end up stuck. Paralysis by analysis is real. Sometimes you can feel the flow slipping away, the more you try to control it.

On the other hand, intuitive creation feels effortless. Not because it's easy, but because you're connected to your emotion, your tools, and your intention. You're not fighting the process—you're moving with it.

My Own Experience

Many of my favorite compositions emerged from a state of pure improvisation. I didn't plan the structure. I didn't aim for a specific emotion. I simply sat down, let go of expectations, and followed the sound.

One of the most powerful shifts in my creative process was realizing that not every decision needs to be justified technically. Sometimes, it just needs to *feel* right. That's enough. For example, I've layered sounds that clash technically but create emotional tension I wanted. If I had followed theory alone, I might have missed the moment.

Trusting intuition also means accepting that your taste will guide you toward decisions that others may question. That's okay. Your uniqueness lives in those choices.

I also have a producer friend who practices the power of intuition. He sets aside dedicated time just to be creative and let things flow. He doesn't focus on perfection—he follows his instincts and avoids tweaking too much. During this time, it's only about the creative moment. Polishing and production are intentionally excluded. He can sometimes write several songs in a week, or even in a single day. The next day, he listens back to the quick ideas he recorded and selects the ones worth developing further into full demos—only then bringing in more musicians, singers, or detailed arrangements.

I'm also a classically trained piano player and even studied church organ for a few years. With all the music theory and knowledge I had, I used to follow these theoretical structures closely when composing. But early in my journey, I worked with a singer who had no formal background in theory. She would simply say things like, "This feels right," or "This doesn't."

Sometimes I would hit what I thought was a wrong note, and she would stop me and say, "Wait, play that again." To her, it wasn't wrong—it was interesting. And often, those moments became the most special part of the song. That collaboration taught me something vital: Music isn't just about following rules. Theory is helpful, absolutely, but it should never override intuition. Happy accidents and unexpected turns often create the most memorable moments. That experience helped me understand how powerful it is to let go of control and trust the feeling.

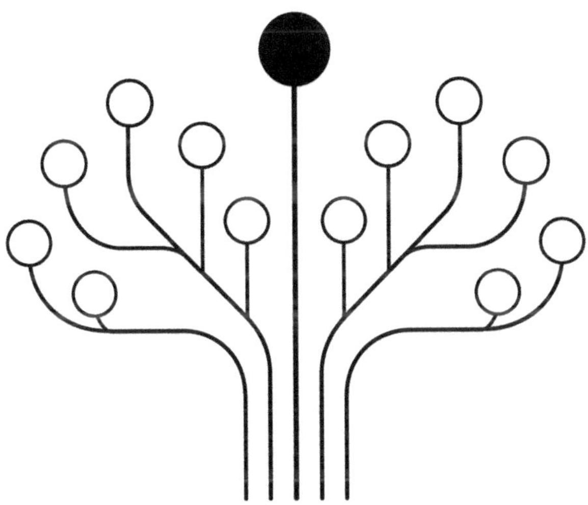

Intuition is the true path among a thousand turns.

Ways to Strengthen Intuition

- **Practice regularly**:
  The more you create, the more intuitive your decisions become.
- **Listen deeply**:
  Pay attention to what moves you emotionally—not just what sounds "good."

- **Reflect**:
  After finishing a track, ask what decisions felt intuitive. Which felt forced? Learn from both.
- **Limit your tools**:
  Too many choices dull your inner voice. Fewer options sharpen it.
- **Embrace imperfection**:
  Don't rush to "fix" everything. Let your instincts guide whether something should stay.

Intuition in Collaboration

Trusting your intuition becomes even more important when working with others. There will be moments when your creative partner suggests something you don't fully agree with. Instead of analyzing it endlessly, ask yourself: *How does it feel?* That emotional check-in often gives you the answer.

Intuition is also what helps you find the right collaborators in the first place. You just *know* when someone aligns with your vision—or when something feels off.

Final Thought

Intuition isn't about rejecting knowledge or skill. It's about blending everything you've learned with everything you *feel.* It's about trusting that inner voice that led you to create in the first place.

The more you trust it, the clearer it becomes. And the clearer it becomes, the more your music sounds like *you.*

Some of my best ideas come when I stop thinking and start feeling.

Action Items

- **Notice your first instinct.**
  During your next creative session, pay attention to your *very first* reaction to a musical idea. Before adjusting, fixing, or analyzing it, pause and ask: *What did this feel like when it first appeared?*
- **Create without justification.**
  Set a short session (20–30 minutes) where you allow yourself to make decisions without explaining them technically. If something feels right, let it stay—no reasoning required.
- **Identify when thinking takes over.**
  After a session, reflect on moments where your flow slowed down. Write a few sentences about whether overthinking, comparison, or technical doubt replaced intuition.

- **Limit your choices on purpose.**
  Choose a small, fixed set of tools for one project or sketch. Notice how reducing options sharpens your ability to listen inward rather than searching outward.
- **Revisit an intuitive decision.**
  Listen back to an older piece where you trusted a "rule-breaking" choice. Reflect on whether that moment still feels emotionally strong—and what it taught you about your instincts.
- **Practice intuitive listening.**
  Listen to a piece of music that deeply moves you and focus only on how it feels in your body and emotions, not on structure or technique. This strengthens the same muscle you use when creating.

Creating for Yourself: Finding Fulfillment in the Process

From External Approval to Inner Compass

When I began my journey in music production, I had little idea of what I was doing. I learned through trial and error, navigating unfamiliar territory. Being inexperienced, I sought feedback from others, showing them my early recordings and asking for advice. However, most of the people I approached weren't involved in the music industry. They weren't artists or producers—they were consumers. I believed their opinions would help me improve my craft, so I began tailoring my work to please them.

What I didn't realize at the time was that I was losing connection with my instincts and my own artistic vision. I became more focused on what others thought, often at the expense of my own voice. Many people evaluated my work from a commercial perspective, offering advice like, "If you do it this way, you'll be more successful." But true art doesn't aim to please others—it's about expressing the artist's personal view of the world. Whether it's music or any other form of art, the creative process must stem from within.

Reclaiming the Process

Over time, I learned that my job wasn't to meet others' expectations but to create the most authentic version of my own vision. By embracing this mindset, I began to find more joy in the creative process. Staying true to myself allowed me to create work that was unique and deeply satisfying. And the irony is that the more authentic I became, the more my music resonated with others—because authenticity naturally draws people in.

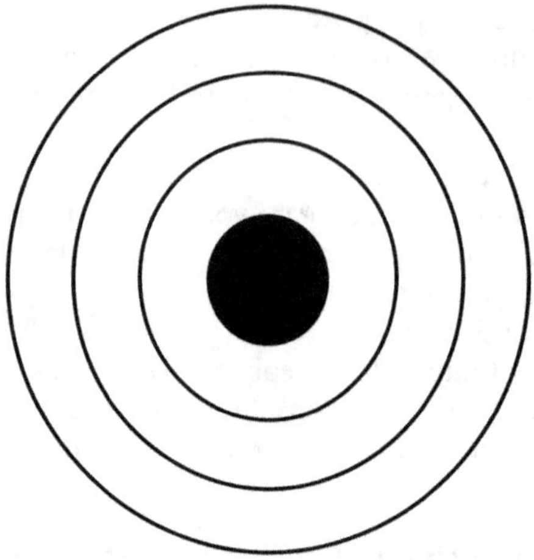

Fulfillment begins within—and its resonance reaches far beyond.

Personal Proof: "Peaceful" and Dreamscapes

"Peaceful" is one reminder of this for me. Written for my son, it was never intended as a strategic release—it was simply a personal moment captured in music. Over time, it seemed to find listeners in a way I hadn't planned, and to me that suggested how far emotional honesty can travel.

Dreamscapes came from a similar place. I wrote it at a time when I needed peace and an escape from the world. The calm, immersive, and reflective nature of the album was part of my own search for restoration, and some listeners have told me they sense that atmosphere in it. From my perspective, both works reflect how a piece can connect more deeply when it begins from something genuine.

Artists Who Chose Themselves—and Connected

This principle is something I associate with artists I admire. When I listen to Brian Eno's *Ambient 1: Music for Airports* or Moby's *Play*, what I hear is commitment to a mood and a personal aesthetic—music that doesn't sound like it was designed by committee. And when I listen to Adele or Billie Eilish, I'm reminded how far emotional directness can carry: the sense that the song is rooted in something real. Those examples help me trust the same idea in my own work.

Why Creating for Yourself Connects More

Creating for yourself gives the music, in my experience, a kind of honesty and individuality that technical perfection alone cannot provide. My own impression is that listeners often respond most strongly when a piece feels genuinely meant, as if the artist truly stands behind every note and lyric. From my perspective, that sense of sincerity can create a deeper and more lasting connection than work shaped mainly by short-term trends.

Practical Tips for Creating for Yourself

- **Set personal goals**:
  Define success on your own terms, not by comparing yourself to charts or trends. These goals can be creative milestones, such as mastering a new instrument, finishing a concept album, or collaborating with someone who inspires you.
- **Create without an audience in mind**:
  Focus entirely on what inspires and moves you. This frees you from second-guessing yourself and allows you to explore unfiltered creativity without worrying about how it will be received.
- **Reflect on your motivations**:
  Ask yourself why you're creating this track and whether it truly serves your own vision. If the answer is simply to please others, it's a sign to pause and reconnect with your authentic purpose.
- **Protect your creative space**:
  Limit outside feedback until you've solidified your own artistic direction. Too many early opinions can dilute your ideas or steer you toward compromises that weaken your original vision.

Create not for applause, but for your own soul's applause—a melody of self-fulfillment and joy.

Action Items

- **Redefine success in your own words**.
  Write down what creative fulfillment means to you *right now*. Avoid external markers like numbers, platforms, or recognition. Focus instead on how you want the process to feel.
- **Create something with no destination**.
  Begin a piece of music with no plan to release, share, or finish it. Let it exist purely as an honest expression of your current emotional state.
- **Notice when approval enters the room**.
  During your next session, observe moments when thoughts like *"Will people like this?"* arise. Gently redirect your focus back to *"Do I like this?"*
- **Protect your early ideas**.
  Choose one project where you delay feedback until you feel emotionally complete with it. Pay attention to how this changes your relationship with the work.
- **Reflect on a meaningful piece you've created**.
  Think of a track or project that felt deeply personal. Write a few sentences about why it mattered to you—and how that sincerity translated into connection with others.
- **Reconnect with your original motivation**.
  Finish this sentence honestly, without editing:

  I create music because…

  Return to this whenever the process feels heavy or externally driven.

Breaking the Rules to Innovate: When to Go Against Convention

Rules in music exist for a reason. They give us structure, guide us through harmony and rhythm, and provide a framework that listeners intuitively understand. But every rule, no matter how fundamental, was once a discovery. And that means rules are not sacred—they're tools. And tools can be reshaped, bent, or even discarded when the moment calls for it.

As artists and producers, innovation often comes from knowing the rules well enough to recognize when breaking them creates something more honest, more emotional, or simply more *you.*

Why Rules Exist: And Why They're Not Enough

In my own musical training, I was taught many conventions about voice leading, harmonic progressions, and rhythmic structure. I came to experience these principles as useful frameworks for creating balance and expectation—but also as something shaped by style, context, and tradition. What feels "right" to me in one genre or moment can feel too expected or too rigid in another.

There's nothing wrong with using these rules. In fact, many great pieces of music follow them. But when you rely on them too rigidly, you risk creating music that feels safe, generic, or uninspired.

Sometimes, the most moving music comes from the cracks—from the moments that don't resolve, from the chords that don't belong, or from the silence where a climax was expected.

Rules are a foundation—but not a ceiling.

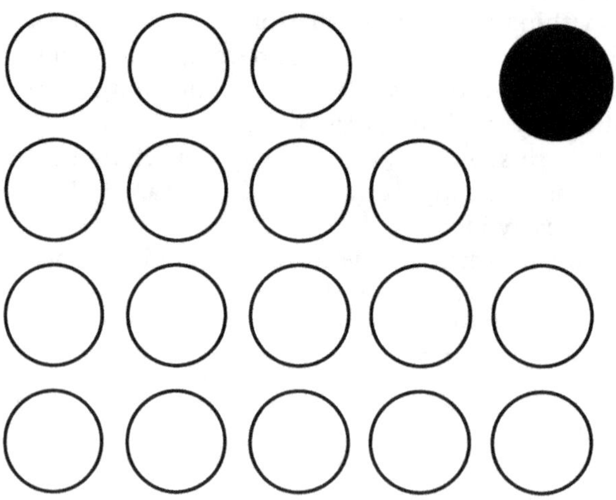

Innovation begins where patterns break.

Trusting Your Ear Over Theory

Academic knowledge is valuable, but it's not the final word. If you're working on a track and the theory says, "not to move from one chord to another," but your ears say it sounds great—trust your ears. Music isn't a math problem to solve. It's a language to express emotion.

I've made many decisions in my compositions that wouldn't pass in a music theory class, yet those were the moments people connected with most. Sometimes a suspended chord that never resolves, or a melody that shifts in unexpected ways, can create the kind of emotional depth that perfect harmony never will.

One thing I've also learned is that musical education—especially early on—can sometimes be a double-edged sword. When I was studying classical piano and organ, I found myself constantly judging whether something was "correct" instead of asking whether it felt right. Over time, I had to unlearn the pressure to follow academic tradition and relearn how to listen intuitively.

Music doesn't care how well you understand it—it only cares how deeply you feel it.

Examples of Rule-Breaking That Worked

- **Radiohead—"Everything in Its Right Place"**
  To my ears, the phrasing and looping feel less like a standard verse/chorus and more like a pattern you sink into—hypnotic in a way that pulls me inward.
- **Björk—*Medúlla***
  What strikes me is how voice-forward it feels. The vocal textures and rhythmic mouth-sounds create an "instrumentation" of their own, and the result lands as both raw and beautiful.
- **Burial—*Untrue***
  I hear it as intentionally rough around the edges: blurred textures, pitchy fragments, and noise that would be "wrong" in a clean pop mix, but somehow carries real emotional weight.
- **John Cage—"4′33″"**
  To me, this piece is a powerful reminder that "music" isn't only the notes we play. When the performer doesn't add sound, your attention shifts to everything that's already there—the room, the audience, your own expectations—and suddenly listening becomes the main event.
- **Marconi Union "Weightless"**
  To me, this track feels less like a "song" and more like an environment: slow-moving harmony, gentle motion, and a pace that encourages my attention to soften. When I listen, I notice how little friction there is—no sudden surprises, no sharp turns—just a steady invitation to settle. It's a good reminder that stepping outside conventional songwriting can be a direct path to emotional effect.

In my own work, I've sometimes taken a finished composition and reimagined it entirely. One example is my track "Serenity (Slowed + Reverbed)." I initially composed and produced it in a traditional way. But when I revisited the finished version, I had the idea to slow the entire piece down and lower the pitch. The result was a warmer, more ethereal piano tone that felt almost otherworldly. I then added even more reverb, washing the entire piece in a deep sense of space and emotion.

This approach goes against many standard production practices. Traditionally, you're encouraged to get the tuning, timing, and clarity just right. But here, I embraced the imperfection that came from slowing and detuning the track. It created a dreamlike atmosphere that gave the song a unique identity—one that might not have been possible if I had simply followed the rules.

Another personal experience that taught me the value of breaking convention dates back to my early career when I was part of the German pop duo *diPOLAR*. I worked closely with Elke, the lead singer, and while I had a formal music theory background, she didn't. During writing sessions, I often played chords I considered "wrong" by the textbook. But Elke would stop me and say, "Wait, play that again!" She didn't know the rules, but she knew what felt good. That freedom led to beautiful discoveries. In fact, we eventually turned it into a creative game—when we were stuck, she'd suggest a completely random chord. More often than not, her intuitive choices sparked a new direction that elevated the song. It taught me that some of the most magical moments happen when we step outside of our expectations.

When I worked on my album *Ambitronic*, I wanted to blend ambient textures with electronic beats—a combination that some people around me felt moved too far from what they considered "pure" ambient music. I trusted my instincts anyway. For me, the experience reinforced a simple lesson: bending genre expectations can open the door to music that feels both more personal and more alive.

When to Follow the Rules

Breaking rules isn't about being rebellious for its own sake. There are situations where structure provides clarity, especially when:

- You're writing for a film or client who expects a certain format.
- You want to ground the listener before leading them into something unusual.
- You're building tension that will later be released by returning to familiar territory.

Understanding rhythm, harmony, arrangement, and dynamics gives you the toolkit. But the art lies in knowing when to step outside of that toolkit.

Sometimes, structure is your ally. It offers comfort to the listener, sets expectations, and provides a canvas on which to surprise them.

Know the foundations well enough that you can stop "following rules" and start making choices.

Final Thoughts

Breaking the rules is not about rejection—it's about *exploration*. It's about being willing to risk imperfection in pursuit of honesty. You don't need to challenge every convention in every track. But when something inside you says, *this doesn't follow the rule, but it feels right*—that's a moment to pay attention to.

Some of the most unforgettable music in history exists because someone dared to go against what was expected. Be willing to be that someone.

Innovation lives where fear of breaking the rules dies.

Action Items

- **Name the rules you usually follow.**
  Write down a few musical rules or conventions you tend to rely on—harmonic habits, arrangement structures, mixing practices, or genre expectations. Simply noticing them is the first step toward creative choice.
- **Break one rule on purpose.**
  In your next sketch or session, choose a single rule to ignore. Let the decision be intentional rather than accidental, and listen closely to what emotional effect it creates.
- **Trust your ear over explanation.**
  When a choice feels right but seems "wrong" on paper, pause before correcting it. Ask yourself whether the emotional impact improves or weakens if you follow the rule instead.
- **Revisit a finished piece differently.**
  Take an older track and experiment with a radical change—tempo, pitch, space, structure, or texture. Treat it as exploration, not revision.
- **Notice where imperfection adds meaning.**
  Reflect on moments in your work where looseness, imbalance, or irregularity created character rather than problems. Write a few sentences about what those moments taught you.
- **Choose structure consciously.**
  Before starting your next project, decide where rules will serve you—and where you're open to letting intuition lead. Innovation often lives in that boundary.

Embracing Failure as a Stepping Stone: Learning from Your Mistakes

Every song you work on is an opportunity for growth. While success can be motivating, it's often the missed notes, rejected ideas, awkward transitions, creative blocks, and even criticism that truly shape us. These moments may sting, but they offer the most enduring lessons.

When I look back at my early works, I see the imperfections and remember the doubt I had. But those so-called "failures" were crucial to my development.

Each misstep was a stepping stone, shaping the artist I am today. I didn't become better by avoiding mistakes—I became better by confronting them, learning from them, and growing through them.

One time, I released a track I had mixed myself, only to find later that it didn't sound quite right on most systems. I felt frustrated. But that experience pushed me to invest time into learning mixing more deeply, to study reference tracks more seriously, and to experiment with more intention. Without that small failure, I may have never developed the mixing style I now rely on.

Many of the most important creative shifts, in my experience, happen after something doesn't work the way I expected. A failed synth patch can lead to a more interesting sound. A melody that falls flat can push me toward something emotionally truer. Again and again, I've found that mistakes can redirect the work in unexpectedly useful ways—not because failure automatically leads to growth, but because it forces a change of attention.

It is easy to focus only on success, but I often feel that creative stagnation begins when we become too cautious. Playing safe can slowly narrow the range of what we are willing to try. For that reason, I see mistakes as part of the process rather than as proof that the process has failed. What matters is not avoiding every wrong turn, but continuing to explore, adjust, and try again. That, at least, is where growth tends to happen in my own work.

And there's something else: You usually do your best with the skills and experience you have at the time. As you grow, improve, and evolve, you gain more perspective.

It's natural to look back at older songs or productions and see imperfections. But that doesn't mean they weren't good at the time. On the contrary, they were honest reflections of who you were and what you knew. With time and distance, you begin to notice what you would now do differently, and that's a sign of growth. Every past song brought you one step further. You learned so much from each of them.

Reframing Failure

Instead of seeing failure as a dead end, see it as a detour full of creative insights. Ask yourself:

- What did this teach me?
- What would I do differently next time?
- Did I discover something unexpected?

Every failed experiment adds to your creative vocabulary. The more you try, the more fluent you become.

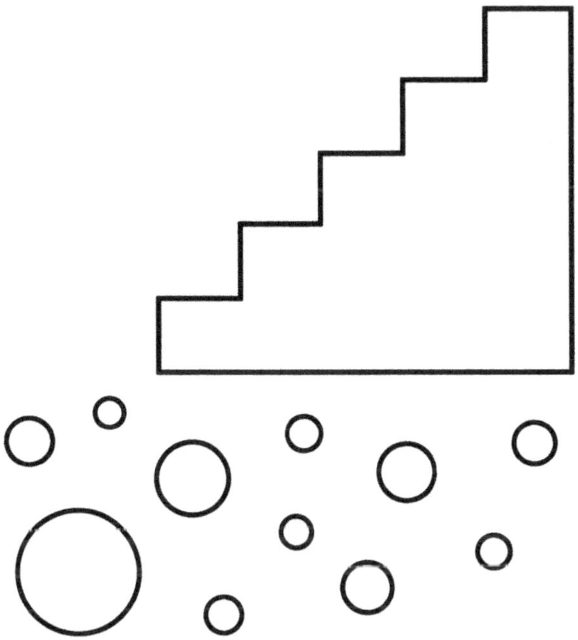

What falls beneath you builds what rises within you.

Turning Mistakes into Momentum

- **Archive your unfinished ideas**:
  What seems unusable now might spark inspiration later.
- **Get feedback early**:
  It can help you course-correct and reduce the fear of judgment.
- **Share your process**:
  Showing not only polished results but also the uncertain parts of the journey can make your work feel more human and relatable.

Final Thoughts

As artists, our goal is not perfection, but evolution. Keep pushing forward, learning from every experience, and remember—failure is not the end, but the beginning of a new chapter in your journey. Don't be afraid to trip. Some of the most beautiful music is born from falling, getting back up, and playing on.

In every off-note lies the possibility of a new harmony. Embrace it.

Action Items

- **Revisit a past "failure" with new eyes.**
  Choose an older track, sketch, or idea you once felt dissatisfied with. Listen to it now and write down what it taught you—technically, emotionally, or creatively.
- **Name the lesson, not the mistake.**
  Think of a recent creative setback and complete this sentence:
  "What this experience showed me is…"
  Focus on insight rather than judgment.
- **Create something you allow to be imperfect.**
  Start a new piece with the clear intention that it doesn't need to be finished, shared, or refined. Let it exist as an experiment rather than a result.
- **Archive instead of deleting.**
  The next time an idea feels unsuccessful, move it to an archive rather than discarding it. Notice how this changes your emotional relationship to unfinished work.
- **Reflect on your growth timeline.**
  Write a short note to your past self at an earlier stage of your journey. Acknowledge what they did well with the knowledge they had at the time.
- **Redefine progress.**
  Ask yourself honestly:

  Am I currently measuring progress by outcome—or by learning?

  Adjust your expectations accordingly for your next creative phase.

Turning Setbacks into Strength: Handling Rejection in the Music Industry

In the music industry, encountering rejection is almost inevitable. Whether you're submitting tracks to a label, seeking a contract with a publisher, or pitching music for a sync placement, you're bound to face moments where your work doesn't receive the response you hoped for. However, embracing these setbacks and reframing them as stepping stones can transform them into valuable lessons that strengthen your career.

Rejection, while disheartening, should never be taken as a personal attack. Music is a subjective art form, and no matter how polished or heartfelt your work is, it may not align with someone else's tastes. This doesn't diminish its value; it simply reflects differences in perception. When I chose to produce ambient and downtempo music, many people around me—who preferred mainstream radio hits—often suggested I change genres. In its own way, this was a form of rejection, but it didn't sway my dedication to my chosen path.

It's important to review any feedback you receive—even if it comes alongside a "no." Sometimes there's nothing actionable, and it's simply a matter of taste or timing. Other times, there may be valuable insights that can help you refine your craft, improve your presentation, or strengthen your communication. The key is to take what's useful and leave the rest, without letting it undermine your confidence.

Personal Story: From Rejection to Opportunity

When I started in the chillout/downtempo scene, I produced the songs for my first album, *Chillout Lounge*. At first, I hadn't decided it would be a self-release—I sent countless demos and letters to labels. Most never replied, and the few that did rejected it.

But I didn't give up. I believed in the music and thought, *If no one is going to release this with me, I'll do it myself.* I had no experience and no idea how much work producing my first physical CD would require. Yet the process taught me invaluable lessons—from understanding a label's perspective to managing production and distribution. Those lessons still serve me today.

About half a year after my independent release, I heard back from Café del Mar—who had received my demo earlier—about licensing one of my tracks, "Fatigué," for their compilation series. Looking back, it felt like the kind of turn that makes rejection worthwhile: it helped me recoup some of my early expenses, it gave me a meaningful boost in confidence and visibility, and it reminded me that I could keep moving forward while still staying in control of my own music.

What began as a series of discouraging rejections turned into a pivotal moment for my career. It taught me resilience, reinforced my creative vision, and showed me that persistence can sometimes turn a "no" into something better.

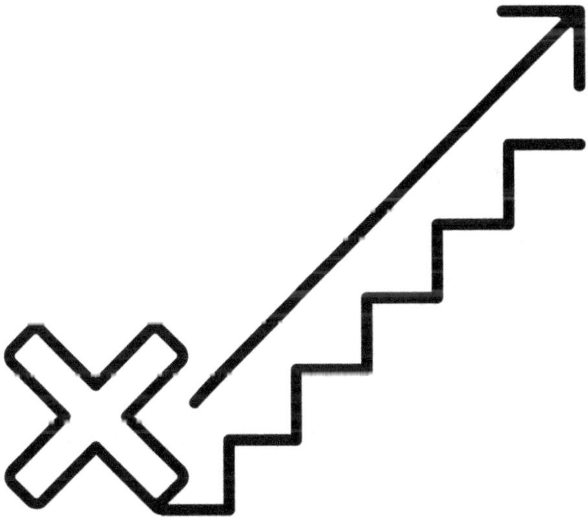

Rejection is the first step that lifts you higher.

Proactive Strategies for Handling Rejection

- **Build resilience and keep creating**:
  The more you submit and create, the more comfortable you become with hearing "no," and the more likely you are to eventually hear "yes." Submitting regularly also helps you refine your pitches and better understand your audience. For example, after multiple submissions, you might notice certain types of tracks receive more responses, guiding your future work.
- **Keep a rejection log**:
  Track when and where you sent your work, the response, and any feedback. Over time, patterns can reveal which styles or approaches resonate more. I've noticed that logging rejections helped me adjust my submission timing to when labels were actively scouting.
- **Network outside of submissions**:
  Attend industry events, engage on social media, or collaborate with peers so that when you submit, your name is already recognized. For instance, meeting a label representative at a music conference can make your later email stand out.
- **Reframe the narrative**:
  View each "no" as a necessary step toward the right "yes." Keeping a record of past rejections can remind you how far you've come and keep motivation high during dry spells.
- **Follow up professionally**:
  A polite, respectful follow-up can leave a positive impression and keep the door open for future opportunities. I once secured a compilation placement simply because I reconnected months after an initial rejection.
- **Seek constructive feedback**:
  Ask for suggestions and listen openly. Even a single comment about mixing balance or arrangement could lead to a noticeable improvement in your next submission.
- **Diversify your approach**:
  Don't rely on one outlet; multiple submissions spread the risk and opportunity. Pitching the same track to both a label and a sync agent increases chances of success.
- **Celebrate small wins**:
  Playlist placements, local gigs, or good reviews all contribute to your growth and morale. Treat them as stepping stones toward larger goals.

The Bigger Picture

Rejections in the music industry happen for countless reasons: a label might have a full roster, your style may not fit their current needs, or timing may be off. The key is to see rejection not as a closed door, but as a signpost pointing you toward a better path. Ask yourself: *Is there something I can improve, or is this simply not the right fit?*

When I read artist stories, I often come away with the personal impression that persistence matters just as much as talent. When I think of names such as The Beatles, Daft Punk, or Lady Gaga, I don't mean to offer them as proof, but as reminders that an early "no" doesn't automatically define the long-term value of the work. For me, the lesson is simple: keep going and keep improving.

The music industry, like any creative field, requires thick skin. Staying balanced and keeping perspective is essential to navigating its highs and lows, and connecting with fellow artists for mutual support can be invaluable.

Ultimately, rejection can either hold you back or propel you forward. The choice is yours. Keep creating, refining, and trusting in your unique voice. When the time is right, your work will find its audience. Until then, let every *no* become fuel for the *yes* that matters.

Rejection can be information—feedback that helps you adjust course.

Action Items

- **Separate rejection from self-worth.**
  The next time you receive a rejection, write down exactly what was rejected: the *song*, the *timing*, the *fit*—not you as a person or artist. This simple distinction helps protect your creative identity.
- **Extract what's useful—and release the rest.**
  Review any feedback you've received alongside a rejection. Ask yourself: *Is there something actionable here, or is this simply a matter of taste or circumstance?* Keep only what helps you grow.
- **Document the journey.**
  Keep a simple record of submissions, responses, and outcomes—not to dwell on rejection, but to gain perspective over time. Notice patterns rather than isolated moments.
- **Create despite uncertainty.**
  Commit to continuing your creative work regardless of external responses. Let the act of creating be the constant, even when validation is absent.
- **Reframe a past rejection.**
  Think back to a rejection that initially felt discouraging. Write a few sentences about how it ultimately redirected you, strengthened you, or led to an unexpected opportunity.
- **Define your personal "yes."**
  Reflect on what kind of opportunity would truly feel aligned with your values and artistic vision. Not every acceptance is a win—and not every rejection is a loss.

Embracing Diversity: What to Do When You Don't Have a Defined Style

Not every artist begins their journey with a crystal-clear sonic identity. In fact, many don't. It's easy to feel pressure to "find your sound," especially in a music culture that often celebrates distinct, recognizable styles. But here's the truth: exploration is part of the process. Not having a defined style isn't a weakness—it's a phase of growth, and for some, it becomes a strength.

Some of the most exciting music, to me, comes from artists who refuse to be pinned down. When I look at artists like Moby, Bonobo, and Four Tet, I hear a willingness to move between moods and approaches without losing a personal thread. Their work reminds me that variety can be a strength when it's guided by curiosity and intention.

Diversity in your sound isn't confusion—it's curiosity in motion.

Genre Blending as a Creative Strength

We live in an era where genres are blurring more than ever. With tools and access at our fingertips, we can pull influences from jazz, hip-hop, cinematic scores, ambient, techno, and classical music within a single track.

In my own work, I've always loved blending elements from different genres. My album *Ambitronic* is a perfect example—it combines expansive ambient soundscapes with electronic beats. At first, I worried it might alienate fans on either side, but the opposite happened: listeners embraced the unexpected fusion. For me, it was a deeply authentic expression, and authenticity is what truly connects people. The album ultimately became a personal success that went far beyond my expectations.

Even if a track doesn't fit into a clean category, if it tells an emotional story and feels coherent within itself, it can resonate deeply.

You don't need to choose a lane. You can build the road.

Genre blending isn't just a creative expression—it can even become your signature. Some artists create a whole new sub-genre by simply staying true to their intuition while drawing from unexpected influences. As long as the emotional thread remains intact, genre fusion can feel both innovative and personal.

When to Separate Identities

Sometimes, exploring diverse styles does raise practical questions: Should I release everything under one name? Or create separate aliases for different genres?

There's no one-size-fits-all answer. I personally work under different names depending on the style. I work mainly in ambient and downtempo genres, but I often mix or go to other genres while still staying true to my mostly electronic/ambient style. This style is often based on piano and rich harmonic structures, even when I work with vocals, use pop elements, or cross borders.

For my lo-fi and beat-driven tracks, I use the alias *MonoCulture*. Each project has its own aesthetic, branding, and musical purpose.

This separation helps manage audience expectations. Fans of ambient music may not be the same as those who follow lo-fi playlists. By giving each project its own space, I can explore freely while maintaining clarity in how the music is presented.

Still, if your work is connected by a central emotional or sonic theme, keeping one identity may work just fine. When I think of artists such as Trentemøller and Jon Hopkins, I'm reminded that it can feel possible to explore different sounds while still maintaining a recognizable artistic thread.

If you do choose multiple identities, consider how you'll balance them. Will you alternate releases? Will one alias be more active than the other? Will you use visuals to differentiate them? Being intentional about these decisions makes the process smoother for both you and your audience.

Artistic Exploration vs. Audience Expectation

It's natural to worry that jumping between genres will confuse your audience. But the truth is: Your audience evolves with you—if you're honest with them.

My impression is that many listeners today move comfortably between different moods and styles rather than staying inside a single genre. Because of that, I tend to feel that the emotional core of the music and the way you communicate it matter more than strict stylistic boundaries.

If you feel the urge to experiment, do it. If a track pulls you toward an unfamiliar sound, follow it. Trying to force yourself into one style for the sake of branding can stifle creativity. Over time, patterns will emerge naturally—and your voice will shine through, even across genres.

There's also beauty in the process of discovery. Being a multi-genre artist can be a lifelong creative conversation. The styles you explore might change depending on your life stage, your collaborators, or even the tools you use. What remains constant is your artistic voice.

Your style may not be a destination—it might be the journey itself.

Marketing a Diverse Sound

Marketing becomes more nuanced when your music doesn't fit a box. But there are ways to navigate this:

- **Build your narrative**:
  Share your story and make your creative choices visible. Let fans in on why you explore different styles. Transparency builds connection.
- **Use playlists wisely**:
  Submit tracks to playlists that fit *that* particular track, not necessarily your overall brand.

- **Visual consistency**:
  Even if the music shifts, keeping a coherent visual or emotional aesthetic can help your audience stay grounded.
- **Segmented communication**:
  Use mailing lists or social media channels to communicate differently to fans of each project or style.
- **Highlight emotional consistency**:
  Emphasize the emotional or thematic thread across your work. If your sound is diverse, your *feeling* can be the glue.

Another helpful tip is to test releases quietly. You can release tracks as singles, under a new alias, or to a select group of fans to see what resonates. You don't have to roll everything out at once. Let the music—and the audience—guide you.

What matters is not that every track sounds the same—but that every track feels *true*. That's what keeps listeners returning.

Final Thoughts

Not having a defined style can be frustrating when everyone around you seems to have a niche. But there's no timeline or rulebook. Some artists evolve into a specific sound over time. Others remain ever-evolving—and that, too, is a signature.

Diversity in your work doesn't mean a lack of focus. It can be a sign of creative vitality. The more you explore, the more your true voice will emerge—not by limiting yourself, but by honoring all parts of who you are.

Don't rush to label yourself. Stay curious. Explore widely. Your sound doesn't need a genre to be valid—it needs to be *yours*.

Your style may not be a destination—it might be the journey itself.

Action Items

- **Release yourself from the need to define your style.**
  Write down any pressure you feel to "label" your music. Ask yourself honestly whether this pressure comes from within—or from external expectations.
- **Look for emotional constants instead of genres.**
  Reflect on your recent work and note recurring emotional qualities (calm, tension, intimacy, melancholy, energy). These often reveal your true artistic thread more clearly than genre labels.
- **Allow one project to explore freely.**
  Choose a track or small series where you consciously allow genre boundaries to dissolve. Let curiosity guide the process and notice what feels most natural.
- **Observe patterns over time.**
  Instead of forcing a definition, look back at several projects and ask: *What keeps returning, even when the style changes?* This is where your voice begins to emerge.
- **Experiment with separation—or integration—intentionally.**
  If you work across styles, reflect on whether they benefit from one identity or multiple ones. There's no correct answer—only what supports clarity and creative freedom for you.
- **Trust the journey, not the snapshot.**
  Remind yourself that a defined style often reveals itself in hindsight. Write a short note affirming that exploration is not delay—it is development.

Authenticity Over Trends: Why Staying True to Your Voice Matters

When I ask myself why I return to certain artists, the answer often lies in a sound or emotional identity that feels immediately recognizable to me. When I think of artists such as Queen, The Beatles, Nils Frahm, Bonobo, or FINNEAS, I'm not trying to prove a rule—I'm describing the personal sense that each of them carries something distinct that keeps drawing me back. To me, that kind of singularity feels closely tied to authenticity.

For me, these artists are a reminder that a distinctive voice can leave a deeper impression than music that simply follows the moment. From my perspective, staying close to your own sound gives your work a clearer identity, and that honesty is often what listeners respond to most strongly.

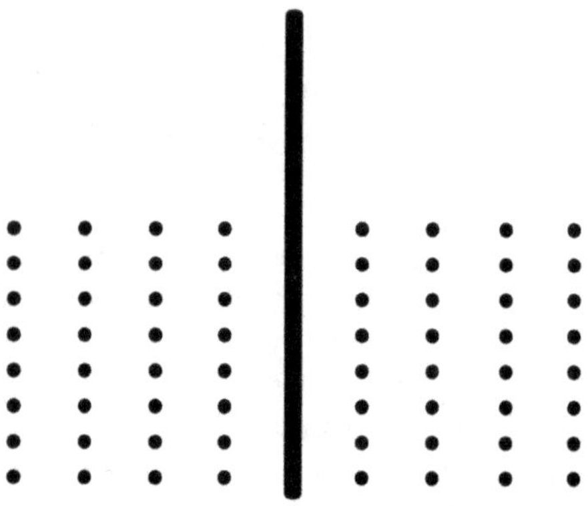

Trends may capture attention for a moment, but authenticity captures hearts for a lifetime.

Authenticity isn't just about originality to me; it's also about emotional honesty. When I listen to Nils Frahm, I hear a very personal meeting point between electronic textures and piano. With Bonobo, I'm drawn to the way live instrumentation and electronic production can feel warm and grounded at the same time. And when I listen to FINNEAS's production work for Billie Eilish on tracks such as "when the party's over," I hear how minimal choices can create a strong sense of intimacy. These are personal listening impressions, not claims I'm trying to prove.

As an artist, you may feel pressure to conform to what's popular or what you believe will get you more streams. But at the end of the day, trends fade, and the only thing that endures is genuine artistic expression. A friend of mine once got caught up in this mindset, focusing solely on creating music to fit a specific playlist algorithm, believing it would propel him to success. Each release left him more frustrated and unfulfilled, as ticking all the algorithmic boxes didn't translate to the recognition he hoped for.

I've experienced this pressure myself. Early in my career, I was tempted to adjust my style to fit what I saw trending at the time. But each time I veered too far from my core sound, the music felt forced and disconnected from who I truly was. It was only when I returned to creating from a place of personal inspiration that I found both fulfillment and an audience that connected with my work.

Creating music that stays true to your vision, rather than fitting into a mold, will provide you with a deeper sense of fulfillment. The artists we admire today aren't remembered for conforming but for forging their own paths, setting themselves apart through their originality. Following your own voice may not always yield immediate success, but in the long run, it is far more rewarding than chasing short-term trends.

Practical Ways to Strengthen Your Unique Voice:

- **Identify your core influences**:
  Reflect on the artists, sounds, and life experiences that have shaped your taste and style. For example, if you grew up with classical piano in your home but spent your teenage years immersed in electronic music, fuse those worlds to create something only you could make.
- **Experiment without expectation**:
  Dedicate sessions purely to creative play without worrying about the outcome. You could try layering the sound of rain you recorded on a road trip over a minimal beat, or pairing a single synth patch with an unconventional chord progression—these moments often become signature elements.
- **Seek honest feedback from the right people**:
  Share your work with trusted peers who understand your vision. A fellow musician might highlight that a track feels too polished in a way that strips away its emotional edge, prompting you to realign with your authentic sound.
- **Document your creative process**:
  Keep notes or recordings of your experiments and sessions. Over time, patterns will emerge in what feels most "you," giving you a roadmap for honing your unique style.
- **Protect your creative boundaries**:
  Say no to projects or collaborations that push you too far away from your core identity, even if they promise quick exposure. This ensures that every release strengthens, rather than dilutes, your artistic voice.

In the end, being true to your voice gives you staying power. Trends may shift and tastes may change, but music created with authenticity has the power to transcend time. It ensures that your audience isn't just hearing a song—they're hearing you. Embracing your unique artistic identity is what will resonate most with listeners, and it's what will ultimately create a lasting impact on the world.

Trends may capture attention for a moment, but authenticity captures hearts for a lifetime.

Action Items

- **Notice where trends influence your decisions.**
  Reflect on recent creative choices and ask yourself where trends, algorithms, or expectations may have influenced you. Write down one instance where you felt slightly disconnected from your own voice as a result.
- **Reconnect with what feels unmistakably yours.**
  Think of a piece of music you created that felt deeply authentic, regardless of its success or reach. Write a few sentences about what made it feel true to you.

- **Create without measuring relevance.**
  Set aside one session where you consciously ignore what is currently popular. Let your taste, mood, and instincts guide the process without asking whether the result fits anywhere.
- **Identify your non-negotiables.**
  Write down two or three artistic qualities you don't want to compromise—emotionally, sonically, or ethically—even if trends suggest otherwise.
- **Reflect on long-term connection.**
  Ask yourself: *What kind of relationship do I want listeners to have with my music in ten years?*
  Let the answer guide your present-day creative choices.
- **Choose fulfillment over immediacy.**
  The next time you feel tempted to chase a trend, pause and ask: *Will this still feel meaningful to me once the trend has passed?* Allow that answer to shape your direction.

Your Signature Sound: Why Personal Decisions Shape Timeless Music

In a world overflowing with presets, samples, and algorithms that promise instant gratification, developing a signature sound may feel like an outdated or even unnecessary concept. But for artists and producers striving to make a lasting impact, it's the most valuable creative asset they can cultivate. A unique sonic identity isn't something you find—it's something you shape, refine, and evolve through thousands of personal choices.

Your signature sound is not simply a plugin chain or a favorite synth patch. It's the sum of your instincts, influences, limitations, and creative decisions over time. It's the feeling that a listener gets when they hear one of your tracks and instantly know it's yours—without needing to look at the credits. And that recognition comes not from sounding like everyone else, but from sounding like yourself.

Beyond Tools: Personal Choices Define the Sound

It's tempting to think that great sound comes from great gear. While high-quality tools can certainly enhance your work, the true differentiator lies in how you use them. Two artists using the same synth can produce completely different results—not because the tools are different, but because their choices are.

What reverbs do you gravitate toward? Do you prefer layering analog warmth or slicing up samples? Is your sense of rhythm tight and quantized, or does it breathe with imperfection? These micro-decisions, repeated across dozens or hundreds of tracks, become your sonic fingerprint.

Even your limitations contribute to your sound. Some of the most iconic music has emerged from necessity. When artists don't have access to everything, they often push what they do have to its creative limits. Limitations force you to focus, commit, and innovate.

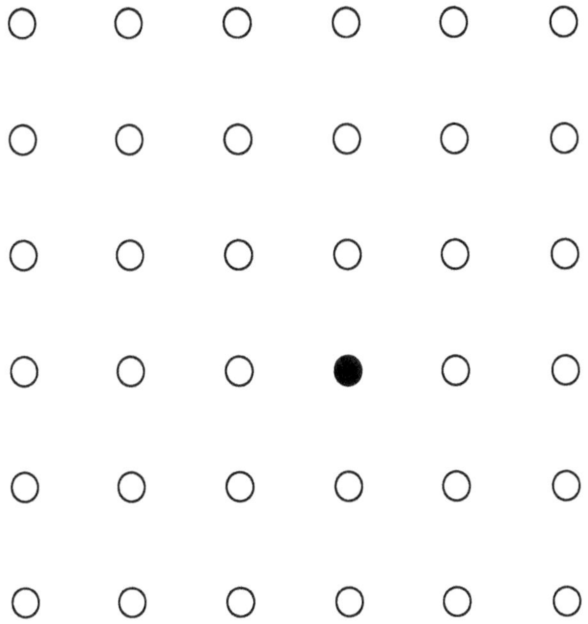

Your signature sound is the sum of countless small decisions only you could make.

Limitations don't restrict your style—they shape it.

Sound Design as Identity

Sound design is one of the most powerful ways to shape a signature sound. Do you create your own presets? Do you resample and process familiar sounds until they become unrecognizable? These creative decisions aren't just technical—they're deeply personal. They reflect your sonic tastes and how you interpret emotion through sound.

Creating your own sample libraries or reusing textures across different projects can also build consistency. You might find that you often gravitate toward specific pads, ambient recordings, or processing chains. Likewise, reusing the same instruments or effects over time—whether it's a trusted synth, a favorite reverb, or a go-to EQ curve—can also shape and reinforce your artistic voice. When these elements resurface organically, they become part of your sonic identity and contribute to the cohesion and recognizability of your work.

Personally, I often use the same synths for specific sounds—like my Moog Sirin that I frequently use for bass sounds, or my Roland Juno 60 for simple pad textures. I also return to the same reverb VSTs, delay units, and other instruments across many of my productions. The key here is that I know the character of these tools. I know immediately which synth to turn to when I have a specific sound in mind. These consistent tools are part of my musical

DNA. But even more important than the gear is my taste, which has been shaped throughout my life. My taste defines the sound that I like, and in the end, it's this taste that forms the core of my sonic identity.

Influence Without Imitation

Inspiration is essential. We all start by mimicking the artists we admire. But at some point, you must translate those influences into something that feels like you. Ask yourself: What do I love about this sound? Is it the atmosphere? The groove? The emotion it evokes? Then, internalize those elements and reframe them through your own creative lens.

Your signature sound isn't a static destination—it's a living process. It grows as you grow. The more music you make, the more patterns emerge. The more mistakes you make, the more you discover what resonates.

Evolution through Repetition

There's power in repetition. The more you create, the more your taste refines. You start recognizing what feels right and what doesn't. Over time, your choices begin to coalesce into a distinct language.

I've noticed that even when I try to explore new styles, my personal sound always comes through—sometimes in the structure, sometimes in the harmonic language, or in how I shape transitions. That's not something you can fake. It's the result of persistent creation and self-awareness.

Your signature sound also helps guide your collaborations. When you're clear on your identity, you become a more compelling collaborator—someone who brings something unmistakable to the table. This clarity can also help in working with vocalists, composers, or even labels, as they begin to trust your artistic vision.

It always fascinates me that my own sonic identity shines through, even in my collaborations—and so does the identity of the people I work with. If you listen to my albums with Andreas Bach or Oine, you can clearly hear my own musical style, but also theirs. The texture, emotion, and compositional flavor each person brings add something beautifully unique. When two strong musical identities meet, the result becomes something that neither of us could've created alone. That's the magic of collaboration.

Recognizable Voices across Changing Styles

When I think of artists such as Bonobo, Ólafur Arnalds, Nils Frahm, Björk, Burial, Max Martin, or Billie Eilish, what stands out to me is not sameness, but recognizability. Even when the tools, textures, or stylistic details shift, I still feel a consistent sensibility underneath. I don't use these names as proof, but as personal listening references for how years of experimentation can still lead to a voice that feels unmistakably one's own.

Trusting Your Instincts

At the heart of developing a signature sound is trust—trust in your ears, your process, and your instincts. You won't get it right every time. But over time, those "wrong" turns become part of your style. They reveal what you care about, what you notice, and what you're willing to let go.

One night, I sat down at my Waldorf Zarenbourg late in the evening, simply capturing ideas with my field recorder. I wasn't planning to compose a full piece—it was just about following a feeling. But somehow, something special happened. I improvised almost an entire track in one take. It wasn't intentional. It just flowed—and it felt right.

The next day, I listened back and realized there was a noticeable noise floor in the recording. I had accidentally used the wrong settings on my recorder. Initially, I was frustrated. I tried fixing the noise using restoration tools, but each time I removed it, the piece lost something essential. The more "perfect" it sounded, the less emotional it felt.

So, I left the noise in. I didn't mention it to anyone. When I sent it to my label, their first comment was how much they loved the character of the recording—that the noise gave it a special, intimate atmosphere. It contributed to the world of music rather than taking away from it. What I had initially seen as a flaw turned out to be one of the track's defining features. It was imperfect—but perfectly imperfect. And that imperfection became part of its soul.

Your voice doesn't come from avoiding mistakes—it comes from embracing them until they sound like you.

Trust that even if your sound doesn't fit into trends, it can still find its audience. In fact, many timeless artists succeeded not because they followed the trends, but because they stayed true to themselves while everyone else chased something else.

Final Thoughts

Your signature sound is the result of hundreds of honest decisions made in the privacy of your creative space. It's not something you force—it's something you reveal. And it's worth the time it takes to find, because once you do, it becomes your compass.

In a world of noise, your personal sound is what cuts through. Make it intentional. Make it yours.

Make enough of your own decisions—and you'll accidentally sound like nobody else.

Action Items

- **Trace your recurring choices.**
  Look back at several of your tracks or sketches and note repeated decisions—specific instruments, harmonic movements, tempos, textures, or emotional moods. These repetitions are not habits to fix; they are clues to your signature.

- **Choose one tool to go deeper with.**
  For an upcoming project, limit yourself to one main instrument, synth, or sound source. Instead of searching for variety, explore depth and nuance. Notice how familiarity sharpens your expression.
- **Listen for taste, not technique.**
  When evaluating your own work, ask yourself: *What do I like about this?* rather than *Is this correct?* Your taste is more defining than any rule or plugin.
- **Preserve an imperfection.**
  In your next piece, identify one element you instinctively want to "fix." Before doing so, listen again and decide whether it adds character or emotional truth. Let at least one imperfection remain.
- **Document your sonic preferences.**
  Write down the sounds, textures, and atmospheres you naturally gravitate toward. Over time, this becomes a personal reference—not to limit you, but to understand yourself better.
- **Trust repetition as evolution.**
  Remind yourself that a signature sound doesn't come from one bold decision, but from many small, honest ones made consistently. Allow your sound to reveal itself gradually.

The Producer's Mindset: Balancing Vision, Emotion, and Execution

Behind every great track is more than just technique or gear—it's a mindset. The producer's role is not just to build beats or mix sounds. It's to shape a vision, navigate emotions, and make hundreds of creative and technical decisions that breathe life into a song. The producer becomes the translator between inspiration and execution.

The Role of Vision

Every track begins with a vision—sometimes clear, other times vague and abstract. It might be a mood, a memory, a sound you heard in a dream, or just a chord progression that feels right. Having an idea is one thing—you can have hundreds of them each day—but the drive to shape an idea into something real, and the determination to follow it through even when the outcome is still nebulous, is what separates mere inspiration from true creation. The mindset of a producer starts with protecting and nurturing that initial spark, and then committing to develop it into something meaningful.

Great producers learn to trust their instincts early on. They ask themselves: What story do I want this song to tell? What emotion should it evoke? What world am I trying to build with sound?

Your job as a producer is to hold onto the essence of the song, even when the production process tries to pull you in a thousand directions.

It's easy to get lost in possibilities. But staying anchored to your vision ensures that every choice serves the music, not just the process.

Emotion as Compass

Music without emotion is forgettable. A producer must constantly ask: Does this move me? Whether it's a sparse piano line or a deep electronic groove, it needs to create a feeling.

That emotional honesty often requires vulnerability. It might mean keeping a take that's technically imperfect but emotionally raw. It might mean removing a sound you love because it doesn't serve the track. Emotional intelligence is as crucial as technical skill.

If it doesn't move you, it won't move anyone else.

Producers aren't just technicians to me—they are emotional guides, shaping how every note, texture, and transition contributes to the larger feeling of a piece. This emotional focus has always been central to my own music. Over the years, my personal impression has been that when I stay true to the emotional intent of a piece, listeners often respond more strongly. One response I received years ago described my music as feeling deeply direct and personal, and that stayed with me. It reminded me that in a world full of distractions, emotion should remain one of the main compasses in the studio.

Balancing Intuition with Craft

There's a delicate dance between instinct and knowledge. While intuition often guides creative breakthroughs, it's technical skill that helps execute those ideas with precision.

A producer's mindset embraces both sides: the wildness of spontaneous inspiration and the discipline of structured editing. Knowing when to flow and when to refine is part of the craft.

Let yourself explore freely in the beginning. Don't judge your ideas too early. Later, switch hats—step back and evaluate. What's working? What's noise? I've found it incredibly helpful to consciously shift roles during the production process. That's why I never mix a song on the same day I arranged or composed it, and I never master it right after mixing. Each stage requires a different mindset—fresh ears, a new perspective, and a different set of creative priorities.

Music is complex, with many layers of emotion, sound design, and technical nuance. Giving each phase its own space and mindset leads to better decisions—and ultimately, better music.

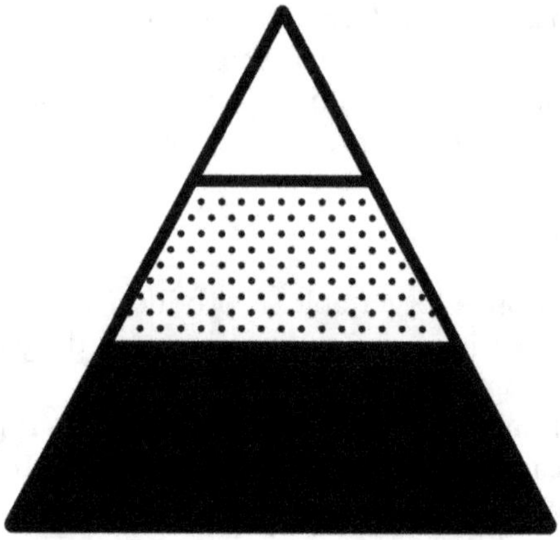

Producing isn't just about making music. It's about building a mindset—layer by layer.

Decision Fatigue and Creative Clarity

Producing a song means making an endless stream of decisions. Sounds, structures, effects, transitions, tempos, and mix choices all add up. It's natural to feel overwhelmed.

To combat this, some producers create rituals or frameworks. They set time limits. They restrict their tools. They break the process into phases: ideation, arrangement, and refinement.

Limitation is not your enemy. It's the frame that helps you focus the picture.

Being decisive doesn't mean always being right—it means trusting that you can revise later. Momentum matters. Indecision can be the biggest creativity killer.

Keeping the Big Picture in Mind

It's easy to zoom in too far—focusing on tiny EQ tweaks or reverb tails for hours. While details matter, producers must frequently zoom out. Listen like a first-time listener. Feel the whole arc. Does it take you somewhere?

I sometimes take my recordings to a different place—outside the studio—just to hear them in a new environment. It gives me a fresh perspective. But perhaps the most powerful test is sharing your track with someone who's never heard it before. Just being in the room with them, observing their reaction, you'll start hearing your own music in a completely different way. Trust me, it's transformative.

The mindset of a great producer involves regularly switching perspective—from granular to global. From artist to audience. From dreamer to editor.

Navigating Doubt

Every producer faces self-doubt. Is this good enough? Will people like it? Should I start over?

The mindset shift comes in realizing that doubt is part of the process—not a sign that you're doing it wrong, but that you care deeply. Let doubt inform your curiosity, not halt your progress.

You won't know if it's great until it's finished. So finish it.

Real-World Inspiration

> One of the clearest lessons I've learned is that reduction can be a form of production. Sometimes the most powerful version of a song is the one where the arrangement steps out of the way and the performance does the talking. If you strip a track down to one instrument and one voice (or one lead element), you immediately hear what matters: phrasing, timing, intention, and emotion. When nothing hides behind layers, authenticity becomes the main "effect."
>
> At the other end of the spectrum, some productions work because they unite big-picture vision with meticulous execution. The strongest records—whether minimal or maximal—feel coherent: every sound supports the same emotional destination. That kind of production is less about showing off technique and more about discipline—making hundreds of small decisions that all point in the same direction, until the listener feels a clear, confident story from the first bar to the last.

Final Thoughts

The producer's mindset is not about perfection—it's about direction. It's about honoring your emotional compass, trusting your vision, and developing the patience to follow a song through its unpredictable evolution. And yes, it's also about delivering a technically perfect result—but always with the focus on what truly matters: the soul of the music.

Sometimes your role is that of the architect. Other times, you're a sculptor chipping away. At your best, you're both a visionary and a craftsperson.

Producing isn't just about making music. It's about making meaning, one decision at a time.

Action Items

- **Clarify the vision before you begin.**
  Before starting your next track, write one short sentence describing its emotional intention or inner image. Return to this sentence whenever decisions start to feel scattered.
- **Check in with emotion first.**
  During a session, pause and ask yourself: *Does this move me right now?* Let emotional response guide whether you continue, simplify, or let something go.
- **Separate creative roles consciously.**
  Try dividing your process into clear phases—exploration, arrangement, refinement. Notice how shifting mindset between these stages improves clarity and reduces frustration.
- **Limit decisions to regain focus.**
  When you feel overwhelmed, reduce your options intentionally: fewer sounds, fewer tools, shorter sessions. Observe how constraints support momentum.
- **Zoom out regularly.**
  At the end of a session, listen to your track without touching anything. Don't analyze—just feel the overall arc. Write down what stands out emotionally.
- **Finish despite doubt.**
  The next time self-doubt appears, acknowledge it without reacting. Commit to finishing the piece anyway. Completion is often what reveals the truth of the work.

What Makes a Song Great: How Music Turns Sound into Emotion

What makes a song truly memorable? What transforms a simple melody and a few lyrics into something that moves people—sometimes even changes them?

The answer isn't singular. Greatness in music isn't defined by one characteristic. It's not just production quality or vocal delivery or lyrical depth. Often, it's a combination of many subtle elements: emotion, timing, vulnerability, contrast, authenticity—and something you can't always explain. A feeling.

Many of the songs that stay with me most don't feel memorable because of technical perfection alone. When I listen to artists such as Nils Frahm or Ólafur Arnalds, I'm drawn to how elements that might seem imperfect can become expressive. And when I hear artists such as Adele or Ed Sheeran, what stands out to me is not technical showmanship but emotional directness. These are personal listening impressions, but they remind me that a song often becomes powerful when it reflects something back to the listener's inner world.

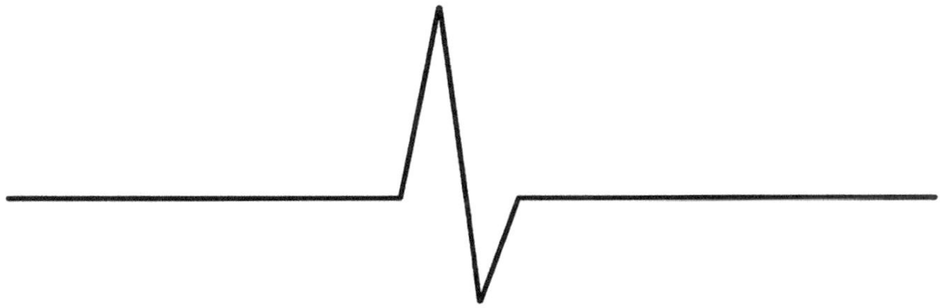

A great song doesn't need to be perfect—it needs to be real.

In my own work, I've noticed that the tracks listeners connect with most are often the ones we didn't expect to stand out. One example is my song "Peaceful." We never positioned it as a single or built a campaign around it, yet it quietly found its audience over time. I wrote it for my son while my wife was pregnant, and perhaps the emotion behind it is what people respond to. It reminded me that emotional authenticity often travels further than "perfect" production.

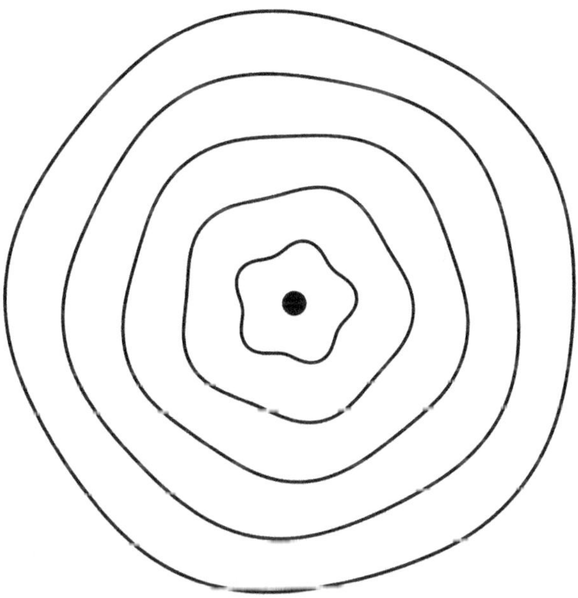

If your song touches one person deeply, it's already succeeded.

Core Elements That Make a Song Great

Over time, both listening and experience have helped me notice several elements that often show up in songs that feel great to me. These elements aren't hard rules, but rather guideposts for emotional impact and musical quality. And while many great songs do include some of these characteristics, there are always notable exceptions—tracks that defy expectations and succeed precisely because they break the mold. It's important to remember that what resonates with one person may not affect another. Greatness is often defined through the ear—and heart—of the listener.

Memorable Melody and Hook

In my experience as a listener and producer, the fastest way a song grabs attention is by giving the ear something to recognize early—an opening motif, a vocal tone, a rhythm, or a signature sound. You don't need a traditional hook in bar one, but you do need a reason to lean in quickly—something that signals, "This is worth your attention."

That said, some songs are loved despite lacking a traditional hook. Think of ambient or cinematic compositions, where the flow and texture matter more than melodic repetition. These pieces still move listeners deeply—just through different means.

Emotional Resonance

Great songs connect deeply with the listener's emotions. The lyrics, tone, tempo, and dynamics all play a part in communicating a specific mood or story. When a song mirrors your feelings or gives voice to what you couldn't say, it becomes powerful.

There's no formula for emotional resonance. Some songs do this with just two chords and a whisper. Others, with grand orchestration. It's not about size—it's about sincerity.

Clear Structure and Repetition

Many songs that stay with me tend to have a structure I can follow, whether that means a familiar verse–chorus shape or some other sense of return and contrast. From my perspective, repetition often helps a musical idea settle in the ear, while variation keeps the experience alive.

At the same time, I'm drawn to songs that move away from standard form. Queen's *Bohemian Rhapsody*, for example, feels to me less like a typical verse–chorus loop and more like a sequence of scenes, and that constant transformation is part of its appeal. John Miles' *Music* gives me a similar feeling—moving between intimate and expansive moments as if the arrangement were unfolding in chapters. To my ears, what keeps these songs engaging is not strict repetition but the sense of forward motion.

Simplicity with Purpose

While complexity can be artistically satisfying, simplicity often results in a stronger emotional impact. A minimal, focused arrangement can leave room for emotion to breathe and shine.

I'm often drawn to records that prove how powerful restraint can be. Norah Jones' early recordings, for instance, feel to me like a reminder that you don't need a crowded arrangement to create depth—sometimes a voice, an honest performance, and a few well-chosen sounds are enough. I feel a similar strength in Billie Eilish's more stripped-back productions: the space isn't emptiness, it's intention. When every element has room to matter, the emotional core can land even harder.

Originality and Surprise

Original chord changes, unique sound design, unexpected lyrics, or structural surprises often elevate a song. These small acts of creative bravery make a piece memorable and fresh.

Sometimes, unpredictability is exactly what draws me in. Björk's genre-bending work is a great reminder that a song can feel alive when it refuses to behave "correctly."

Phil Collins' *In the Air Tonight* is another example I often think about—not because of a rulebook, but because of how it *feels*: the long build creates a kind of suspense, and when the drums finally arrive, the release is physical.

Queen's *Bohemian Rhapsody* works on me in a different way: the constant shifts keep my attention because each section feels like it belongs to the same emotional story. And John Miles' *Music* has that same theatrical quality—moving between delicate and expansive moments in a way that keeps you listening for what's around the next corner.

Lyrics That Connect

Strong lyrics tend to feel most powerful to me when they are both relatable and emotionally honest, even if they are expressed in very simple language. I often notice that a song stays with me when a line seems to meet me at exactly the right emotional moment—when it gives shape to something I have been feeling but have not yet found words for. In that sense, lyrics don't need to be complicated to go deep. Sometimes their strength lies in how directly they speak.

That is especially true when a song seems to echo an inner state with unusual clarity. A line about heartbreak, longing, hope, or emotional confusion can suddenly feel intensely personal, not because it was written specifically for one listener, but because it touches something recognizable. In those moments, music can stop feeling like entertainment alone and start feeling more like an emotional mirror.

Yet sometimes, songs without clear lyrics—like Sigur Rós—can still convey deep emotion. To my ears, the voice becomes an instrument first: syllables, tone, and phrasing carry the feeling even when the words aren't the point. When I listen to tracks like *Hoppípolla*, I notice how the emotional meaning comes through dynamics and delivery, leaving space for the listener to project their own story into the music.

Expressive Performance

How a note is played or sung can be just as important to me as what note it is. Dynamics, phrasing, and even rough edges often carry emotional weight that technical perfection alone cannot. When I think of voices such as Adele, Whitney Houston, or Freddie Mercury, what stays with me is not flawlessness, but the distinct character of the delivery—the sense that phrasing, force, fragility, or intensity become part of the song's identity. These are personal listening impressions, but they remind me that expressive detail often matters more than technical polish.

Strong Production Quality

While not a prerequisite for greatness, thoughtful production helps translate emotion. Good mixing and mastering help the message of the song reach the listener without distraction. In fact, great production can elevate a song to an entirely new level—adding depth, clarity, and dimension that enhance the emotional experience without overshadowing it.

There are songs with minimal arrangements and raw delivery that affect me far more deeply than highly polished productions. I often feel that sincerity can matter more than polish, and that a stripped-back acoustic performance can sometimes feel more intimate and human than something far more elaborate.

Johnny Cash's version of *Hurt* comes to mind for me here—not as evidence I'm trying to prove, but as a personal listening reference. What stays with me in that recording is the exposed quality of the performance: the bare vocal, the sparse accompaniment, and the sense that very little stands between the song and the listener. I hear weight, vulnerability, and reflection in it, and that is exactly why it stays with me so strongly. Its power, in my ears, comes less from production complexity than from how direct and unguarded it feels.

I notice something similar in rough demos, live takes, voice memos, freestyle recordings, stripped-back country performances, sparse indie arrangements, or understated jazz and acoustic moments. Again and again, I find that when less is competing for attention, the emotional center can come through more clearly. What matters most to me is whether I believe what I'm hearing. If the performance feels lived-in and sincere, simple or unconventional production can become a strength rather than a limitation.

Silence and Space

I don't hear silence as the absence of music, but as part of the music itself. Space between notes can let emotion breathe and give the listener room to reflect and absorb what is being heard. When I think of a piece such as Max Richter's *On the Nature of Daylight*, I'm reminded of how powerful slow pacing, restraint, and space can feel in practice. In that kind of writing, the distance between notes can begin to matter almost as much as the notes themselves.

In ambient or cinematic music especially, I often experience silence as a kind of canvas that holds the color of everything around it. A pause before a chord change, a lingering breath, or an unplayed beat can create tension, intimacy, and openness without needing to announce itself. Silence doesn't feel empty to me; it feels charged with presence, possibility, and attention.

Timelessness Over Trendiness

Some songs feel dated to me after a few years, while others seem to deepen with time. My own impression is that music often lasts longer when it feels rooted in emotional truth rather than in whatever happens to be fashionable at the moment. Songs that stay with me usually seem anchored in feelings that remain easy to recognize—love, loss, hope, longing, conflict, or release—even when the production style belongs to a particular era.

When I think of songs such as Whitney Houston's *I Will Always Love You*, Queen's *Don't Stop Me Now*, The Beatles' *Let It Be*, or U2's *With or Without You*, I'm not presenting evidence so much as naming personal reference points: songs that still feel emotionally alive to me because their core feeling continues to come through. That is what makes music feel timeless in my own listening. It is less about sounding current and more about expressing something that still feels true whenever I return to it.

Context and Timing

Sometimes a song feels significant not only because of how it sounds, but because of when it is heard. A piece of music can gather extra meaning when it becomes tied, in the listener's mind, to a wider public moment, emotional climate, or shared atmosphere. That doesn't mean a song has to chase headlines, only that timing can shape the way it is experienced.

In moments like that, a song can begin to feel larger than its structure alone. It may come to carry associations that reach beyond melody, lyrics, or production, simply because it becomes connected to a particular mood, time, or collective feeling. What matters here is not making a historical claim, but recognizing how strongly context can shape the emotional life of a song.

It's about Connection

The best songs make us feel seen. They narrate something we couldn't express ourselves. They become soundtracks to moments in our lives—good or bad. That's the true magic of music: it becomes part of our emotional memory.

What you write and what your listener hears may not be the same—and that's the beauty of it. Each person brings their own story to the music, completing the emotional picture in their own way. A song is never just yours—it becomes a shared canvas.

Sometimes, I ask myself after finishing a track: "Would I want to hear this again in five years? Would it still mean something to me?" If the answer is yes, that's usually a sign I've touched something real.

You know a song is great when it stops being yours and becomes someone else's story.

Technical Brilliance vs. Emotional Honesty

Of course, production matters. Mixing, mastering, and arrangement—all of it contributes to how a song is experienced. But these are tools in service of something greater: the emotional arc. A perfect mix that lacks soul will never outshine a rough demo that makes you cry.

That's why I often let emotion guide the final decisions. Should the vocal stay a bit rough? Should I keep the ambient noise in the piano recording? If it adds to the feeling, I leave it. That's where the magic is.

A Balance of Structure and Surprise

Great songs typically find a balance between familiarity and unpredictability. The listener feels grounded, but also intrigued. There's a hook—but also a twist. The rhythm feels right—but then it breaks pattern just enough to awaken your attention.

One listener once told me that one of my songs felt instantly familiar—and yet strangely new at the same time. That's a sentence I'll never forget, because it captures what great songs do: they comfort you with something recognizable, while still opening a door you didn't know was there.

Music Is Subjective

What makes a song great is deeply personal and subjective. One person might be deeply moved by a minimal piano piece, while another prefers a heavy, driving techno track. Some people love the storytelling in country music, while others are touched by abstract ambient soundscapes. This variety in perception is not only normal—it's what makes music so powerful.

Music taps into individual experiences, tastes, and memories. That's why a song that means everything to you might not affect someone else in the same way—and that's perfectly okay. It's not about universal appeal, but emotional truth.

And sometimes, what makes a song great—at least to me—is that it doesn't follow the expected rules. It's the outliers that grab my attention and linger in my memory. Billie Eilish's close-up vocal style, to my ears, can make a pop track feel unusually intimate, like you're standing right next to the singer. And when I listen to Gotye's *Somebody That I Used to Know*, I hear a song that doesn't "behave" like a typical mainstream single—its choices feel slightly sideways in a way I find refreshing. These songs stand out to me because they take a risk. They don't play it safe.

If your song touches one person deeply, it's already succeeded.

Songs That Stayed with Me

When I think of songs that still feel alive years later, a few titles come to mind—not as a claim about history, but as my own reference points for how far music *can* travel in a person's life.

- **Imagine—John Lennon**
- **Smells Like Teen Spirit—Nirvana**
- **Someone Like You—Adele**
- **Hey Jude—The Beatles**
- **What a Wonderful World—Louis Armstrong**
- **I Will Always Love You—Whitney Houston**
- **Gymnopédie No. 1—Erik Satie**

What connects these songs for me isn't genre or era—it's that they feel emotionally direct. They leave enough space for listeners to place their own stories inside the music, and that's often how a song can feel "bigger than itself."

Courage, Vulnerability, and Letting Go

Being vulnerable in a song is scary. You're putting a piece of yourself out there—something raw and unfiltered—and once it's out, you can't take it back. But that's also where the power lies. The most touching songs often come from a place of uncertainty, from daring to be emotionally exposed. The listener doesn't want perfection; they want truth.

Many times, the fear of judgment holds back the creative spark. But the moment you stop writing for approval and start writing from truth, something changes. You create something with heart—and that's what lingers.

Creative Compass—A Checklist for Emotional Impact

When working on a track, these are some questions I ask myself. They're not rules, just gentle guideposts to help ensure the emotional core stays intact:

- Does this feel emotionally honest?
- Would I want to listen to this five years from now?

- Will someone recognize the hook within 15 seconds?
- What's the emotional journey—where does the song begin, and where does it take the listener?
- Is there a moment of surprise, tension, or contrast?
- What would happen if I removed one element—would it hit harder?
- Am I saying something that matters to *me*?

Behind the Song: The Power of Stripping Back

I once wrote a piece called *Nocturnal Embrace* that started with a rich arrangement—layers of pads, drums, and textures. It was technically solid, but something felt distant. So I removed nearly everything. I left just the piano and a cello, carefully recorded with space and intention. Suddenly, the emotion surfaced. This stripped-down version not only felt more honest—it later won a German Songwriting Award in the **Music for Motion Picture** category.[1]

It taught me something I carry into every project: sometimes, the most impactful thing you can do isn't to add, but to *subtract*. Let the silence speak. Let the vulnerability lead.

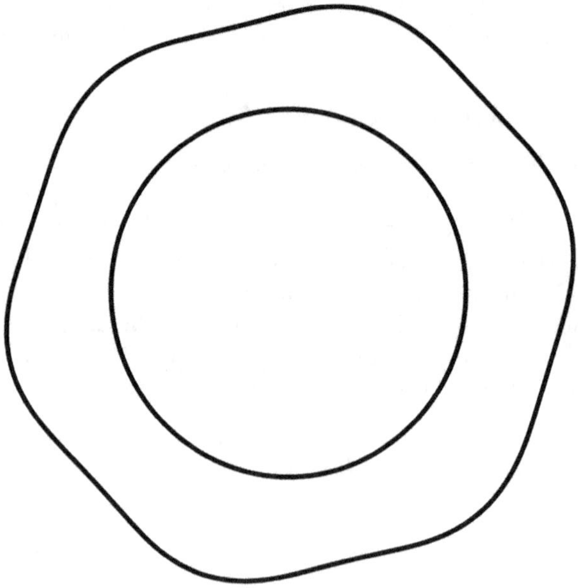

What we leave out often speaks louder than what we put in.

Embracing the Mystery

And then, there's the part of songwriting we'll never fully explain—the moment when it just *works*. You don't always know why. That's the mystery of music. It slips past logic and enters a space beyond language.

Some songs are born from a clear idea. Others emerge from improvisation, instinct, or even accident. And occasionally, when everything aligns—when the song touches you first—it goes on to touch others.

Trusting Your Instincts

In the end, what makes a great song also depends on you as the creator. If it moves you, it will likely move others. Trust that. Don't chase trends—chase truth. The more personal and honest your work, the more universally it will resonate.

The more I trust my own taste, the more timeless the music becomes.

So what makes a great song? It's not a checklist. It's a moment of honesty. A spark of emotion. A piece of your soul turned into sound.

And when it lands in someone else's heart, it becomes great.

The songs that last are the ones that feel like they've always belonged to us—even if we just heard them for the first time.

Action Items

- **Identify the emotional core.**
  Before working on your next song, pause and write one sentence answering:
  What do I want someone to feel when this ends?
  Let this guide all further decisions.
- **Listen beyond technique.**
  Choose a song that deeply moves you. Listen once without analyzing structure, sound, or production. Focus only on *where* and *how* it affects you emotionally.
- **Strip something back.**
  Take a current or finished piece and remove one element—an instrument, a layer, a section. Notice whether the emotional impact becomes clearer, weaker, or stronger.
- **Embrace one honest imperfection.**
  In your next recording or performance, allow a moment of rawness to remain—an unpolished vocal, a breath, a slight timing shift—if it supports the feeling.
- **Ask the five-year question.**
  After completing a song, ask yourself: *Would this still mean something to me in five years?*
  Reflect on what that answer reveals about the song's depth and truth.

- **Redefine success emotionally.**
  Write down what it would mean for a song to succeed *without numbers, charts, or validation*. Let emotional connection be a valid outcome in itself.

Note

1 German Songwriting Awards (official website), winners list (Music for Motion Picture: Thomas Lemmer), accessed March 5, 2026.

Section 2

Emotional Sound

Expressing Feeling through Music

Focused on emotion, aesthetics, vulnerability, and minimalism in musical storytelling.

Focusing on the Essence: Conveying Emotion through Music

Music, at its core, is a vehicle for emotional expression. As producers, we often get caught up in perfecting every detail—adjusting a single frequency, tweaking effects, or endlessly revising arrangements. While striving for quality is valuable, it's essential to remember that the listener connects first with the emotion, not the technique.

Shaping the Emotional Narrative

When we step back from the technicalities, the song's emotional message becomes clearer. Consider the story the music is telling—whether personal, abstract, or simply evoking a mood. Each sonic element should support this narrative. If something feels out of place or doesn't serve the emotion you're aiming for, don't be afraid to remove it. Often, less is more, and stripping away the excess can reveal the heart of your work. For example, while reworking an ambient track, you might find that removing an elaborate synth line allows the gentle piano to shine and carry the mood more effectively.

Power in Space and Restraint

In ambient and cinematic music, space and subtlety often speak louder than dense arrangements. A pause, a gentle fade, or a soft transition can evoke deep emotions. Pay attention to dynamics—how energy ebbs and flows—to shape the listener's experience.

DOI: 10.4324/9781003710622-2

I've often been moved by pieces built from remarkably little—slow strings, a small set of chords, and enough air between the notes to let the listener breathe. When the harmony evolves patiently and dynamics are handled with care, the music feels human, intimate, and cinematic without needing dense layering. In these moments, restraint becomes the "arrangement," and phrasing becomes the hook. The same is true for minimalist piano- and texture-based writing. A repeating figure, a subtle change in touch, or a gradual shift in timbre can carry enormous weight when you give it time. This is why space matters: tone, texture, and patience can communicate more than complexity ever could, especially when the goal is emotional resonance, not spectacle.

My Experience: "Nocturnal Embrace"

While creating "Nocturnal Embrace," I originally shaped it as a kind of lo-fi track with drums, bass, and multiple textured layers, believing that adding richness would make it more engaging. However, the more elements I introduced, the more the original emotion seemed to fade. One night, I made the bold decision to remove almost everything—stripping away the beats, pads, and extra melodies—and returned to the vulnerable solo piano with the cello ending I had started with. This slower, more spacious version carried the honesty and fragility I'd been searching for all along—and it was in that minimal form that the true essence of the track finally emerged. The piece later won a German Songwriting Award in the **Music for Motion Picture** category.[1]

Focus on the core, for the essence of music is the emotion it carries and shares.

Practical Ways to Find the Essence

- **Mute and compare**:
  Mute certain layers and listen again. I've found entire synth pads unnecessary once I heard how much more direct the piece felt without them.
- **Limit your palette**:
  Choose fewer instruments or sounds and explore how deeply they can convey the emotion.
- **Test in context**:
  Play the track in varied settings—through speakers, headphones, or in the background—and note when the emotion feels strongest.
- **Ask "Does this serve the story?"**:
  Every sound should have a purpose. If it doesn't enhance the emotion, it may be better left out.
- **Return to your first take**:
  Sometimes the earliest recording holds the raw emotion that later revisions dilute. Revisit it before finalizing.

Essence Over Perfection

Ultimately, essence in music isn't about simplicity for its own sake—it's about intentionality. Every note, pause, and texture should serve the emotion, story, and experience you want to share. Letting go of unnecessary complexity not only clarifies your creative vision but also strengthens the bond between your music and its audience.

Focus on the core, for the essence of music is the emotion it carries and shares.

Action Items

- **Name the emotional story**.
  Before continuing work on a piece, write one short sentence describing the emotional journey you want the listener to experience—from beginning to end.
- **Listen with closed eyes**.
  Play your track once without looking at the digital audio workstation (DAW). Notice which moments move you emotionally—and which feel distracting or unnecessary.
- **Remove before adding**.
  Choose one element in your current project and mute it completely. Ask yourself whether the emotional message becomes clearer, weaker, or unchanged.
- **Return to the fragile version**.
  Revisit the earliest recording or sketch of a piece. Listen for raw emotion that may have been softened or obscured during later refinements.

- **Let space speak.**
  Pay attention to silence, pauses, and decay tails in your music. Ask yourself whether allowing more space could deepen the emotional impact.
- **Choose intention over perfection.**
  Reflect on one technical imperfection you're tempted to fix. Decide consciously whether fixing it serves the emotion—or whether leaving it strengthens the song's honesty.

Creating Meaning Without Lyrics: Telling Stories with Sound

When Music Speaks Without Words

Music doesn't need words to speak. In my experience, it is fully capable of carrying meaning through mood, melody, rhythm, and dynamics. Some of the compositions that have affected me most, old and recent alike, have communicated deep emotion, vivid imagery, and even a sense of narrative without a single line of text. From sweeping orchestral works to minimal ambient textures, instrumental music can create emotional connections that seem to go beyond language.

Inner Narrative in Instrumental Music

Instrumental storytelling has been part of music for a long time. In classical music, pieces are sometimes discussed in narrative or scene-based terms—but to me, storytelling can also be purely emotional and internal. When I listen to Beethoven's *"Moonlight" Sonata* (Piano Sonata No. 14), I'm not following a literal plot; I'm noticing how strongly a piece can suggest mood and inner movement without saying a single word. It leaves me picturing scenes and emotions even though nothing is spelled out.

And when I hear Vivaldi's *Four Seasons*, I naturally associate the shifting gestures and energy with changes in weather and atmosphere.

To me, that's the beauty of instrumental music: it can hint at a narrative without explaining it. The listener isn't handed a script—they're given space to build their own images and emotions from melody, rhythm, and timbre.

Music can tell a story without using words.

How Listeners Create Their Own Stories

I remember a conversation I had with a DJ while discussing my album *PURE*. I was especially proud of the vocal collaborations on that record—tracks I had carefully crafted with vocalists to express specific emotions. But the DJ surprised me. He told me, quite honestly, that he wasn't interested in the vocal songs. He focused entirely on the instrumental tracks because, for him, they offered something far more powerful: imagination. They left space for his own interpretations, thoughts, and emotions. That conversation changed the way I viewed instrumental music.

Until then, I had assumed that vocal songs were more relatable for most people. After all, lyrics guide the listener, right? But here was someone who valued the open-ended nature of instrumental work—music that doesn't dictate, but invites. It opened my eyes to how deeply people connect with sound when they're given the freedom to make it personal.

Today, I appreciate both vocal and instrumental music, but I share his perspective. There's something magical about music that doesn't need to explain itself. It can be ambient, classical, cinematic, or any genre that speaks without words. And when you think of the emotional power behind film scores, it becomes clear: instrumental music is anything but limited.

When there are no lyrics to define the message, I often notice myself creating one. Instrumental music can invite images, moods, and emotional associations—a swelling string section may feel hopeful to me, while a descending piano melody can suggest loss. Artwork, titles, or a short description can also gently shape how I hear a piece while still leaving room for personal interpretation.

The absence of lyrics doesn't leave a void—it creates space for the listener's own story to unfold.

Techniques for Instrumental Storytelling

There are many tools available to composers and producers to craft meaning without words:

- **Motifs**:
  Repeating musical phrases that evolve, mirror characters, or reflect emotional changes.
- **Dynamics and tempo**:
  Use contrast to build tension or create calm.
- **Instrumentation**:
  A cello might suggest warmth or melancholy. A plucked harp can feel magical or fragile.
- **Sound design**:
  Natural elements—wind, footsteps, distant thunder—can be mimicked or embedded for cinematic effect.
- **Arrangement and structure**:
  Like a screenplay, a song can follow a story arc: introduction, development, climax, and resolution.

Modern Examples

Contemporary artists continue to tell stories with purely instrumental work. When I listen to Explosions in the Sky, Ólafur Arnalds, or Nils Frahm, I often experience the music as an emotional arc—even without lyrics. For me, it's the pacing, the texture, and the way tension builds and releases that carry the "narrative."

And when I listen to film music by composers like Hans Zimmer or Max Richter, I'm reminded how much can be communicated through dynamics, recurring motifs, and sonic color. In ambient or cinematic music, the story can live in texture and time. Sometimes a single sustained note, a gradual crescendo, or a well-placed silence says more to me than a line of text.

Improvisation as Emotional Narrative

Improvised music often carries a raw, authentic emotional signature. A spontaneous piano piece, a jazz solo, or a live ambient session can capture the feeling of a moment in a way that no pre-written lyric could. The story isn't scripted—it unfolds as it is being created. In my own work, I've experienced this firsthand. One example is my track "Sweet Longing—Late Night Live Improvisation," which appears on my album *Ambient Nights*. I recorded it late at night, playing it entirely on my Waldorf Zarenbourg with a KORG M1 layered on top. There were no overdubs, no edits—just a single take, capturing exactly what I felt in that moment. The mood, the energy, the vulnerability—it's all preserved in the performance. For me, this kind of raw, unfiltered improvisation tells a story that's deeply personal and emotionally honest. It's a sonic photograph of a feeling, frozen in time.

Improvisation reveals the sound of the soul in real time.

Exercises to Try

- **Title first**:
  Choose a title like *The Long Goodbye* or *Into the Light*. Compose a short instrumental piece that matches the emotion or imagery of the title.
- **Emotional arc**:
  Structure your song like a film—start small, build intensity, introduce tension, then resolve.
- **Sound palette limitation**:
  Use only three instruments to tell your story. Restriction encourages creative choices.

Conclusion

Lyrics are powerful—but not required. Instrumental music invites listeners to experience something personal and unique. It doesn't tell you what to feel—it gently opens the door for your own story to unfold. It offers space rather than instructions, and freedom rather than direction. This openness is what allows instrumental music to feel so intimate and profound. And when crafted with clear emotional intent, it can be just as moving—if not more—than any lyrics could ever be.

When music is honest, it doesn't need to speak. It already knows how to be felt.

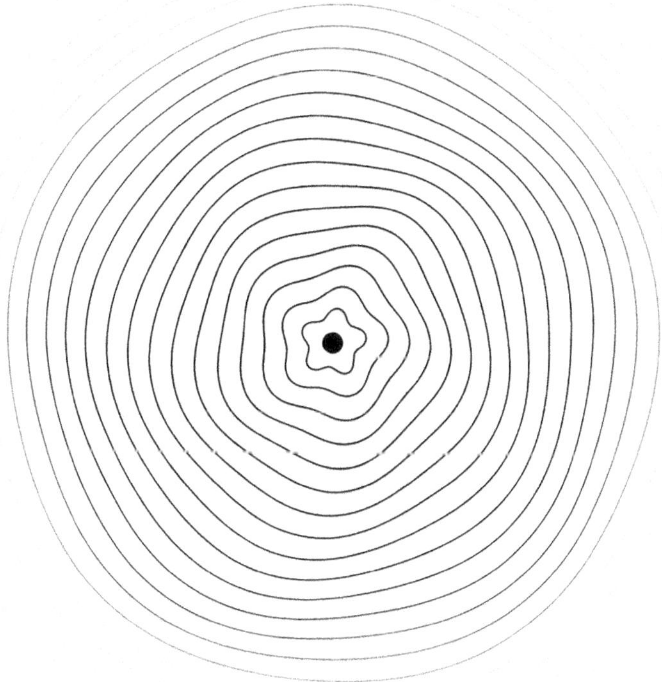

Music has long been a powerful medium for storytelling beyond words.

Action Items

- **Start with an image or feeling.**
  Before composing, write down a single image, memory, or emotion you want to explore. Let this be the silent "story" behind the music.
- **Compose without explaining.**
  Create a short instrumental piece without trying to clarify its meaning. Trust that the emotion will communicate itself without guidance.
- **Listen as a first-time listener.**
  Play your track and imagine you don't know why it was written. Notice what images, moods, or narratives naturally arise.
- **Use restraint to invite imagination.**
  Limit your sound palette or arrangement and observe how fewer elements create more space for interpretation.

- **Let structure tell the story.**
  Reflect on whether your piece has a sense of beginning, development, and release—even without lyrics. Adjust only if the emotional arc feels unclear.
- **Accept multiple meanings.**
  Remind yourself that instrumental music doesn't need a single interpretation. Let listeners complete the story in their own way.

Soundtrack of the Soul: Why Music Moves Us

More Than Just Sound

Music has the uncanny ability to make us cry, dance, remember, or feel understood—often without a single word being spoken. But why? Why does music have such a powerful grip on our emotions and memories? In my experience, the answer lies somewhere between emotion, memory, attention, and human experience.

In this chapter, we'll explore the deeper forces that make music emotionally resonant—and why it has become the emotional language of our lives.

How Music Shapes Feeling and Attention

When I listen to music, it can feel surprisingly physical—like my mood and attention are being guided in real time. Certain passages pull me in, build tension, and then release it in a way that feels genuinely satisfying. That's one reason I take emotional pacing so seriously as a producer: the shape of a piece can affect how the listener experiences time, expectation, and relief.

Interestingly, this can still happen even when we know what's coming. In my experience, the anticipation of a musical climax can feel almost as emotionally powerful as the climax itself. It's the musical equivalent of knowing the punchline of a joke and still laughing.

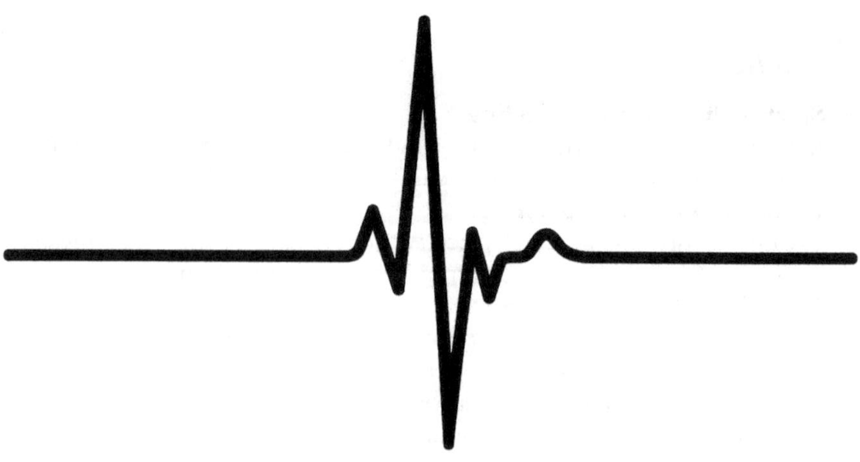

Music doesn't just move your heart—it can reshape how a moment feels and how your attention settles into it.

Music as Emotional Mirror

One reason music is so powerful, in my experience, is that it can mirror our own emotional states. When I'm heartbroken, I often find myself drawn to sad songs. When I feel euphoric, I'm more likely to reach for anthems. Music doesn't tell me how to feel—it meets me where I am. And sometimes, it seems to express emotions I didn't even know I was carrying.

Lyrics can amplify this effect, but even instrumental music can capture the nuances of joy, longing, grief, or wonder. The emotional color of a minor chord, the urgency of a crescendo, or the stillness of a piano solo can all speak very directly to our emotional core.

Music and Memory

Have you ever heard a song and been instantly transported back in time? I've noticed that music can latch onto memory in a way that still surprises me. One track can summon a feeling—or a whole moment—with intense clarity.

A familiar song can bring back images and emotions with a speed that catches me off guard. In that sense, music doesn't just remind us of a moment; it can feel like the moment returns.

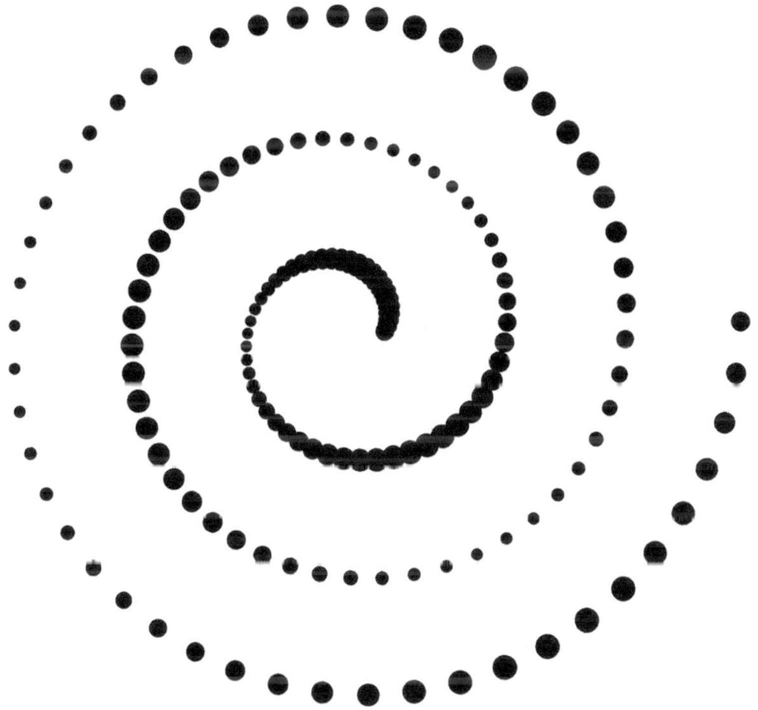

Some songs don't just remind us of moments—they are the moments.

Universal and Cultural Language

To me, music often crosses language and context more easily than words do. I've heard melodies move people who don't share the same background, even when the style is unfamiliar. At the same time, I'm aware that culture shapes what we expect and how we interpret rhythm, harmony, and instrumentation.

What still feels consistent in my own listening is how contrast communicates: tension and release, soft and loud, fast and slow. Those simple musical opposites can carry emotion even when the "meaning" isn't explained.

Music as Identity

Music can become part of how we define ourselves. Our playlists, favorite artists, and even the genres we reject can say something about who we are—or who we want to be. Music can become part of our emotional autobiography. It can express things words don't fully capture.

As artists and producers, recognizing this emotional bond can help us create more honestly and connect more deeply. We're not just making tracks—we may be shaping experiences, soundtracking someone's memory, or giving voice to what they feel.

Composing for the Heart

Music moves us because it bypasses logic and speaks straight to our emotional core. It's not just entertainment—it's emotional communication. When you create music that resonates, you're not just filling a playlist—you're becoming part of someone's internal world.

To me, music is emotion made audible.

And perhaps that's the most powerful role a music creator can play: not just to be heard, but to be felt.

A Personal Reflection

As someone who's lived and created music for decades, I'd like to share what this emotional connection means to me personally.

I've always felt a deep connection to music—not just as a listener but as someone who lives and breathes it. Growing up, I mainly listened to pop music, but what mattered most wasn't the genre—it was the feeling. I was so often so moved by music that I would listen to it loudly, immersing myself in the emotion it evoked. I used to sing with my brother in our childhood room, mimicking Beatles songs even though we didn't understand the lyrics. We didn't need to. We *felt* the music. Even as kids, the emotion carried through the melody and sound.

Later, through classical piano lessons, I learned to truly listen—to details, to dynamics, to the emotional current hidden in a phrase. That training didn't just teach me how to play—it sharpened my emotional ear. It shaped my taste and deepened the way I connect with music to this day.

When I compose, I don't just write notes—I follow my feelings. A track has to move me first. If it resonates with me deeply, I trust that it might do the same for someone else. In that way, music becomes a direct line from one soul to another.

Over time, all my experiences—the songs I've loved, the skills I've developed, the emotions I've explored—have shaped my musical identity. Creating music is, for me, an emotional mirror. It reflects who I am in that moment. And that reflection, in turn, becomes part of the emotional journey of someone listening.

That's the creator's perspective. The deeply personal one. And it's incredible to think that what I create in isolation might one day mean something powerful to a stranger on the other side of the world. Because music, when it's honest, speaks in ways nothing else can.

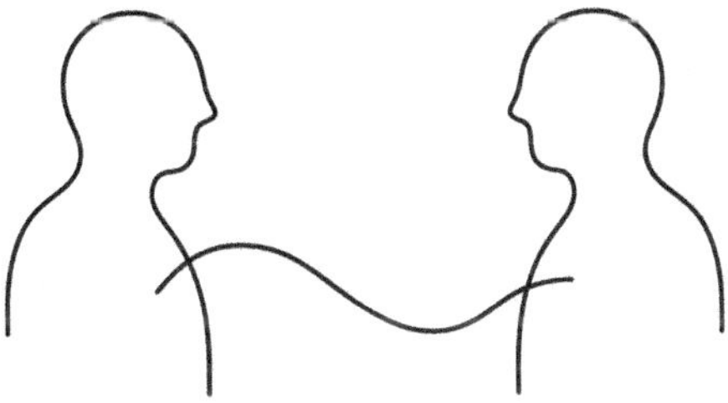

The most beautiful thing about music is that it connects people—heart to heart, without saying a word.

Action Items

- **Recall a defining musical moment.**
  Think of a song that is inseparably linked to a memory, place, or person in your life. Write a few sentences about *why* it affected you so deeply—not musically, but emotionally.
- **Listen for emotion, not preference.**
  Choose a piece of music outside your usual taste. Instead of judging whether you like it, focus on what emotion it conveys and how your body reacts.
- **Notice music as an emotional mirror.**
  Pay attention to what kind of music you're drawn to over the next few days. Ask yourself what emotional state it reflects or supports in you.
- **Create from feeling, not intention.**
  Sit down to make music without a concept or goal. Let your current emotional state guide the first sound you choose, and follow it without overthinking.

- **Observe how music shapes identity.**
  Reflect on how your musical tastes have changed over time. Write down what those shifts say about who you were—and who you are now.
- **Trust the emotional transfer.**
  Remind yourself that if a piece of music genuinely moves you, it doesn't need explanation or justification. Emotional honesty is often the strongest connection you can offer a listener.

Listening as a Creative Skill: From Passive Hearing to Intentional Sound Design

In the journey from silence to sound, listening is not merely a step—it is the very bridge that carries you across. While music production is often associated with creation, manipulation, and performance, listening is the hidden discipline that powers it all. And yet, few producers actively train their ears beyond technical feedback.

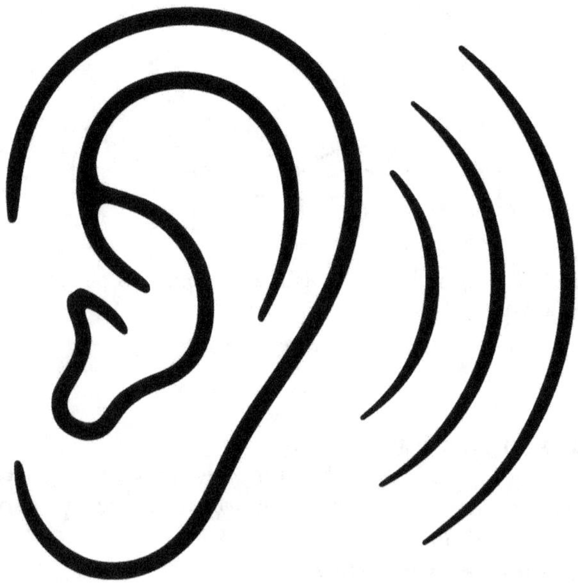

Listening is not passive—it's the most powerful creative act you have.

We often spend years refining our skills in synthesis, recording, or mixing, but overlook the foundation they rest upon—deep, intentional listening. Listening isn't something you just do with your ears; it involves the brain, the body, and often, emotion. It is both an instinct and a learned craft, and over time, it can become one of the most valuable tools in your creative process.

Listening Is a Skill, Not Just a Reaction

Many people confuse hearing with listening. Hearing is passive. Listening is intentional. In music production, it means tuning into not just what is loudest, but what is meaningful.

To become a better producer, you must become a better listener. This means not only identifying frequency imbalances or phase issues but also:

- Understanding the emotion in a performance
- Noticing how space is used (or unused)
- Recognizing when something feels cluttered or too sparse
- Picking up on what isn't said, what isn't played—the silence

Intentional listening also improves communication in collaborative settings. By being able to describe what you hear and feel, you're able to give better feedback and also receive it more openly. Listening becomes an act of respect—not just toward the music, but toward your collaborators and your audience.

As you develop as a producer, your ears evolve. What once seemed complex may become obvious. What once impressed you might now sound overdone. Each phase of your journey will invite a different relationship with listening. The key is to stay curious, critical, and open.

Hearing is automatic. Listening is a decision—and it's the decision that makes me a better producer.

Different Modes of Listening

Each phase of your creative process benefits from a different listening mindset. There are several ways to listen, and each reveals a different layer of understanding:

Emotional Listening

This mode is all about how music makes you feel. It bypasses the technical and speaks directly to your emotional core.

I remember once listening to the song "Just to Let You Know" by Cultured Pearls. My girlfriend at the time had just left me, and the emotional impact of the song was overwhelming. Still today, when I hear that track, it transports me back to that raw, emotional moment. This might be an extreme example, but any song evokes—or should evoke—some emotion. Absorb this and analyze what moved you the most.

When the emotion is strong enough, even imperfections disappear.

Analytical Listening

This is where your inner audio engineer steps in. You listen for EQ balance, compression artifacts, stereo imaging, phase issues, transients, and more.

For example, when I'm finalizing a mix, I often solo different frequency bands to analyze clarity and separation. This kind of listening is demanding and often best done in short, focused sessions to avoid ear fatigue.

You can have all the gear in the world, but if you can't hear what's wrong in a mix, it doesn't matter.

Referential Listening

This listening mode helps you compare your track with other professional productions in your genre.

Sometimes I listen to a well-mixed Daft Punk track to recalibrate my ears, especially for punch, groove, and dynamic balance. I also recommend creating playlists over time with tracks that you personally love and that you think sound absolutely perfect. If they fit the genre you work in, you can use them as references. I have such lists on Apple Music and Spotify, and they help me a lot in referential listening.

A trusted reference track can be your north star in the mix.

Exploratory Listening

This is about discovery. It's when you listen to new or unfamiliar genres without judgment, only curiosity.

While I'm mainly a music producer in the ambient/downtempo scene, I listen to other genres on purpose that I don't really like or wouldn't usually choose. I've discovered ideas that—when transformed—fit beautifully into my own work. It could be a texture, a sound effect, or an arrangement style that sparks a new direction.

Unexpected ideas show up more often when your ears are trained—and your musical diet is wide.

Narrative Listening

This mode involves following the structure and arc of a song. Is it telling a story? Is it keeping the listener engaged?

I often use this method when finishing a track. I close my eyes, listen from start to end, and ask: Am I still emotionally involved? If I lose interest, I revisit the arrangement and make adjustments. It's not about complexity—it's about flow.

A great song is a journey—it must take you somewhere.

Physical Listening

Music has a physical component—it moves you, literally. In this mode, you listen with your body.

For instance, I was once working on a song with a drum loop. It had a nice groove, but the dynamics lacked punch. I refined the mix so the drums hit with more impact. In the end, I had a version that didn't just sound better—it made me want to move. That's physical listening.

You don't just hear a groove—you feel it. That's when you know it's right.

Intuitive Listening

This approach involves stepping back. Put on the track quietly while doing something else. What sticks? What disappears?

One practice I use is listening at very low volume while doing something ordinary—washing dishes, making coffee, walking around the room. In that state, I'm not "analyzing," but I still notice what pulls my attention (or what disappears). It's a simple way to sense what's working without overthinking it.

Sometimes you need to stop listening with your mind and start listening with your instincts.

Critical Listening

Involves rigorous evaluation of sonic accuracy—how well the mix translates on various systems.

Producers often use critical listening when bouncing between studio monitors, car speakers, headphones, or even phone speakers. The aim is to catch flaws in balance, tonality, or presence that only appear in certain contexts.

Your mix isn't finished until it sounds good everywhere.

Environmental Listening

This tests how your track performs in real-world situations. Play it in a car, a shop, or in a playlist alongside others.

Sometimes I'll sneak one of my tracks into a public playlist and listen while driving or working out. Hearing it out of context offers a fresh perspective on energy and flow.

Music doesn't just live in the studio—it lives in the world.

Metacognitive Listening

This mode is less about the sound and more about how you're listening. Are you distracted? Biased? Overly critical?

For instance, if I'm listening in a bad mood, I try not to make final decisions. Metacognitive listening is about being self-aware—recognizing that your mindset affects your perception.

To truly listen to the music, you must also be listening to yourself.

Summary Table of Listening Modes

Listening Mode	*Short Description*
Emotional Listening	Focuses on the feelings and emotional response the music evokes
Analytical Listening	Examines technical elements like EQ, compression, stereo image, and clarity
Referential Listening	Compares your music to reference tracks for sonic quality and genre alignment
Exploratory Listening	Engages with unfamiliar genres to discover new textures and structures
Narrative Listening	Observes the song's story arc, transitions, and ability to maintain interest
Physical Listening	Listens to how music physically feels—groove, impact, body reaction
Intuitive Listening	Relies on instinct and subconscious impressions when casually listening
Critical Listening	Evaluates tonal balance and translation across playback systems
Environmental Listening	Assesses how a track feels in real-world settings like cars, cafes, or background
Metacognitive Listening	Reflects on how you're listening and identifies biases or habitual patterns

Listening Forward

Listening isn't just a passive act. It's an artistic decision, a craft, and a mirror. The better you listen—in all these modes—the better you will produce. These listening styles are not mutually exclusive. They overlap, evolve, and deepen over time. Rotate between them consciously. Train your ears like you train your instruments. Listening, truly listening, is what turns noise into music—and music into emotion.

Learn to listen deeply. Listening is the most important skill you have as a musician.

Action Items

- **Practice one listening mode per day.**
  Over the next week, choose one listening mode (emotional, analytical, narrative, physical, etc.) each day and apply it consciously to a single piece of music. Notice how your perception changes depending on *how* you listen.
- **Listen without fixing.**
  Play one of your own tracks from start to finish without touching the mouse, keyboard, or screen. Resist the urge to correct anything. Simply observe what holds your attention—and where it fades.

- **Train your emotional ear.**
Listen to a song that once moved you deeply. Ask yourself what creates that emotional impact: harmony, timing, silence, performance, texture, or memory. Write down what you discover.
- **Use low-volume intuition.**
Play a work-in-progress quietly while doing something else. Notice which elements still reach you and which disappear. Let this guide your next production decisions.
- **Expand your listening horizon.**
Intentionally listen to a genre you normally avoid. Don't judge whether you like it. Instead, listen for one sound, idea, or structural detail you could translate into your own work.
- **Reflect on how you listen.**
Before making important creative decisions, check in with yourself: Are you tired, distracted, emotionally charged, or overly critical? Sometimes the most important adjustment isn't in the mix but in your mindset.

The Art of Tempo and Groove: Why Timing Shapes Emotion

Tempo and groove are not just technical decisions—they are the pulse of emotion in music. Whether it's the driving energy of an uptempo dance track or the slow, meditative calm of ambient music, tempo can strongly shape how a piece feels. Groove, on the other hand, is about how rhythm breathes, moves, and carries us. Together, they can create a powerful emotional framework that shapes the listener's experience from the very first beat.

Why Tempo Matters

Tempo sets a track's energy and expectation. In my own listening, slower pacing often *feels* more introspective or tender, faster pacing more urgent, and mid-tempo grooves more balanced—reflective, but still moving forward. I don't treat these as fixed rules, just patterns I notice when I'm deciding how a piece should feel.

I've noticed that tempo can feel "body-aligned." Some tempos feel naturally grounded—neither rushed nor dragging—as if they match a comfortable pace of breathing and movement. When a track sits in that zone, it often feels easier for me to settle into it emotionally.

I often notice a similar pattern in film music and in record production: slower pacing can feel tender, reflective, or tragic to me, while faster rhythms tend to create urgency and forward motion. I don't hear this as a fixed rule, but as a useful emotional cue when shaping tempo.

But tempo is not just about beats per minute (BPM). It's about intention. Some producers set tempos intuitively based on what feels right rather than relying on a predefined BPM. Starting with a tempo that matches your emotional intent can help guide arrangement, instrumentation, and dynamics from the ground up.

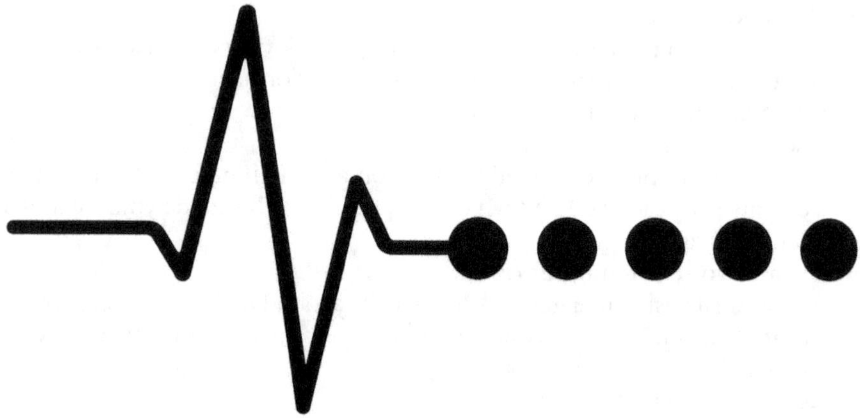

Tempo is the heartbeat of your track. When it aligns with your emotional message, the entire production falls into place more naturally.

Another powerful tool at your disposal is tempo modulation. Slowing a track at the end, much like a musical ritardando, can feel deeply emotional to me—almost like a breath out. I often hear that kind of deceleration as a signal of reflection, closure, and release. In Marconi Union's *Weightless*, I hear a gradual sense of slowing and settling across the piece, which to me feels like a gentle invitation to let tension dissolve.

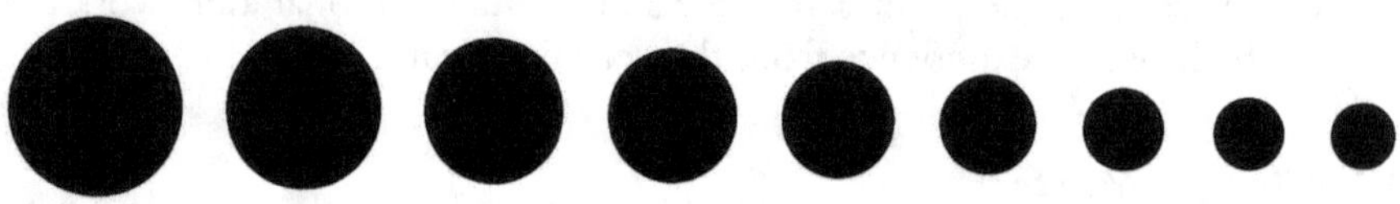

A subtle slowing down, like a ritardando, signals reflection and release—it can be more emotional than any chord change.

To my ears, that kind of tempo movement can change the *felt* emotional state of a piece without changing harmony or melody—simply by reshaping time.

The Subtle Power of Groove

Groove is not limited to genres like funk or hip-hop; it can be felt in almost every kind of music, including ambient and cinematic work. I think of groove as the way time moves inside a piece—the subtle placement of notes, the push and pull of timing, and the relationship between instruments.

What makes a rhythm feel alive is often not strict precision, but the small shifts within it. Perfectly quantizing everything to the grid can sometimes flatten that sense of movement. Tiny timing differences—when one element sits slightly behind or pushes a little ahead—can create depth, tension, and flow. Even a minimal beat can become hypnotic when those details are allowed to breathe.

In the end, feeling matters more than perfection. A perfectly aligned rhythm may sound clean, but it does not always create the strongest emotional response. Much of the magic lies in those slight imperfections and human nuances that make the music breathe.

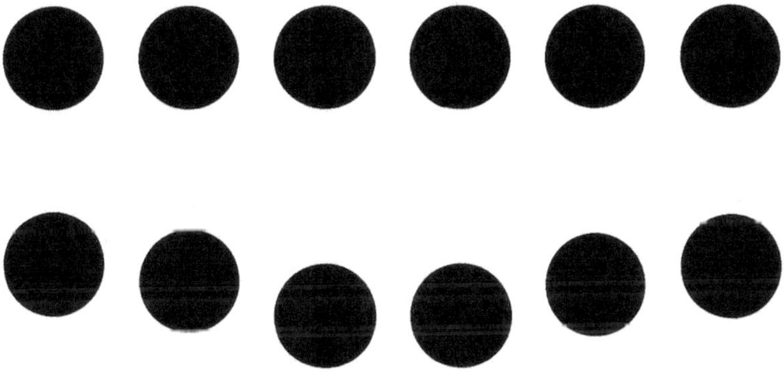

Groove lives in the spaces between the beats—it's what turns rhythm into emotion.

Real-World Examples

In electronic music, Bonobo's *Kerala* is one example that stands out to me. To my ears, the syncopation and off-beat movement create a kind of swirling momentum. The chopped vocal fragments and rhythmic push-pull give it a hypnotic forward drive that feels emotional as much as it feels rhythmic.

In ambient-influenced electronic music, I'm drawn to artists like Brian Eno and Tycho because the sense of "groove" can be extremely subtle. To my ears, the rhythm sometimes barely announces itself—yet the repetition, the pacing, and the small shifts still create emotional flow. With Tycho in particular, I associate the sound with spacious textures and gentle downtempo motion, where tiny changes in motif and delay make the music feel like it's moving even when nothing dramatic happens.

One example of tempo manipulation that stands out to me is Marconi Union's ambient track *Weightless*. As the piece gradually slows—almost like a long-form ritardando—I experience it as a soft landing. It's a reminder, to my ears, that subtle changes in pacing can shift the emotional weight of a track without changing a single harmony.

In a lot of pop and R&B, groove is what tells my body how to feel the track. With some Billie Eilish songs, what stands out to me is the use of broken, minimalist grooves—rhythm that leaves gaps on purpose. Those spaces create tension and shape the mood as much as any chord or lyric.

Groove and Human Feel

Some of the most emotional performances feel alive because they are slightly imperfect. Think of a live drummer's subtle swing or how a pianist pulls back a millisecond before striking a chord. These moments create connection. That's why many producers add swing, humanize MIDI performances, or even record real percussion or hand claps.

As a producer, you have the power to manipulate timing for emotional effect. You can intentionally offset elements to create tension or unity. You can slow a chorus slightly to make it feel heavier, or shift percussion ahead of the beat to lift the energy.

Don't underestimate the power of not quantizing everything. Keeping certain elements free of rigid timing preserves the expressive, human feel of your track.

Music is complex, with many layers of emotion, sound design, and technical nuance. Timing is one of those layers that touches both the technical and the emotional side. Getting it right doesn't mean making it perfect—it means making it feel true.

Personal Reflection

When I start a new piece of music, I often find myself tapping out a tempo before anything else—feeling it in my body and not just hearing it in my ears. That tempo becomes the anchor. Many of my most emotionally resonant songs started with a groove, not a melody. The moment I feel the tempo and the pulse working together, I know I've found the emotional entry point.

Some of my work in ambient music, for example, is built entirely around slow-evolving grooves. The repetition and subtle shifts become meditative—like breathing. It's amazing how much emotion you can communicate without a single lyric or chord change, simply by shaping time.

Sometimes, I even choose to slow a track down at the end, using tempo automation or ritardando-like structures. This gentle deceleration invites the listener to breathe, reflect, and land softly in silence.

Final Thoughts

Tempo and groove are the unsung heroes of emotional storytelling in music. They are not just structural choices—they are expressive tools. They shape how a track feels, how it moves, and how it resonates.

Trust your body when setting tempo. Listen to your emotional response when crafting groove. Let timing be not just technical, but intentional.

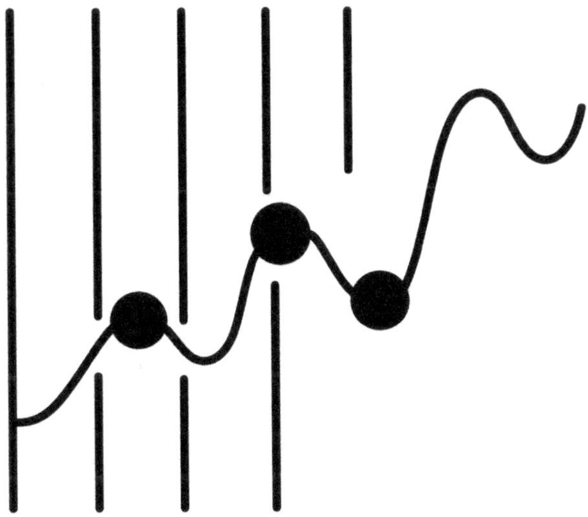

Groove is the soul's sense of time. Get the timing right, and the emotion will follow.

Action Items

- **Find the tempo in your body first.**
  Before opening your DAW, tap a tempo with your hands or feet that matches the emotion you want to express. Only then translate it into BPM. Notice how different it feels compared to choosing a tempo numerically.
- **Change nothing but the tempo.**
  Take an existing track or loop and try it at ±5–10 BPM. Observe how the emotional character shifts—calmer, heavier, more urgent, or more playful—without changing a single note.
- **De-quantize with intention.**
  Choose one rhythmic element (hi-hats, percussion, or piano) and slightly loosen its timing. Listen for when the groove starts to feel alive rather than messy. Stop there.
- **Listen for groove, not accuracy.**
  Close your eyes and listen to a rhythm without watching the grid. Ask yourself a simple question:
  Does this make me want to move, breathe, or lean in? Trust the answer.
- **Experiment with slowing down.**
  Try a subtle tempo slowdown toward the end of a track—or remove rhythmic elements entirely in the final section. Notice how this affects the sense of closure and emotional release.

- **Let repetition become meditation.**
  Create a short loop with minimal variation and let it run for several minutes. Instead of adding elements, focus on how tiny timing changes alter the emotional flow over time.

Building Emotional Connections: The Power of Vulnerability in Music

Why Vulnerability Matters

To me, music often crosses language in a way words can't. It can connect people emotionally and reveal things that are hard to say out loud. One of the most powerful tools in creating that connection is vulnerability. When an artist opens up and shares something honest, it invites the listener into an inner world—and that's when music stops being "just sound" and becomes an emotional journey.

It's the cracks in our walls, not the perfect facade, that let others truly see us.

A Personal Example

As a producer and artist, I've often found that my most meaningful pieces are the ones where I allow myself to be completely open—where the emotion is central to the listener's experience. Take my track "Peaceful," for example. I wrote it for my son as a private, deeply personal expression of what I felt in that moment. It wasn't created as a strategic release; it was created as truth.

Another example is my album *Dreamscapes*, composed during a time when I needed peace and solitude. I wrote what I felt—immersive music that helped me step away from the noise of the world. In both *Peaceful* and *Dreamscapes*, vulnerability isn't just a theme; it's the intention behind the sound. And over time, I've noticed that listeners tend to respond most strongly when that intention is real.

More Than Sadness

Vulnerability in music isn't limited to pain or hardship. It can be joy, hope, love, or even uncertainty. What matters, to me, is that the emotion feels unfiltered. I often sense when something is genuine, and I'm naturally drawn to songs that choose truth over polish.

When I listen to Adele's *Someone Like You*, the performance feels exposed—like nothing is hidden. And when I listen to Coldplay's *Fix You*, I hear how simplicity and restraint can carry comfort and hope. I'm not claiming one "formula" here—only that, as a listener, I connect most when the song invites me to feel with it, not just admire it.

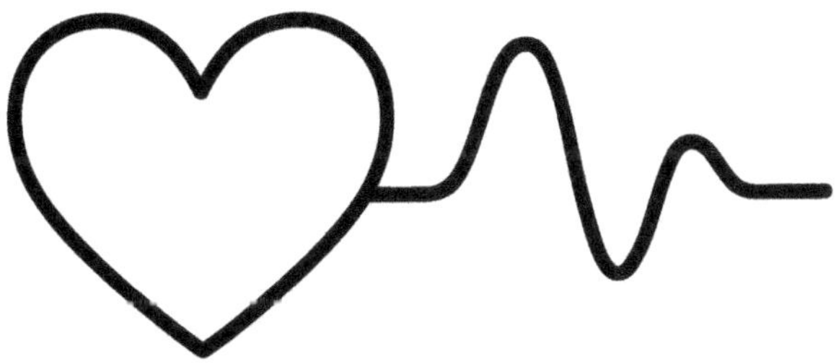

Every heartbeat carries music within it—vulnerability lets it be heard.

The Artist–Listener Bond

When you allow yourself to be vulnerable, you give your audience permission to feel deeply as well. They may be experiencing similar emotions, or they might simply be drawn to your openness. In my experience, songs tend to stay with people longer when that honesty is present—when the track feels like it was made from something real, not performed at a safe distance.

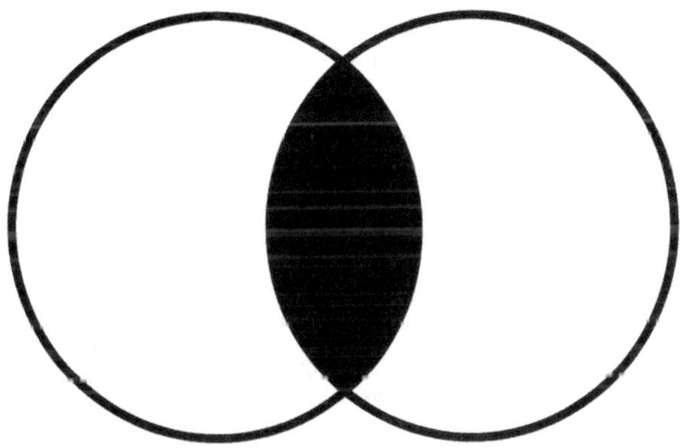

Vulnerability is the bridge where the artist and listener meet.

Risks and Rewards

Openness can feel exposing, especially when you fear criticism or misunderstanding. Yet music born from an honest place can carry a unique kind of power—it can feel healing, hopeful, and deeply comforting in ways words alone sometimes cannot. When a song carries genuine emotion, listeners may recognize something of themselves in it, and that recognition can build trust and empathy. Over time, this shared vulnerability can become the foundation for a deep emotional connection that keeps people returning to your music.

Practical Ways to Embrace Vulnerability

- **Write from real life**:
  Draw on both personal milestones and challenges so your songs carry authentic depth. This could be as simple as reflecting on a quiet morning with a loved one or processing a major life change—and don't filter the emotion to fit expectations.
- **Capture genuine moments**:
  Record during times of real emotion, even if technically imperfect. A slightly shaky vocal take can often carry more impact than a polished but detached performance.
- **Create space for feeling**:
  Leave room in arrangements for emotion to breathe. A stripped-back piano interlude or minimalist synth pad can give listeners space to absorb the feeling.
- **Shape emotion with dynamics**:
  Use volume, pauses, and textures to reflect mood—for instance, silence before a chorus can build anticipation, while soft strings can convey tenderness.
- **Collaborate with like-minded artists**:
  Work with others who understand your vision. They can help you uncover new emotional layers you might not explore alone.

Final Thought

In the creative process, don't shy away from the emotions that make you uncomfortable—lean into them. Listeners aren't looking for perfection; they're seeking authenticity. By embracing vulnerability and tying it directly to the emotional heart of your songs, you create the kind of depth that makes music unforgettable.

In vulnerability lies the deepest connection in music—share your soul, touch a heart.

Action Items

- **Identify the emotion you're avoiding.**
  Before starting a new piece, ask yourself quietly: *What feeling am I not sure I want to show right now?* That emotion is often the one worth exploring.
- **Create once without protection.**
  Set aside one session where the goal is not quality, release, or usefulness—but honesty. Don't ask whether it's "good." Ask whether it's *true*.
- **Keep the take that feels uncomfortable.**
  When a performance feels slightly exposed—too quiet, too fragile, too personal—don't delete it immediately. Listen again later and notice whether it carries more emotional weight than the safer alternatives.
- **Remove one layer instead of adding one.**
  If a track feels emotionally distant, resist the urge to enrich it. Strip something away and listen to what suddenly becomes audible: breath, space, intention.
- **Write for one person, not an audience.**
  Imagine a single listener—real or imagined—who matters to you. Let that person guide your choices, instead of an abstract idea of "listeners" or "success."
- **Notice what resonates after release.**
  Pay attention to which pieces people connect with emotionally, not numerically. Often, these are the tracks where you were most honest—not most polished.

Reflections Through Time: Revisiting Old Work with New Perspectives

As artists, we grow and evolve continuously. One of the most fascinating parts of this journey is returning to earlier works and seeing them in a new light. Revisiting old compositions often brings a mix of emotions—nostalgia, pride, perhaps some embarrassment—but most importantly, a deeper understanding of how time has reshaped our perspectives.

Recognizing the Emotional Core

When you revisit a piece years later, you're not just hearing the sound—you're engaging with a moment in time. Every note becomes a time capsule, carrying the mindset, emotions, and creative limitations of when it was made. I've looked back at older tracks with a critical ear, convinced that my newer productions better reflect my abilities. Yet, many still resonate on an emotional level, reminding me that technical skill is only one piece of the puzzle.

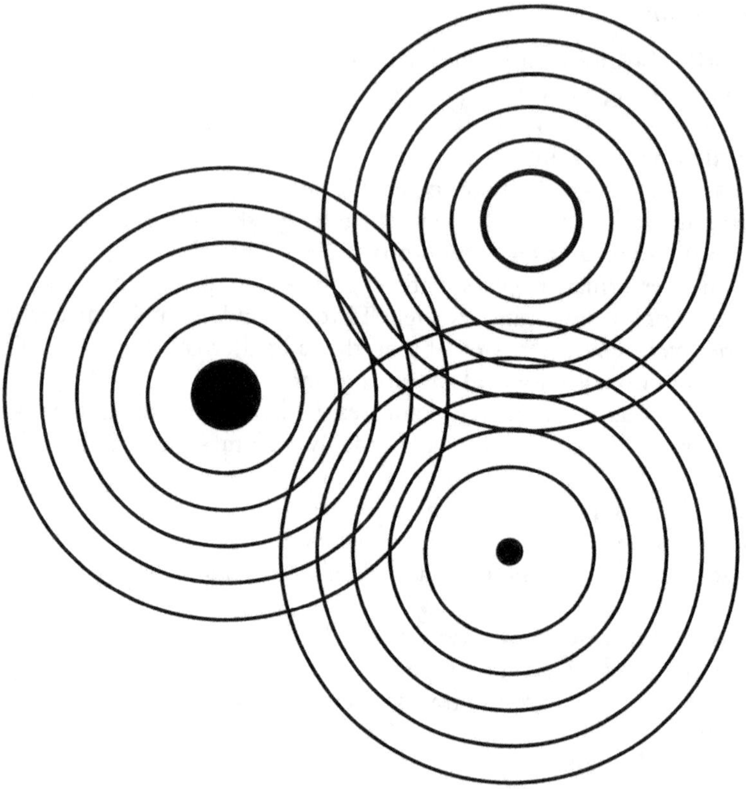

Every note is a drop in time—its ripples carry forward, shaping how we hear it years later.

Take my track *Peaceful*, for instance. Written for my son, it captured a deeply personal moment. Revisiting it, I was reminded that the connection listeners feel often has little to do with technical perfection—what seems to carry through is the emotion woven into the music.

The Magic in Limitations

Older works reveal the gap between who you were and who you've become. Songs once deemed imperfect may now show an authenticity that's difficult to recreate. Sometimes, the limitations of your younger self created a kind of magic—unexpected melodies, unique chord progressions, or raw production choices that feel fresh years later. These quirks often came from experimenting without the weight of industry expectations, producing results that were deeply personal and creatively free.

Breathing New Life into Old Creations

Revisiting older material can be a chance for transformation. With new tools, skills, and perspectives, you can enhance the original without losing its essence:

- **Remixing**:
  Add new layers, rhythms, or arrangements to shift the track's mood while keeping its core intact.
- **Remastering**:
  Improve clarity, depth, and balance with modern tools, aligning the mix with current sonic standards.
- **Alternative versions**:
  Create acoustic, orchestral, or stripped-down interpretations to highlight new emotional dimensions.
- **Genre reinterpretations**:
  Reimagine the piece in a different style—turning chillout into deep house, or reshaping an upbeat track into a cinematic slow-burn.
- **Self-covers**:
  Perform your own song anew with different instrumentation, tempo, or mood.

For example, I revisited my earlier piano piece "Serenity" and transformed it into an ambient interpretation with richer textures, additional layers, and a slower, more atmospheric feel in a "Slowed + Reverbed" version. This process allowed me to preserve the emotional spark of the original while applying the refined production skills I had developed over the years.

Knowing When to Leave Things Untouched

Sometimes, the best choice is to preserve an older work exactly as it is. Its imperfections may be the very reason it resonates. Leaving a track untouched can keep it as a pure snapshot of your creative journey at that time.

In the end, your past work captures where you were—creatively, emotionally, and personally. Revisiting it can reveal growth, inspire new directions, and remind you that the past often holds the seeds of your future.

Looking back with today's eyes, old melodies can sing new truths.

Action Items

- **Revisit without judgment**.
  Choose one older track and listen to it without the intention to fix or improve it. Ask only: *What emotion was I expressing back then?* Let that answer stand on its own.

- **Identify what still works.**
  Instead of focusing on what you would do differently today, note what still feels alive: a melody, a texture, a pacing choice. These elements are clues to your enduring artistic voice.
- **Separate emotion from execution.**
  When something feels "weak," ask whether it's technically outdated—or emotionally misaligned. Often, the feeling remains strong even when the production doesn't.
- **Decide consciously: evolve or preserve.**
  For each old piece you revisit, make a clear decision: *Am I honoring this as a time capsule—or allowing it to evolve?* Avoid changing it halfway without intention.
- **Use limitations as guidance, not embarrassment.**
  Notice what you *couldn't* do at the time—fewer tools, less knowledge, tighter constraints. Ask yourself how those limitations shaped the music in ways you might be missing today.
- **Let the past inform, not define, your present.**
  Don't measure old work against current standards. Instead, let it remind you how growth actually happens: step by step, song by song, without knowing where it leads.

The Art of Silence: Making Space Speak in Your Music

Silence as a Musical Force

In a world overflowing with noise, silence can be one of the most powerful tools in music production. To me, silence isn't "nothing"—it's a deliberate space where meaning can gather. Used intentionally, it creates contrast, tension, intimacy, and breath. It gives music shape, invites the listener to lean in, and can turn even the simplest notes into something profound. Music is, at its core, a dialogue between sound and space.

Silence in Music History

When I think about silence as part of music, John Cage's *4'33"* is one reference point that comes to mind—less as "a song" and more as a frame that makes the room itself audible. More broadly, I notice (as a listener) how pauses can punctuate phrases, build anticipation, and let dynamics breathe.

In film music, I often feel the emotional weight most strongly when everything goes still for a moment. And in contemporary pop and electronic music, I hear artists like Billie Eilish and James Blake using space in a similar spirit—pulling elements away so tension and fragility can sit in the foreground.

How Silence Shapes Attention and Emotion

I've noticed that when sound breaks into silence, my attention often sharpens. A rest or pause can create anticipation, reflection, or release. To me, silence functions like punctuation: without it, the musical "sentence" can feel rushed or unclear.

In ambient, neoclassical, or minimalist music, silence isn't just background—it's part of the composition. The spaces we leave unfilled invite imagination, giving listeners room to interpret and feel more deeply.

Silence can function like punctuation, shaping musical phrases and giving time its meaning.

Using Silence as a Creative Tool

Silence is never passive—it's an active compositional choice that shapes perception of rhythm, phrasing, and emotion. Here are key ways to harness it:

- **Breathing room**:
  Leave space between notes or sections so the music can settle. A single note can feel surprisingly powerful when it's given time to resonate. Sometimes space carries more weight than motion.
- **Dropouts**:
  Sudden removal of elements can heighten attention. A brief gap—or even a thinning of texture—can make the return of a full arrangement feel larger and more emotionally charged.
- **Isolated sounds**:
  Let a single resonant sound—a piano note, bell, or percussive hit—stand alone. Long reverbs and decays make silence feel expansive. These moments slow time, inviting reflection and intimacy.
- **Negative space**:
  Frame delicate moments with silence. A whispered vocal line or solo instrument in stillness can strike deeper than a full arrangement.
- **Silence as build-up**:
  A complete stop before a chorus or drop can create suspense. Silence (or near-silence) right before a reveal often makes the next moment feel larger through contrast.

The Power of Stripping Back

Producers often fall into the trap of adding layers, believing more equals better. Yet clutter can dilute emotion. Knowing when not to add is as important as knowing what to include. Before introducing a new element, ask: *Does it serve the song's message?* Sometimes it's absence, not presence, that heightens emotion.

When I listen to Ólafur Arnalds or Max Richter, I'm reminded how powerful restraint can be. Pieces like Arnalds' *Near Light* or Richter's *Horizon Variations* make me notice the role of space—the feeling that emotion can "breathe" when the arrangement doesn't rush to fill every moment. To my ears, that kind of silence reads as clarity.

Silence in My Own Music

In my own productions, I've often found that silence isn't just a break—it's a decision. In my cover of "The Power of Love," I began with just piano and vocals, letting vulnerability shine through minimalism. As the arrangement built to an orchestral climax, the initial restraint gave the ending more weight. Listeners frequently tell me that they return to my ambient tracks not just for the sounds, but for the spaces between them. Those quiet moments often leave the deepest impression.

Mixing with Space in Mind

Silence can act like an additional instrument. Build tracks around one or two core elements, ensuring every added layer enhances rather than competes. In mixing, prioritize clarity and let dynamics breathe through automation. For example, using volume automation to fade elements in and out, or creating sudden dropouts, can enhance tension and give the music room to breathe. When every sound has its space, the mix feels alive.

Less Can Say More

To me, silence is expressive. It gives listeners space to process, reflect, and connect. Used well, it can amplify intensity and clarity—like a breath in conversation that makes the next words land. I think of silence as the background your notes can stand against; it's where meaning has room to form.

Silence isn't the lack of sound—it's the presence of space, attention, and possibility.

Action Items

- **Listen for what isn't there.**
  In your next listening session, focus deliberately on the spaces: pauses, decays, breaths, transitions. Ask yourself where silence already works—and where it might be missing.

- **Remove before you add.**
  Before introducing a new layer, mute one existing element instead. Notice whether the emotional message becomes clearer rather than weaker.
- **Create one moment of intentional silence.**
  In a current or upcoming track, design a pause on purpose: before a chorus, after a climax, or between phrases. Treat it as a compositional decision, not an accident.
- **Let one sound stand alone.**
  Choose a single note, chord, or texture and give it full space—no accompaniment, no rhythm underneath. Listen to how its decay and resonance carry emotion on their own.
- **Use silence as an emotional signal.**
  Ask yourself what each quiet moment communicates: anticipation, intimacy, reflection, release. Silence should say something, even when nothing is played.
- **Trust restraint as strength.**
  When a piece feels "almost too empty," resist filling it immediately. Sit with that discomfort. Often, that edge is exactly where honesty and depth live.

The Art of Sonic Minimalism: Doing More with Less

In an age of unlimited plugins, endless tracks, and infinite sonic possibilities, one of the boldest creative choices you can make is to do less—but achieve more. Sonic minimalism isn't about restriction—it's about refinement and intention. It's the art of creating space for meaning, allowing each element in your track to speak with clarity and emotional resonance. By stripping back the excess, you make room for focus. You let the soul of the music breathe.

It's not just about fewer notes or layers—it's about using fewer tools, fewer instruments, and still making something emotionally rich and deeply resonant. With intention, even a single synth, a simple vocal, or a minimal beat can deliver what no vast wall of sound ever could.

Why Less Often Says More

Minimalism in music isn't about making things sound empty or unfinished. It's about making *room*—room for the listener to breathe, to feel, to interpret. Every sound has a job to do. If it doesn't serve a purpose—emotionally, rhythmically, or texturally—it risks becoming clutter.

When you pare back your arrangement to its essentials, something beautiful happens: the few sounds that remain start to shine. The groove deepens. The emotion becomes more immediate. The listener is invited into an intimate conversation rather than a crowded room.

Clarity through Contrast

Sonic minimalism creates contrast—not just in volume or frequency but in meaning. A sparse, dry vocal can feel more exposed and vulnerable next to a lush pad. A single piano note in a quiet moment can land harder than a full chord in a wall of sound.

It's this contrast—between presence and absence—that draws the ear in. Silence, decay, space—these become as important as the notes themselves.

Focus and Emotional Weight

When you limit the number of elements in a track, you give each one more weight. A single delayed guitar becomes not just a texture but a character. A filtered synth becomes the emotional lead. The listener starts to notice details: the tremble in a note's tail, the grit in a sample, the rhythm of a delay. Minimalism invites attention.

Too many ideas in one track can cancel each other out. But when you give space to one idea, it often becomes unforgettable.

Minimalism doesn't remove emotion—it concentrates it.

Famous Examples of Sonic Minimalism

When I listen to artists like Nils Frahm, Brian Eno, or Ólafur Arnalds, I'm reminded of how much can be done with very little. With Eno's ambient work, I often experience just a few slowly shifting textures as enough to hold my attention. And with Arnalds, the sparse combinations—piano, subtle strings, small electronic details—feel emotionally weighty to me precisely because there isn't much competing for space.

Coldplay is another reference point for me. In songs like "The Scientist or Fix You," I notice moments where simplicity does a lot of emotional work—where a few essential elements set the tone before the arrangement expands. To my ears, that restraint makes the later build feel more meaningful. I'm not presenting this as a universal rule, only as an example of how minimal choices can carry a lot of emotional weight.

When I listen to Billie Eilish's "when the party's over," what stands out to me is how little is needed: sparse piano, soft textures, and an intimate vocal that leaves space for vulnerability. To my ears, the restraint is what makes the track feel so close-up—proof that minimalism can be bold when the emotional focus is clear.

Sonic minimalism isn't limited to instrumentation. It also includes the choice to limit gear. In my experience, working with fewer tools can sharpen my attention and push me deeper into the sounds I already have. When I know my tools deeply and use them intentionally, I often discover things that a larger arsenal might distract me from finding.

Escaping the Gear Trap: Overcoming Gas

One of the biggest obstacles to sonic minimalism is the urge to believe that more tools will make the music better. In my experience, it often does the opposite: too many synths and plugins can become a burden instead of a boost.

With endless options, it's easy to fall into tweaking, preset-surfing, and distraction. You end up choosing tools instead of making music. The result can be overwhelmed, unfinished tracks, and a scattered sonic identity.

When I work with fewer tools on purpose, my focus sharpens. I stop chasing the next thing and return to listening, exploring, and expressing.

Intentional limitations foster resourcefulness. They make you a better producer—not because you have more, but because you do more with what you have.

In my own production workflow, I try to get the sounds I need from my hardware synths first. This approach not only reinforces a consistent sonic identity—since familiar instruments and timbres thread through my productions—but it also enhances my creativity and efficiency. By focusing on a few trusted tools, I avoid distraction, make decisions faster, and achieve more cohesive results. For example, in mastering, I rely primarily on a handful of carefully chosen plugins. Over time, I've developed a deep understanding of how they behave, allowing me to shape the sound with precision and confidence. Working consistently with these familiar tools has deepened my connection to my own sound. It strengthens my workflow and creative identity.

This approach helps me maintain a consistent sonic fingerprint that listeners can recognize and feel.

Think back 30 years—before the era of virtual instruments and countless plugin options. When I think about earlier production eras, I'm reminded how creatively rich work can emerge from a much smaller set of tools. You don't need 30 compressors or dozens of EQs to make great music. What truly matters, in my experience, is knowing how to use the tools you have—and how that use reinforces your sonic identity. Working consistently with a familiar set of instruments, effects, and plugins can help you craft a signature sound that listeners may connect with. It's not just about making do with less—it's about making more of what you already have. The knowledge and experience you bring to the process can matter far more than the gear you collect.

After all, what's the use of owning a Steinway grand piano if you don't know how to play?

The Courage to Stop Adding

Sometimes the hardest part of producing isn't starting—it's stopping. The temptation to keep layering, tweaking, and polishing can dilute the soul of a track. Sonic minimalism requires the courage to say, "This is enough."

It's not laziness. It's mastery. Knowing when to stop is a creative decision that requires awareness, restraint, and trust in the emotional power of your core idea.

The real discipline isn't what you add—it's what you have the courage to leave out.

Action Items

- **Reduce before refining.**
  Take a current track and mute at least one element you like. Don't replace it. Sit with the result and notice whether clarity, focus, or emotional impact increases.
- **Limit your palette on purpose.**
  For your next piece, commit to a maximum of three core sound sources (for example: one synth, one rhythmic element, one melodic voice). Let depth come from interaction, not quantity.
- **Choose familiarity over novelty.**
  Work with tools you already know well. Avoid adding new plugins or instruments for this project. Observe how confidence and speed increase when you stop searching and start listening.
- **Identify the emotional lead.**
  Ask yourself: *What is the one element carrying the emotional message?*
  Shape everything else around supporting—or getting out of the way of—that element.

- **Practice intentional stopping.**
  Set a clear endpoint for your session. When you reach it, stop adding. Listen once more and ask: *Does this already say what I want it to say?* If yes, trust it.
- **Notice where space does the work.**
  Pay attention to moments where silence, decay, or restraint communicates more than another layer ever could. These moments often define your signature sound.

Creative Routines and Rituals: Cultivating Consistency, Inspiration, and Flow

One of the most persistent myths about creativity is that it requires inspiration to strike first. In my experience, it often works the other way around: inspiration follows action. This is why routines, habits, and rituals matter so much. They're not constraints but creative scaffolding.

Whether you're composing ambient textures or building a dance floor banger, having a regular, intentional practice can open space for new ideas and deepen your creative flow. A consistent practice can help signal to your mind and body that it's time to enter a creative headspace. It's not about waiting for a flash of genius—it's about showing up consistently so that inspiration has somewhere to meet you.

Creativity is not a lightning bolt. It's a doorway you unlock each day by showing up.

Rituals That Ground and Guide

A creative ritual can be as simple as turning on a favorite lamp before starting, or as elaborate as a soundwalk in the forest with field recording gear. What matters is that the ritual cues your brain: "Now it's time to create."

A simple method I recommend is using "creative prompt" cards—short, slightly cryptic instructions you draw at random when you feel stuck. The point isn't that the prompt is "correct," but that it interrupts your default habits. A random nudge can break the loop of overthinking, shift your attention to a new angle, and get your hands moving again. Once you're in motion, intuition has something to react to, and the next decision starts to feel obvious.

Rituals can also build creative momentum. They remove friction. Instead of waiting for motivation, you're already moving. Just lighting a candle, opening your DAW, or tweaking a synth patch can get you into a creative mindset.

You don't find your flow. You create the conditions where flow can find you.

I've also found value in switching roles—or switching hats, so to speak. When I'm arranging a song, I try to stay in that creative, intuitive mindset. But when it comes time to mix or master, I deliberately approach the session with fresh ears—sometimes even the next day. The mindset required for mixing is very different from composing. You need distance. Perspective. Sometimes I even take my track out of the studio—listen in the car or on a walk—or better yet, I play it for someone who's never heard it before. The moment they're listening, I hear it with completely new ears. It's one of the best reality checks for whether something truly works.

Daily Practice: The Power of Showing Up

You don't need to wait for big, uninterrupted blocks of time. In my experience, doing a little bit each day—even if it's only 15 minutes—can be more powerful than waiting for ideal conditions. It's not about output—it's about consistency. And over time, consistency often beats intensity.

One approach I find helpful is the 1% method: instead of pushing for huge leaps, focus on getting just a little better each day. It might seem small in the moment, but those micro-improvements can accumulate over time. Like compound interest, daily creative practice can build into something meaningful and lasting. It's not just about skill—it's also about action. You don't need to finish a masterpiece every session; just do one thing that moves your project forward. Each tiny step adds up. The key is showing up and making steady movement—even if it's just a small brushstroke in a much bigger painting.

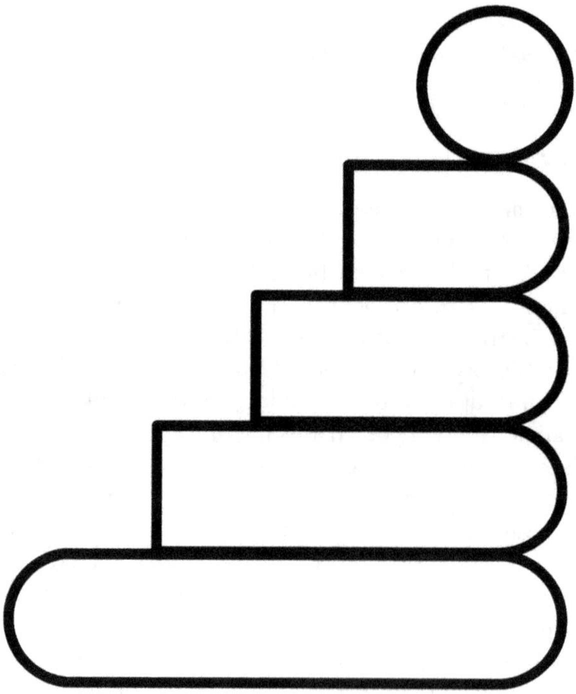

Consistency compounds—step-by-step, small daily actions rise into lasting creative growth.

Only finished ideas make it into the world. Let your routine be the bridge between inspiration and realization.

Micro-routines can help here:

- Set a specific time each day for creative work—even if just 10 minutes—so your brain knows when to prepare.
- Keep a "scratchpad" project open at all times, where you allow yourself to play freely without judgment.
- Always end your session by leaving a small note for tomorrow—what you were thinking or where you left off.
- Create a ritual of exporting a daily "audio sketch"—no matter how rough.
- Do a 5-minute listening session to your favorite track before starting to tune into the mood.
- Start your DAW by loading a random sample or preset and responding to it with curiosity.
- Save unfinished ideas in a dedicated "sketches" folder so you can revisit them without pressure.
- Build a 'creative warm-up' routine, such as finger exercises on a MIDI controller, or sound design play.
- Set a timer for 20 minutes and noodle with no goal.
- Start each session by remixing a favorite loop or preset.
- End each day by exporting a rough bounce, no matter what stage you're in.
- Begin sessions with 3 minutes of silence to reset your focus.
- Open an old project just to explore and learn from it.
- Record a short vocal memo describing what you're trying to create.
- Spend five minutes naming and organizing files to reinforce your project's importance.
- Review your last session's bounce and journal your immediate reaction.

A page stays empty only until you begin.

Ideas show up constantly—but finishing is what makes them real. After a stretch of unfocused creativity, that lesson becomes obvious: half-built thoughts rarely leave a mark. It's refining and completing that turns potential into something people can actually feel. Let this be your nudge to choose one idea and carry it all the way to the end.

These actions build creative muscle memory. They also reduce the fear of the blank page.

Creative Environment: Shape Your Space

Your workspace matters. It's not about fancy gear—it's about how the space makes you feel. A cluttered desk may drain you. A well-lit corner with your favorite headphones might uplift you. Consider your environment an extension of your creativity.

Some suggestions:

- Use lighting and plants to make your space inviting.
When I created my studio space, I made sure I really felt comfortable with everything and that it looks clean and inviting. I even have a little sofa in the corner to relax or listen from a distance instead of always sitting in the sweet spot between my studio monitors. That simple touch helps shift perspective and makes the space more human and flexible.
- Keep the tools you use most within reach.
I, for example, have my favorite synths positioned around my workspace in the studio. If I turn my chair, I can immediately reach and play one of them. I've noticed that the gear that's easily accessible gets used far more often—those synths become part of my creative flow. The others, placed out of reach, tend to gather dust. This setup makes a big difference in how spontaneously and often I create.
- Remove distractions—physically and digitally.
I like it clean and tidy so that I can focus on my art purely. Cluttered spaces are distracting to me for some reason. Even on my computer, I keep a well-organized file system so that I can easily find my files, samples, and projects. I always use the same naming patterns and folder structures to stay fast and efficient.

A clear space creates a clear mind.

When your space is primed, your focus sharpens. You'll spend less time fiddling and more time flowing.

My Own Experience

I take time every day to just do a little bit—no pressure, just showing up. Most of the time, this naturally turns into doing more. I play around with sounds, improvise, and often find that the sound itself sparks inspiration. In fact, I'd say sound is one of my greatest sources of inspiration. Exploring a new synth, hearing a surprising texture, or just sitting at the piano and letting my fingers wander—all of this often leads to new ideas.

Sometimes I deliberately listen to a specific genre or artist to set a mood or create a certain energy. With that inspiration in mind, I start experimenting with similar sounds or ideas. It usually evolves into something completely different, but it gives me a point of departure.

I've also learned to stay open to whatever happens. I might sit down intending to create an ambient track, but end up producing something that leans more toward downtempo or even cinematic. That's perfectly fine. Don't force yourself into a predefined idea. Let the flow dictate where you go. When you allow the creative process to unfold naturally, the result is often more authentic and compelling.

Sound is a conversation partner. If you listen closely, it always has something to say.

The most important insight I've gained from this routine is that inspiration doesn't come before the work—it arrives while you're in the process. Each time I engage, even for a short while, something creative is set in motion. That's the power of simply starting.

Final Thoughts

Routines and rituals are not about control; they are about cultivation. When you craft intentional habits around your creative process, you remove resistance and increase your receptiveness to new ideas. Whether through a walk, a single synth patch, or a random card draw, your creative self responds best when it knows when and where to show up.

Inspiration isn't something I wait for—it's something I meet halfway, through rhythm, curiosity, and simply showing up every day. When you understand this, you stop looking for perfect conditions and instead create them. Creative momentum builds not from occasional intensity but from consistent effort over time. It's about building trust with your creative self—showing up regularly, even when it feels uncertain, and letting that repetition shape your confidence and output.

What you do every day matters more than what you do once in a while. Make creativity part of your rhythm.

I don't wait for inspiration—I invite it by showing up, even on the days I don't feel ready.

Action Items

- **Design a personal start ritual.**
  Choose one simple, repeatable action that signals "creative time" to your brain—lighting a lamp, opening a specific project template, or listening to one reference track. Use it every session.
- **Commit to showing up, not finishing.**
  Define a daily minimum (10–20 minutes). Treat presence as success. If inspiration comes, let it extend the session—but never require it.
- **Separate creation from evaluation.**
  Clearly divide composing sessions from mixing or refining sessions. Avoid technical judgment while generating ideas. Distance creates clarity.

- **End every session with a breadcrumb.**
  Before stopping, leave a short note, marker, or audio memo describing what comes next. This removes resistance when you return.
- **Create a "no-pressure" sketch space.**
  Maintain a dedicated project or folder for rough ideas only. No expectations, no finishing—just exploration. This protects curiosity.
- **Use micro-routines to defeat inertia.**
  Start sessions with a fixed, low-effort action:

  - 5 minutes of sound design
  - Playing one synth patch
  - Free improvisation
  - Momentum often follows motion.

- **Limit session goals to one intention.**
  Decide in advance: *today is for rhythm*, *today is for harmony*, or *today is just for listening*. Narrow focus increases flow.
- **Shape your environment intentionally.**
  Adjust lighting, clutter, and accessibility so your most-used tools are within reach. Make your space invite creation rather than demand effort.
- **Trust sound as your guide.**
  Begin sessions by exploring sound without a plan. Let texture, tone, or rhythm suggest direction instead of forcing an idea.
- **Track consistency, not output.**
  Keep a simple log of days you showed up—not what you made. Over time, consistency becomes visible motivation.

Creating with Constraints: The Power of Limits in a World of Infinite Options

In today's world of music production, we are surrounded by endless possibilities. Thousands of sample libraries, synthesizers, effects plugins, virtual instruments, and presets lie at our fingertips. With just a few clicks, we can access sounds that once required entire studios to produce. This abundance can feel like a blessing—but it can also become a burden. In my experience, with so many options, decision fatigue, perfectionism, and creative paralysis can creep in.

Paradoxically, having too many choices can sometimes make it harder to create.

That's where creative constraints come in. Setting boundaries—whether in tools, time, structure, or process—can actually expand creativity rather than limit it. Constraints create focus. They remove the overwhelming need to try everything and instead invite you to go deeper with what you have.

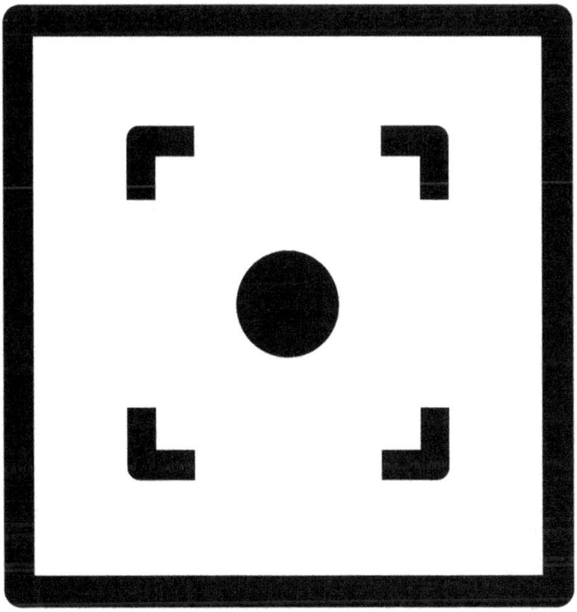

Within limits, creativity finds its sharpest focus.

Why Constraints Work

Constraints can remove distractions. In my experience, they reduce decision overload and help me stay in a creative flow. When I limit my palette, I tend to think more inventively about how to use it. Instead of spending hours scrolling through sounds, I'm more likely to shape them myself. Instead of waiting for the perfect sample, I'm more likely to commit to making something unique.

Here are a few examples:

- **Creative prompt cards**:
  A small set of short, intentionally open-ended prompts you draw at random to interrupt creative autopilot. Used as a quick reset when a session stalls, they introduce gentle constraints that shift perspective, reframe decisions, and often reveal fresh solutions—simply by forcing your next move to come from a new angle.
- **The Beatles (early tape-era limitations)**:
  When I think about recordings made under tighter technical limits, I'm reminded that committing early and using arrangement as a creative tool—can sharpen an idea.

- **Daft Punk's album *Homework***:
  As a listener, I associate this album with a raw, focused character—music that feels committed to a clear palette rather than to endlessly expanded options.
- **Lo-fi music aesthetics**:
  By embracing imperfections, limited gear, and noise artifacts, producers create a warm, nostalgic atmosphere that wouldn't exist with pristine high-end tools.

How Constraints Support Creativity

There's a mental side to this, too. When I give myself fewer options, I notice that I hesitate less. Limiting tools or setting a time boundary creates a simple framework that narrows focus and leaves more space for imagination.

For me, creativity tends to thrive when there's some structure—enough boundary to give the work direction, without boxing it in.

Types of Constraints in Music Creation

Type of Constraint	*Description*	*Musical Example*
Tool Based	Restricting yourself to a single instrument, plugin, or sound source	Producing an entire track using only a single hardware synth or sampler
Time Based	Working within a fixed time frame to limit over-editing or procrastination	Finishing a track sketch in one hour or mixing a song within two sessions
Harmonic Constraints	Composing with limitations in key, mode, or chord progressions	Writing a track that stays entirely in D minor or uses only three specific chords
Rhythmic Constraints	Using fixed tempos, time signatures, or rhythmic motifs	Composing a track in 3/4 or basing it entirely on a triplet groove
Textural Constraints	Limiting the types of textures or sonic layers used	Using only percussive sounds or only ambient pads in a composition
Recording Constraints	Using only live recordings or acoustic sources	Creating a track using only field recordings or one vocal take without edits
Performance Based	Writing music you must be able to perform without editing	Only recording compositions you can play live from start to finish
Conceptual Constraints	Centering a track around a single emotional, visual, or narrative idea	Composing an ambient piece inspired by a painting or a memory

Practical Ways to Create with Constraints

Here are some ways you can introduce healthy creative boundaries:

- Use only one synth for an entire track.
- Limit yourself to five plugins or effects.
- Set a time limit (e.g., write a full sketch in one hour).
- Use only sounds you record yourself.
- Choose one key, tempo, or rhythmic motif and build around it.
- Force yourself to finish a track without using your go-to tools.
- Try composing without the screen—on an acoustic instrument or on paper.

The result? You stop tweaking and start creating. You get to know your tools better. And you often end up with something more original and personal.

My Own Experience

To be honest with you, I've collected so many plugins over the years that I sometimes don't even know what I have anymore. I'm a victim of the plugin industry too, I must admit. It's so tempting to grab the latest tool, thinking it will be the one that makes everything easier or better.

Over time, however, I found that using external equipment—actual instruments and hardware synths—is more creatively fulfilling for me. It slows me down just enough to think. And more importantly, it contributes to "my own" sound. When I use certain synths repeatedly, I not only know them better and can work faster with them, but I feel more connected to the sound they produce. Their unique tonal qualities have become part of my signature. Coming back to these instruments feels like coming home. The sound is familiar, and often, I instinctively know which synth to reach for when an idea hits.

In contrast, when I use plugins, I often feel overwhelmed by thousands of presets and menus. I know my hardware synths also offer endless possibilities, but interacting with a physical instrument—turning real knobs, playing real keys—feels entirely different from clicking around with a mouse. That tactile engagement makes me more creative in the end.

That said, I absolutely use VSTs too. They're amazing tools and sometimes just the right thing for a particular task. But I try to stay aware of how I use them and not let them lead the process.

Another example of how I apply constraints: for my EP *In Silence*, I set myself a very clear rule. I wanted to write every song purely on the piano—no computer composition allowed. My goal was to internalize each piece to the point where I could play it by heart before even thinking about recording. This constraint had a huge impact on the outcome. By the time I entered the studio, I had rehearsed the songs so many times that I could focus entirely on the feeling and nuance during recording rather than on hitting the right notes.

Over time, I've noticed the same pattern in many great performances: the more the material is internalized before recording, the freer the delivery becomes. When the lyrics, melodies, or parts live in your body—rather than on the screen—you can focus on emotion, timing, and presence instead of "getting it right." That idea stayed with me, and it's one reason I love constraints: they reduce mental noise and make room for real performance.

Final Thought

Too many choices can lead to hesitation. Too many tools can distract from expression. When you create limits, you often unlock a deeper creative voice. Don't fear working with less. Embrace it—and you might discover more of yourself in the process.

Constraints are not the enemy of creativity. They are its catalyst.

Action Items

- **Define one clear constraint per session.**
  Before you start, decide on *one* boundary—tool, time, key, or concept. Do not stack multiple constraints unless you're experienced with the approach. One limit is enough to sharpen focus.
- **Commit to a single sound source.**
  Create a full sketch or track using only one synth, one piano, or one sampler. Explore its full expressive range instead of reaching for alternatives.
- **Set a time boundary—and respect it.**
  Use a fixed window (30, 60, or 90 minutes). When the timer ends, stop. This trains decision-making and reduces overthinking.
- **Remove choice before you create.**
  Temporarily hide or disable plugins you don't plan to use. Fewer visible options reduce cognitive load and keep you in flow.
- **Work without the screen.**
  Compose one piece away from the DAW—on piano, guitar, paper, or voice memo. Focus on emotion and structure before production.
- **Limit harmonic or rhythmic material.**
  Write a track using:

  - one key only
  - three chords maximum
  - one rhythmic motif

  This forces depth over variety.
- **Finish something imperfect.**
  Choose a sketch and finish it without switching tools or rethinking the concept. Completion under constraint builds confidence and momentum.

- **Rotate constraints weekly**.
  For one week, limit tools. Next week, limit time. Another week, limit structure. This keeps the practice fresh and trains adaptability.
- **Identify tools that feel like "home."**
  Notice which instruments or methods consistently lead to flow. Prioritize these in future sessions to reinforce your sonic identity.
- **Reflect after each constrained session**.
  Ask:

  - What did the limitation remove?
  - What did it reveal?
  - Did I go deeper instead of wider?

  Write one sentence. That's enough.

Embracing Mistakes as a Creative Tool: Turning Accidents into Art

In the controlled world of DAWs, plugin chains, and automation curves, it's easy to think that every sound must be meticulously planned and polished. But sometimes, the most inspiring breakthroughs don't come from perfect planning—they come from imperfection. From noise and glitches to human error and technical malfunctions, mistakes can transform a sterile production into something deeply alive and emotionally resonant.

From Error to Emotion

One example that often comes to mind for me is the unexpected use of instruments and gear. When I think of machines like the Roland TR-808 or TB-303, I think less about their original purpose and more about what can happen when artists use tools in ways they were never expected to be used. For me, that is a powerful reminder that unusual sounds can become emotionally defining.

Sometimes a rough, unstable, or imperfect texture gives a track its identity. What first seems like a flaw can turn out to be the very thing that makes the music feel human, alive, and memorable.

I have often found that an emotionally convincing idea matters more than technical polish. A fragile take, an unintended distortion, or an awkward detail can carry a truth that a more refined version might lose. Not everything needs to be corrected. Sometimes the original spark lives precisely in what was unplanned.

These moments remind me that mistakes are not always problems to solve. They can open new creative paths, interrupt habit, challenge control, and lead us closer to something honest. What begins as an error can become the emotional center of a piece.

Perfection gives order. Mistakes give life.

My Own Experience

When I recorded one of my piano ideas on the Waldorf Zarenbourg, the internal noise from the instrument—something I usually would filter or edit—suddenly became part of the emotion of the piece. The ambient hiss and mechanical resonance gave it a cinematic, almost nostalgic texture that a pristine recording couldn't replicate. Rather than re-recording it, I leaned into the imperfection. What was originally a flawed take turned out to be a defining sound for the entire track. It helped the music breathe, live, and connect on a deeper level.

When I worked with Andreas Bach on our song "Embracing Love," we used a Kalimba toy instrument in a different way. We turned the Kalimba around and hit the side with our thumbs. The resulting sound was a collection of overtones from the Kalimba. It was a very low sound, but it had an interesting timbre to it. We analyzed the overtone spectrum and discovered that hitting the left and right sides created slightly different resonances. We recorded both into a sampler, analyzed the tonality, and realized we essentially had two different chords to work with. That signature, self-made sound became the sonic foundation of the entire song—and something truly unique that could only come from experimentation.

Since then, I've trained myself to listen not just for what went wrong but what went *right in the wrong*. A pop in the audio, an unquantized hit, or a misplayed chord might seem like mistakes at first—but in the right context, they become the exact thing that makes a track feel human.

Embracing the Unexpected

Mistakes force us to confront our expectations. In a world where so much music is polished to the point of perfection, leaving in a rough edge or unintended texture can set your work apart. It makes the listener *feel* something real.

Here are some ways to embrace creative accidents:

- **Leave the mic rolling**:
  Capture the in-between moments. You never know when a background noise, spoken word, or tuning drift might add unexpected charm.

- **Record in imperfect environments**:
  Room noise, environmental ambiance, and natural reverb can bring authenticity.
- **Experiment with "wrong" takes**:
  Keep alternate versions or "mistake" bounces. Revisit them later with fresh ears.
- **Let sounds bleed**:
  Sometimes, mic bleed or overlapping frequencies create beautiful chaos. Don't fix it too soon.
- **Allow for limitations**:
  Use outdated gear, old plugins, or unconventional workflows to invite surprises.

I can't prevent every flaw in a recording—but I've learned not to erase it too fast. Sometimes the "problem" is the personality.

Final Thoughts

In a perfection-driven culture, learning to embrace mistakes is a radical act of creativity. The artist's job is not just to control sound, but to *listen differently*—to hear value where others might hear noise. Often, what we dismiss as failure holds the seed of something unforgettable.

In the right context, a mistake isn't failure—it's an opportunity.

Action Items

- **Delay correction on purpose**.
  When something sounds wrong, resist the impulse to fix it immediately. Let the mistake live for a while and listen again later. Ask yourself: *What would be lost if I removed this?*
- **Create a safe space for imperfection**.
  Dedicate at least one session per week to exploration without judgment—no editing, no quantizing, no cleanup. Let the goal be discovery, not polish.
- **Archive your "mistakes"**.
  Save flawed takes, glitches, and odd bounces in a separate folder. Revisit them weeks or months later. Distance often reveals emotional value you couldn't hear before.
- **Listen emotionally, not technically**.
  When an accident happens, don't analyze it first. Ask only one question: *Does this make me feel something?* Emotion comes before explanation.
- **Intentionally break a rule**.
  Choose one technical rule you normally follow—clean signal, perfect timing, pristine sound—and consciously violate it in a controlled way. Observe what changes emotionally.

- **Redefine success for the session.**
  Instead of asking "Did I get it right?," end the session by asking: *Did I discover something I wouldn't have planned?* Let discovery be your metric.

The Art of Completion: Finishing Songs with Confidence and Clarity

In a world of infinite plugins, endless tweakability, and constantly shifting standards, one of the hardest questions a music producer can face is: *When is this song finished?*

The journey from idea to release often begins with energy, inspiration, and clarity. But somewhere in the middle—or worse, toward the end—we hit resistance. We wonder: Should I tweak the EQ on the snare one more time? Should I replace the synth lead? What if I added another vocal layer? The rabbit hole of possibilities opens wide, and the finish line seems to blur.

The Myth of Perfection

Perfectionism is often disguised as professionalism. We think we're improving a song, when in fact, we're avoiding letting it go. But the truth is, no song is ever "perfect." Even your favorite artists likely hear things they would change in their most successful tracks.

Perfection, in music production, is not a destination. It's a moving target. What mattered yesterday might not matter today. And that's okay. Art isn't about perfection. It's about communication, emotion, and resonance.

There's also a danger in perfecting the life out of your work. The longer we stay in the polishing phase, the more we tend to erase the spontaneous and emotional magic that made the track special in the first place. We smooth over the texture. We correct the quirks. And slowly, the track may lose the essence that made it feel alive.

I often think of it this way: finishing music is not about arriving at perfection. It's about capturing a moment. Letting it breathe. Letting it live in the world.

What Finished Feels *Like*

So how do you know a song is done? Often, it's not about ticking every box on your production checklist. It's about a feeling. A sense of arrival. A moment when listening back makes you feel something—and nothing feels missing.

Here are a few signs that a song might be finished:

- You can listen from start to finish without reaching for the mouse.
- The track holds your attention, emotionally and sonically.
- Feedback from trusted collaborators points to clarity, not confusion.
- You're no longer changing things to improve the song, but to avoid releasing it.

If that last one resonates—pay attention. That may be your cue to let go.

Completion is the moment when fragments stop searching and become whole.

Tools to Help You Finish

- **The 24-hour rule**:
  When you think you're done, step away. Come back the next day. If nothing screams for change, it's probably ready.
- **Export and walk away**:
  Bounce the track as if it's final. Listen to it casually over the next few days. Does it hold up?
- **Mix to emotion, not perfection**:
  If the energy is right and the feeling translates, don't obsess over surgical detail.
- **Use a checklist**:
  Have a defined set of steps (gain staging, mastering prep, arrangement check). Once complete, commit.
- **Create version milestones**:
  Instead of one endless session, make clear checkpoints: V1 (idea), V2 (production), V3 (mix), V4 (final master). It brings clarity.
- **Time-limit revisions**:
  Give yourself a set window for revisions. Then stop. Too much tweaking often leads to confusion and fatigue.

Letting Go Is a Skill

Finishing isn't just a task. It's a creative muscle. The more you practice letting go, the easier it becomes to move forward. Finishing one song makes space for the next. Without that closure, your creative pipeline becomes blocked by half-finished ideas and open sessions.

I've met incredibly talented producers with hundreds of unfinished tracks—each one paused just before the finish line. Why? Because finishing is vulnerable. Releasing something means it's no longer just yours. It's out there. And that takes courage.

But here's the paradox: If you never finish, no one will hear what you truly have to say.

My Own Experience

Like many others, I've spent days—sometimes weeks—trying to decide if a track is really done. I'd sit at the piano or in front of my DAW and tweak minor elements endlessly. Over time, I realized that the more I forced a track toward perfection, the more I disconnected from its original emotional intent.

What helped me was creating deadlines, not just for release schedules, but for creative phases. I allowed myself time to explore, to refine, to mix—but also made peace with the moment I had to call it done. When I trusted that inner voice that said "*This feels right,*" the results often connected better with listeners.

There's a kind of relief—and power—that comes from letting a song go. From giving it wings, even if it's not flawless. And each time I do that, I become a better, braver artist.

Sometimes the most magical parts of a song aren't the ones that are technically perfect. They're the ones that happened in a moment of feeling. A spontaneous harmony, a vocal take full of emotion, or a synth texture that wasn't planned but somehow glued everything together. Those moments don't survive endless revisions.

Learning to recognize those moments—and protect them—can help you finish with integrity.

Final Thought

The point of music is not to make something perfect. It's to make something meaningful.

Your song is done not when nothing more can be added, but when nothing more needs to be said.

A song is finished the moment it stops asking questions and starts giving answers.

Action Items

- **Define what "finished" means *before* you start.**
  At the beginning of a project, write down one sentence describing what the song should *feel like* when it's done. Let that sentence—not endless options—be your finish line.
- **Notice when tweaking turns into avoidance**.
  If you find yourself changing details without improving the emotional impact, pause. Ask honestly: *Am I refining the song—or protecting myself from releasing it?*
- **Practice listening without intervention**.
  Play the track from start to finish with your hands off the mouse or keyboard. If you can stay present and emotionally engaged the whole time, you're closer to completion than you think.
- **Create a personal "enough" rule**.
  Decide in advance how many revision passes a song is allowed (for example: one emotional pass, one technical pass). When those are done, commit.

- **Finish one song before starting the next.**
  Resist the urge to open a new project when things get uncomfortable. Completion builds confidence. Momentum grows from closure.
- **Release the song as a snapshot, not a monument.**
  Accept that every finished track is a reflection of who you were at that moment—not a final statement of who you are. Let it go so the next chapter can begin.

Note

1 German Songwriting Awards (official website), winners list (Music for Motion Picture: Thomas Lemmer), accessed March 5, 2026.

Section 3

Creative Growth

Overcoming Blocks and Evolving

These chapters address personal and creative challenges—like burnout, growth, physical and mental well-being, and staying inspired over time.

Balancing Beats and Emotions: Navigating Mental Health in Music Production

The Hidden Struggles Behind the Music

In the world of music production, the journey from conception to completion is filled with exhilarating highs and inevitable lows. To outsiders, the life of a music producer may appear endlessly rewarding, characterized by creativity and sonic exploration. Yet, the reality is often a mix of emotional turbulence and sustained effort that goes unseen.

From the outset of my career in music production, I've encountered numerous challenges. Crafting music involves moments of doubt where ideas seem elusive, and the production process feels stagnant. The act of creating music isn't just about spontaneous bursts of inspiration but also about enduring periods of meticulous refinement, and sometimes disheartening setbacks.

I also know from personal experience that I tend to take on too much at once, which sometimes leaves me with chaos in my head. What helps me in these situations is creating to-do lists, organizing them by importance, and then taking things one step at a time. Focusing only on the most important task at hand helps me regain clarity and move forward steadily without overwhelming myself.

The Pressures of the Digital Era

Music production, particularly in a digital era marked by relentless comparison and competition, can feel mentally demanding in my experience. The constant

DOI: 10.4324/9781003710622-3

exposure to the achievements of others through social media can, from my perspective, amplify feelings of inadequacy and foster a counterproductive habit of self-comparison.

When I began my journey, isolated in a studio with just a tape recorder, my only competition was myself. Now, social media platforms expose us to a myriad of talented individuals, each showcasing their best work, which can skew our perception of our progress and achievements. While these platforms are invaluable for learning and can inspire creativity, they also pose risks to our mental health. Observing others who might seem more successful or creatively fulfilled can lead to frustration and self-doubt. It's crucial to shift this perspective and use these insights constructively rather than destructively.

Building Resilience and Perspective

Building mental resilience involves recognizing your unique journey in music. Each producer has their timeline and distinctive voice. Embracing your individuality and focusing on personal growth rather than external validation is key to maintaining mental wellness. It's about understanding and leveraging your strengths, not fixating on how you measure up to others.

Learning to detach your sense of self-worth from external measures of success, such as streams, likes, or followers, is an important step. True fulfillment comes when you find meaning in the act of creating itself, rather than in how others react to it.

Real-World Examples of Artists and Mental Health

The challenges of balancing creativity and mental wellness are not unique to unknown producers—they affect even the most famous artists:

- **Avicii (Tim Bergling)**
  Avicii's public story is, for me, a powerful reminder that relentless pace and pressure can collide painfully with well-being. I read his trajectory less as a legend of endurance than as a cautionary reflection on how costly constant output can become.
- **Robbie Williams**
  Robbie Williams's public openness around struggle reads, to me, as a reminder that success and inner stability are not the same thing. What stays with me is not a celebrity narrative, but the sense that honesty about difficulty can coexist with an ongoing creative life.

- **Adele**
  Adele's public candor around nerves and self-doubt is, for me, a useful reminder that visibility does not cancel vulnerability. I hear that kind of openness not as weakness, but as part of what can make an artist feel human.

These examples remind me that mental and emotional struggle can remain part of the human experience, regardless of how successful someone may appear. I take them as invitations to respond with honesty and compassion, both toward artists and toward ourselves.

Practical Strategies for Mental Wellness

Practical steps can make a real difference in sustaining both your creativity and your well-being:

- **Set realistic goals**
  Break large projects into smaller, manageable steps to avoid overwhelm and maintain motivation. Celebrate milestones along the way, no matter how small. A structured approach provides clarity when chaos threatens to take over.
- **Seek feedback constructively**
  Ask for feedback from trusted peers who understand your artistic vision, and remember that it's a tool for growth, not a verdict on your worth. Learn to filter advice so it aligns with your goals and doesn't derail your confidence.
- **Take regular breaks**
  Step away from the studio to reset your mind. Go for a walk, listen to unrelated music, or simply rest. Fresh perspectives often arise when you give yourself space, and your creativity benefits from mental breathing room.
- **Build in quiet moments**
  For me, even a few minutes of stillness, breathing, or simply stepping back from the noise can change the tone of a day. These small pauses help me feel more present and make it easier to return to music with a clearer mind.
- **Stay connected to other people**
  I've found that honest conversations with other musicians can make difficult phases feel less isolating. Simply knowing that others understand the highs and lows of creative work can bring perspective, encouragement, and a sense of shared experience.
- **Protect a life beyond the studio**
  Music matters deeply to me, but I've learned that it cannot be the whole of life. Time with family, movement, hobbies, and everyday routines often bring me back to the studio with more energy, gratitude, and emotional balance.

Balance isn't only found in music—it's essential for your well-being too.

Sustaining Passion through Balance

The life of a music producer, while artistically enriching, demands a careful balance of mental and emotional well-being. By acknowledging the pressures and implementing strategies to manage them, you can not only sustain your passion for music but also enjoy a more fulfilling career. Balance doesn't mean perfection—it means creating space for both your art and your well-being to coexist.

In the rhythm of production, balance your beats and your emotions for a symphony of mental wellness.

Action Items

- **Separate your creative worth from external metrics.**
  Remind yourself regularly that streams, likes, and algorithms measure visibility—not value or depth.
- **Create structure when your mind feels overloaded.**
  Use simple to-do lists or priority sorting to reduce mental chaos and focus on one meaningful task at a time.
- **Limit comparison by curating your input.**
  Be intentional about how and when you consume social media, especially during vulnerable creative phases.
- **Build recovery time into your creative routine.**
  Schedule breaks, walks, or non-musical activities as deliberately as studio sessions to protect your mental energy.

- **Talk openly with trusted peers about struggles.**
  Sharing doubts and pressure can, in my experience, make them feel more speakable and less isolating during difficult creative periods.
- **Define success in personal, internal terms.**
  Decide what fulfillment means to you—emotionally, creatively, and sustainably—so your career supports your well-being rather than undermines it.

Your Body Is Part of the Instrument: Physical Health for Creative Longevity

Your physical state is part of your creative setup—ignore it and the work gets harder.

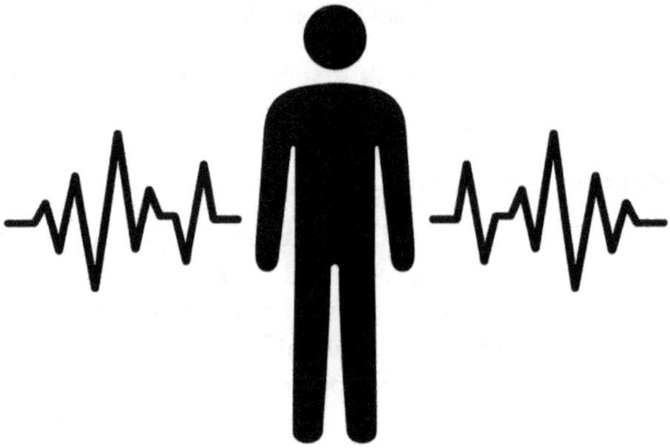

There is a quiet irony in modern music production: we spend hours shaping tone, resonance, and balance—while our own physical balance slowly disappears.

What I've come to notice is that creative momentum can be worn down by physical strain long before inspiration disappears. The shift is often gradual: a tight back, irritated wrists, poor sleep, a body that feels overstimulated for too long. It rarely announces itself dramatically; more often, it becomes normal by slow degrees.

And once my body starts to protest, creativity becomes harder for me to access. Not because I have suddenly lost my musical identity, but because the physical foundation that carries focus, patience, and emotional bandwidth no longer feels stable.

This chapter isn't about becoming a fitness expert. It's about becoming aware. Because your creative life is not only written in melodies and mixes—it is written in posture, habits, recovery, and the way you treat yourself between sessions.

The Producer's Physical Reality

In my experience, body and mind are hard to separate in the studio. When I'm physically tense, my thinking often feels narrower and less patient. And when discomfort lingers, the emotional space I need for creative work feels smaller too.

Sitting for long periods, staring at bright screens, repeating small hand movements, living on caffeine, and working at odd hours may feel like part of the lifestyle. But over time, it becomes a cost.

If you want a long creative life, you need a workflow that doesn't slowly break the body you depend on.

Common Physical Traps in Music Production

Some physical issues are so typical in studios that people treat them as inevitable. They are not.

Repetitive Strain and Overuse

In my own studio life, I've learned to watch for strain in the hands and forearms, especially during long periods of mouse work, editing, MIDI programming, piano playing, or controller performance.

Static Posture and Neck Tension

I also notice how easily tension builds when I lean toward a screen, raise my shoulders without realizing it, or stay turned slightly toward a controller for too long.

Lower Back Fatigue

Long sitting sessions can gradually wear me down physically, especially when I've been working for hours without enough movement or support.

Eye Fatigue and Headaches

Bright screens, small interface elements, and extended concentration can leave me feeling visually tired and mentally dulled.

Sleep Disruption

Late-night sessions can feel productive in the moment, but I've often found that they affect how steady, patient, and clear I feel afterward.

The point is not to fear these risks. The point is to notice them early—when small adjustments still have a big impact.

The Studio Is a Physical Environment

A studio is not only a creative space. It is a place where your body repeats the same positions thousands of times. That repetition either supports you—or slowly trains you into tension.

Ergonomics doesn't need to be perfect. But it does need to be intentional.

Simple studio adjustments that matter more than you think:

- Place your screen so you don't constantly tilt your head down.
- Keep your keyboard and mouse close enough that your shoulders can relax.
- Sit so your feet can rest flat on the ground.
- Angle your chair and controller so you don't twist your spine for hours.
- It's easy to obsess over the "right" chair or the "perfect" desk. But the biggest shift usually comes from something simpler:
- Stop treating posture as a static position—and start treating it as a dynamic awareness.

Micro-Recovery: The Missing Skill

Producers often develop incredible skills in sound design, arrangement, and mix translation. But many never develop a basic recovery skill: knowing when the body is asking for a reset.

For me, this often means leaving the studio entirely—especially after long piano sessions or hours of detailed editing.

When I feel tension building or when a mix starts to feel flat or overworked, I step outside. I breathe fresh air. I move my body. Sometimes it's just a few minutes of stretching, sometimes a longer walk in nature. I don't bring music with me. I don't analyze. I let the nervous system slow down.

Almost without exception, something shifts. What felt heavy at the piano suddenly feels light again. What sounded unresolved in a mix begins to reveal its solution.

Ideas appear while I'm not looking for them. Melodies reorganize themselves. Arrangements simplify. I stop forcing answers and start recognizing them. Musical decisions that felt complicated suddenly feel obvious. When I return to the studio, my ears are fresher, my perspective wider, and my relationship to the music softer. I hear balances more clearly. I trust my instincts again.

This distance is not time lost. It is part of the process—just as essential as sound design, editing, or mixing.

Over time, this idea became even more concrete for me through a simple agreement with a producer friend of mine.

We both noticed the same pattern: too many hours in the studio, too much sitting, and the same physical complaints repeating themselves. Instead of just talking about it, we decided to act. We made a plan to go for one long walk together every week.

These walks are not short breaks. They are long—often around twelve kilometers, sometimes lasting two hours. We walk, we breathe fresh air, and we talk about music. We discuss what we're currently working on, where we feel stuck, what excites us, and what doesn't. We challenge each other, give advice, and often arrive at insights we never would have reached sitting in front of a screen.

What started as a response to physical discomfort quickly became one of the most valuable creative tools I have.

When we return to our studios after these walks, decisions feel clearer. Problems feel smaller. And the music benefits directly from the distance we allowed ourselves.

This experience taught me something very simple and very important: ignoring your physical health always comes at a creative cost. Taking it seriously may sound counterintuitive in a culture obsessed with constant output—but it will make you a better producer in the long run.

The best strategy is not heroic discipline. It's gentle consistency.

Stand up more often than you think you need to. Change your position before your body forces you to. Move even when you feel "in the zone."

Counterintuitively, short breaks can, in my experience, deepen focus. They keep fatigue from stacking up unnoticed.

A simple guideline that works well in real studio life is a rhythm like this:

Work focused for a while, then interrupt the pattern with movement.

Not a big workout. Just a physical reset.

Sleep, Food, and the Nervous System Behind Your Sound

For me, creativity is closely tied to the condition I'm in physically and mentally, and that includes sleep, food, hydration, and the overall level of stimulation I carry into the studio.

When I haven't slept well, I may still be able to work—but I notice that my choices often become tighter and less generous. I tend to lose patience more quickly, second-guess myself more often, and drift toward control when what the music may actually need is feeling.

When my eating is irregular or careless, I often feel that instability in the way I work. What looks at first like a creative block can sometimes feel more like low energy, restlessness, or the urge to push through with stimulants rather than real clarity.

And when I'm physically depleted, even small things can start to feel disproportionately difficult. Details become irritating, concentration feels fragile, and the work demands more effort than it otherwise would.

By contrast, when I'm rested and feel more physically steady, I usually notice a wider emotional range in myself and a calmer, clearer relationship to decision-making.

Exercises to Try

You don't need a complex health routine. You need small habits that are easy enough to repeat.

- **The 60-second posture check**
  Before you start a session, pause for one minute.
  Relax your shoulders. Let your jaw soften. Breathe slowly. Notice whether you're already tense before the first note.
- **The eye reset**
  Every so often, look away from the screen and focus on something far away. Let your eyes relax. Return with a softer gaze.
- **The end-of-session release**
  When you stop producing, don't immediately collapse into the next screen. Stand up. Walk for a moment. Stretch lightly. Signal to your body: the session is complete.

These tiny rituals don't just protect your health—they create transitions. And transitions are often where clarity returns.

Final Thoughts

A producer is not only a mind. A producer is a whole human being.

If your workflow slowly damages your body, your creative life becomes shorter than it needs to be. But if you build simple, supportive habits, you gain something rare in modern art: longevity.

You can learn new plugins at any age. You can rebuild a studio. You can reinvent your sound.

But your body is the one instrument you cannot replace.

Care for the body, and the music will have a home to live in.

Action Items

- **Treat your body as part of your studio setup.**
  Notice posture, tension, and fatigue with the same care you give to sound balance and mix decisions.
- **Interrupt long sessions before your body forces you to stop.**
  Stand up, change position, or move briefly even when you feel "in the zone," to prevent invisible fatigue from stacking.
- **Build micro-recovery into your workflow.**
  Short walks, light stretching, or fresh air resets often unlock clearer musical decisions than pushing through tension.
- **Design your studio for awareness, not perfection.**
  Small ergonomic adjustments and dynamic posture matter more than expensive furniture or idealized setups.
- **Respect sleep, hydration, and nourishment as creative tools.**
  In my experience, a calmer and more physically steady state supports emotional range, patience, and intuitive decision-making in music.
- **Create a simple physical closing ritual after sessions.**
  Stand up, move, and signal completion so your body and mind can fully recover before the next creative cycle.

Embracing the Void: Strategies to Break Creative Blocks

Creative block is the shadow that looms over every artist, a presence both dreaded and often inevitable. Every new project begins with a blank canvas—a prospect that is both exhilarating and intimidating. While the blank page holds the promise of something remarkable, it also stirs fears of not living up to past work, or simply of not knowing how to begin. Sitting down without being able to move forward or find an idea can feel like a daunting challenge.

Over time, I've learned that creative blocks are not signs of failure, but part of the natural rhythm of creating. They are moments that invite us to pause, adjust, and find new entry points into our work. Personally, I've experienced these moments often—sometimes overwhelmed by too many ideas, other times stuck in silence. One practical tool that helps me is writing to-do lists, organizing tasks by importance, and then taking them step by step. Focusing only on the most important thing brings clarity, reduces pressure, and helps me move forward. Alongside this, I've discovered other strategies that turn blocks into opportunities for growth and exploration.

Creative block is not a failure—it's part of the rhythm of making art.

Shift Your Mindset

An open mindset is one of the most powerful antidotes to creative block. Not every day will bring groundbreaking ideas, and that's okay. Accepting this reduces pressure and makes it easier to experiment. Ideas that first seem weak often reveal their potential later. Allowing yourself to create "bad" work opens the door to unexpected gems and lets creativity flow without judgment.

Change Space and Tools

Sometimes a change of scenery refreshes creativity. I often move from my studio to my living room, where my piano is waiting. Different instruments, acoustics, or simply a new space can shift perspective and inspire new ideas. Exploring unfamiliar genres or instruments also broadens your palette and challenges your habits, opening doors to new sounds and approaches.

Collaborate with Others

Working with others provides fresh ideas and encouragement at times when motivation runs low. My album *One Vision*, created with Oine, is a strong reminder that collaboration not only expands sound but also helps overcome creative blocks. The right collaborator can offer perspectives you may not see yourself, unlocking stalled projects and bringing renewed excitement.

Harness the Power of Constraints

Ironically, limitations can set creativity free. Restricting tools or imposing small rules forces you to think differently.

For my EP *In Silence*, I worked almost exclusively with a Waldorf Zarenbourg e-piano, a Roland Juno-60, and a string sample library. These boundaries shaped the project and gave it, in my view, a unique intimacy. When I listen to artists like Ólafur Arnalds and Nils Frahm, I hear how minimal setups can still lead to deeply powerful results.

Play Without Pressure

Improvisation and unstructured play can be a gateway to new ideas. Recording spontaneous sessions without judgment often reveals starting points for future projects. Returning to the childlike joy of creation—simply playing without expectation—helps bypass the inner critic and invites surprise. Some of my best ideas have emerged during moments when I wasn't trying to achieve anything at all.

Take Purposeful Breaks

Sometimes the best way forward is to step away. Walks, exercise, cooking, or other hobbies allow your subconscious to process ideas. When you return, you may find that what felt like a block has transformed into clarity. Purposeful breaks are not wasted time—they are investments in creative recovery.

Use Tools and Keep Learning

Technology and knowledge can also serve as allies. Plugins, chord generators, or curated sample libraries can break cycles of repetition. Expanding musical knowledge through theory or studying global scales and rhythms provides new possibilities to draw from. Just as importantly, seeking inspiration beyond music—in art, films, or nature—fuels creativity from unexpected directions, keeping your artistic perspective fresh.

Practical Tips to Break Through

- **Start small**:
  Begin with a short loop or phrase, no matter how simple. Starting creates momentum and helps overcome the fear of the blank page.
- **Set micro-goals**:
  Break large projects into small, achievable steps. This prevents overwhelm and gives you quick wins that build confidence.
- **Switch instruments or methods**:
  Pick up a guitar instead of a synth, or sing a melody instead of programming it. Different methods lead to fresh approaches.
- **Remove pressure**:
  Create with no audience in mind. Free yourself from expectations and reconnect with the joy of making music for its own sake.
- **Keep a creative journal**:
  Save fragments, riffs, or unfinished sketches. Revisiting them later often sparks breakthroughs you couldn't see before.
- **Limit distractions**:
  Protect your attention by turning off notifications, closing apps, and dedicating uninterrupted time to creating.
- **Use rituals**:
  Small habits like lighting a candle, tidying your desk, or meditating signal to your brain that it's time to focus.
- **Look outside music**:
  Read, watch films, or spend time in nature. These experiences feed your imagination and echo back into your music.

Creative struggles are universal—but so are the ways through them. With the right mindset, tools, and habits, every block can become less a wall and more a doorway to new creative possibilities.

In the face of creative voids, stepping back can illuminate new paths, turning apparent blocks into gateways of innovation.

Action Items

- **Redefine creative block as a signal, not a failure.**
  Treat moments of resistance as invitations to pause, reframe, or change approach rather than proof of lost ability.
- **Change your physical or sonic environment deliberately.**
  Move rooms, switch instruments, or alter your listening context to interrupt habitual thinking patterns.
- **Introduce gentle constraints when momentum disappears.**
  Limit tools, instruments, or time to reduce overwhelm and force focused, creative decisions.
- **Return to play without outcome or expectation.**
  Record improvisations, explore sounds freely, and allow yourself to create without judging usefulness or quality.
- **Use purposeful breaks as part of the creative process.**
  Step away to let subconscious processing occur, trusting that clarity often arrives when effort pauses.
- **Lower the entry threshold to begin again.**
  Start small—one loop, one sound, one gesture—so action replaces hesitation and momentum can rebuild naturally.

Creative Burnout and Recovery: Finding Your Way Back to the Music

Creativity is powerful—but it's also demanding. While moments of flow and inspiration can be exhilarating, they often come with long hours, pressure to deliver, self-doubt, and comparison. These forces can quietly accumulate until the spark that once drove us dims or vanishes altogether. That's burnout—and it doesn't mean you've failed. It means you're human.

Recognizing the Signs

When I think about burnout in creative life, I think less of one dramatic crash than of a slow dimming: opening the DAW with resistance, feeling strangely numb toward work I usually care about, second-guessing everything, or drifting away from music altogether. Those are the kinds of states I've learned to take seriously in myself.

How Burnout Happens

In my experience, burnout often begins when the way I'm working drifts too far from what actually nourishes the work. For me, that drift can show up in different forms:

- **Perfectionism**:
  The feeling that every note, every mix, or every release has to be flawless before it can be allowed to exist.
- **Overproduction**:
  Working without enough pause, pushing for constant output, or feeling pulled by expectations that leave little room for breath.
- **Comparison**:
  Measuring myself against other people's visible milestones, polished highlights, or imagined momentum.
- **Isolation**:
  Spending too long alone in the work without enough feedback, collaboration, or emotional connection.

In music, I've found that the pressure to keep delivering can quietly overpower the original joy of discovery and play that made creating feel alive in the first place.

Don't wait until you're empty to rest. Step back while you still have energy to recover with ease.

Rest Is Part of the Process

One of the most radical ideas in a hyperproductive world is this: **doing nothing is part of creating**. Rest is not a pause—it's a vital part of the cycle.

Just as our ears need breaks to reset after long sessions, our minds and emotions need downtime to recover and regenerate. You can't pour from an empty cup.

Inspiration fades when you run on empty. Rest brings it back.

Allowing yourself to step away—even for days, weeks, or months—can renew your clarity and sensitivity. You may come back with new ideas, a sharper sense of what matters, or a different relationship to your craft.

My Own Experience

I've had times when music became work in the worst sense—when projects felt like obligations, not expressions. The more I pushed, the less joy I felt. I've learned that when creativity starts feeling like a weight instead of a release, that's my signal to slow down.

Sometimes, I simply stop producing and go for walks. Other times, I spend time listening to music I normally wouldn't, reading, or doing something completely unrelated to sound—like photography, writing, or even organizing my studio. These things may seem far from "being productive," but they're often what bring me back with energy and perspective.

Most importantly, I've stopped feeling guilty for needing a break. Recharging is not a luxury—it's essential.

Ways to Recover and Reconnect

Here are a few approaches that I've found genuinely helpful when I feel depleted.

Digital Detox

Take a break from screens, plugins, and social feeds. Step away from the noise and reconnect with silence or nature.

Change Your Input

Listen to new genres. Go to a gallery. Watch films you wouldn't normally watch. Creative burnout often reflects creative stagnation—new stimuli can wake up dormant parts of you.

Connect With Others

Talk with fellow musicians. Join a group. Share your feelings with someone you trust. Sometimes, simply realizing you're not alone can be healing.

Move Your Body

For me, physical movement can have a strong impact on emotional well-being. Dance, walk, stretch, swim. Let your body help reset your mind.

Reflect Without Judgment

Write in a journal. Ask: *What's draining me? What do I miss about creating? What am I afraid of?* Honest reflection often reveals the root cause of burnout.

Redefine Success

What does success look like for you—not in numbers or followers, but in how you *feel?* Shift the focus from outcome to experience.

Rebuild Rituals

Return gently. Light a candle in your studio. Play a sound you love. Create for just 10 minutes. Let joy—not pressure—be the guide.

A Personal Note and Disclaimer

Everything I share in this chapter comes from my personal experience as a music producer and artist. I am not a psychologist, therapist, or mental health professional. If what feels like burnout begins to deepen into depression, anxiety, or chronic exhaustion—or starts affecting other areas of your life—I encourage you to seek support from a qualified professional.

I am not speaking here as a clinician, but as an artist who takes these experiences seriously. Creative exhaustion can sometimes reach beyond music and begin to shape everyday life in heavier ways. When that happens—when it feels persistent, overwhelming, or too difficult to carry alone—I believe it is wise to reach out to a doctor, therapist, counselor, or another trained professional.

Final Thoughts

Burnout doesn't mean the end of creativity. In fact, it can be a powerful invitation—to pause, recalibrate, and rediscover your voice. Like seasons, your creative energy will shift. The key is to honor that rhythm instead of fighting it.

Rest. Reflect. Reimagine.

Then return—with fresh ears, open hands, and a renewed heart.

Music will always wait for you. But it needs the real you to return.

Action Items

- **Learn to recognize burnout early and name it honestly.**
  Notice emotional fatigue, avoidance, or numbness as signals to slow down rather than reasons for self-criticism.
- **Allow rest to be part of your creative cycle.**
  Step away without guilt, trusting that recovery is essential for long-term artistic clarity and sensitivity.
- **Change your creative input before forcing output.**
  Introduce new stimuli—music, art, movement, or silence—to gently reawaken curiosity and inspiration.
- **Reconnect with others instead of isolating yourself.**
  Share experiences with fellow musicians or trusted people to regain perspective and emotional grounding.

- **Return to music through low-pressure rituals.**
  Start with short, gentle sessions focused on enjoyment rather than results to rebuild trust with the process.
- **Seek professional support when burnout goes beyond creativity.**
  If exhaustion, anxiety, or emotional numbness persist, asking for help is a strength—not a failure.

The Power of Incremental Progress: Embracing the 1% Approach

The Myth of Overnight Success

In music, I've often felt how easy it is to be seduced by the idea of overnight success, especially when public stories are told in a way that makes breakthroughs look sudden and almost effortless. It can be tempting to imagine that one song, one lucky connection, or one moment of visibility will change everything at once.

What I return to, though, is a different picture—one that feels far more honest to the creative life as I know it. What appears sudden from the outside often seems to rest on a much longer private stretch of practice, uncertainty, trial and error, and slow refinement.

To me, the most meaningful progress rarely arrives as a dramatic leap. More often, it grows quietly through repetition, patience, and the willingness to keep going long before anything outward suggests that the work is "paying off."

What looks like a sudden breakthrough is usually the result of years of quiet work.

The Reality of Creative Careers

From what I've seen, building a life in music is often more complex than it appears from the outside. In my experience, many creative lives are shaped through a mix of artistic work, related activities, and different responsibilities. That reality does not make the path less meaningful, but it does make it more layered than the dream version often suggests.

This does not mean success is unattainable. It simply highlights the importance of persistence, adaptability, and steady development over time.

The 1% Approach Explained

One of the most effective approaches to creative growth, in my experience, is what I think of as the 1% approach. The idea, as I use it, is that rather than focusing on instant results, I aim to improve by just 1% at a time. Over time, those small, incremental gains can add up to meaningful growth.

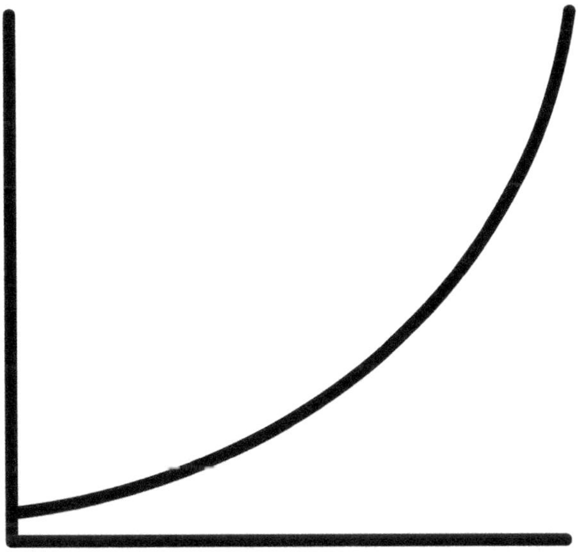

Consistent, small improvements are the heartbeat of every lasting career.

When I speak about the 1% approach, I'm not referring to a formal system so much as a way of working that has gradually become important in my own life. For me, it comes down to three simple ideas:

1 **Small habits make a big difference.**
I've often found that even very small steps, repeated consistently, can change far more than dramatic bursts of effort. What matters is not whether the progress feels impressive in the moment, but whether it keeps the work moving and deepening over time.
2 **Sustainable systems are more powerful than short-term goals.**
I still value goals, but I've learned that routines, structures, and repeatable habits carry me further than moments of intense motivation. They help me continue even on days when energy is low or inspiration feels distant.
3 **Creative routines shape and reinforce your identity as an artist.**
The way I return to practice, writing, listening, or sound design does more than improve technique. Over time, it also shapes how I hear, how I decide, and how my own voice becomes clearer to me. In that sense, I don't feel that I simply reach goals—I slowly grow into them through the patterns of work I choose to keep.

You don't just achieve your goals—you grow into them through the systems you build.

Applying a 1% Approach to Music

For musicians, this approach can take many forms: practicing consistently, exploring new production techniques, building relationships within the industry, or staying meaningfully connected with listeners. Instead of waiting for a single big break, it is about showing up regularly and improving your craft one step at a time.

Lessons from Sports

An example of this philosophy in action comes from the world of sports. Consider how athletes train: they don't expect to become champions overnight. Instead, they put in consistent effort day after day, building their strength, refining their technique, and mentally preparing themselves for success. Musicians can adopt a similar mindset, understanding that slow, consistent progress often leads to the most sustainable results.

Consistent, small improvements are the heartbeat of every lasting career.

My Personal Journey with the 1% Approach

In my own career, I've found that the 1% approach has been key to my growth. Whether it's refining the sound of a synth or learning a new mixing technique, focusing on small improvements has allowed me to continually evolve and produce work that I'm proud of.

One example comes from my album *Hope*, where I spent days perfecting the synth solo for the track *Focus*. Initially, I thought I had captured the sound I was looking for, but with patience and persistence, I realized there was still room to elevate the track. In the end, those extra hours of refinement led to a piece I'm proud to share with others—one that resonates deeply with my listeners.

This method is more than a productivity strategy—it's a mindset. It's how I've approached writing and producing music over many years. Across albums, EPs, collaborations, and side projects, I've come to see this approach as foundational. Not every day was spectacular, and not every session led to magic—but each small step was part of a larger journey.

It's not the hours you work in a day—it's the days you keep showing up that shape a career.

Learning through Incremental Steps

I've also applied this mindset to learning new tools and evolving my sound. Sometimes, I dedicate a day to learning one new feature in my DAW, or try one new plugin in a mix. These small, deliberate choices often ripple into big breakthroughs months later. It's not about quantity—it's about consistency.

When I learned mastering, I attended mastering courses and earned a certification as a mastering engineer. But the real progress came through small steps over a long period. I committed to learning every day—reading books, listening to mastering-focused podcasts, and watching tutorials on YouTube. Over several months, I steadily built a strong foundation. Combined with years of practical experience, this knowledge now gives me the confidence to master music at a professional level.

Writing this Book with the 1% Approach

Even this book was written with this method. One sentence here, one paragraph there, often late at night after a long day of producing music or parenting. I didn't block out huge stretches of time—I simply committed to showing up regularly. That same consistency that helped me finish albums also helped me complete this book. The principle applies to everything: creative output, learning, and even confidence. The more you build, the more you trust your ability to keep going. One paragraph at a time, one chapter at a time, I made space for daily progress. It would've felt overwhelming to write an entire book all at once—but broken down into daily creative sessions, it became not only achievable, but enjoyable.

Don't wait for big breakthroughs. Build them—one focused moment at a time.

Practical Tips: Embracing the 1% Approach

- **Set micro-goals**:
  Break large projects into tiny, achievable steps. Instead of aiming to finish a track in one sitting, focus on perfecting a single melody, adjusting one sound, or refining one verse. These small wins compound over time into something much bigger.
- **Track your progress**:
  Keep a journal, checklist, or project log where you note your daily improvements. Seeing a month of consistent entries builds confidence and reminds you that growth is happening—even when it feels slow.
- **Create consistency cues**:
  Anchor your creative work to existing habits, like sitting down to write lyrics after morning coffee or practicing scales right after dinner. Attaching creative work to routine actions makes consistency easier and automatic.
- **Celebrate small wins**:
  Don't wait for a finished album to celebrate. Acknowledge the completion of a demo, a new sound design experiment, or a productive writing session. Celebrating reinforces motivation and helps you enjoy the journey.
- **Stay patient**:
  Progress through the 1% approach can feel invisible in the short term, but compounding only reveals its power over weeks, months, and years. Stay patient and keep showing up—real progress compounds over time.

Small Steps Lead to Big Achievements

In conclusion, while the allure of instant success is strong, it's important to recognize that true, lasting success in music is often built on years of effort, consistency, and small, daily improvements. By embracing this method and focusing on continuous growth, artists can achieve their long-term goals and build sustainable careers.

Remember, progress doesn't have to be dramatic—it just has to be steady. And over time, those small improvements will lead to something remarkable.

Every day, aim to improve just a little; these small gains accumulate into massive achievements over time.

Action Items

- **Shift your focus from breakthroughs to consistency.**
  Measure progress by how often you show up, not by how dramatic the result feels in a single session.
- **Define daily 1% improvements instead of vague long-term goals.**
  Choose one small, concrete action per session that slightly improves your skills, workflow, or understanding.
- **Build systems that work even when motivation is low.**
  Anchor your creative work to routines and habits so progress continues regardless of mood or inspiration.
- **Track small wins to make progress visible.**
  Use notes, journals, or simple checklists to remind yourself that growth is happening over time.
- **Apply the 1% mindset to learning, not just creating.**
  Dedicate short, regular sessions to mastering tools, techniques, or concepts rather than trying to learn everything at once.
- **Practice patience and trust the compounding effect.**
  Accept that meaningful creative growth unfolds over months and years, not days, and stay committed to the process.

The Virtue of Patience: Cultivating Depth in Musical Expression

Why Patience Matters in Creativity

Patience is a vital element in the creative process, often underestimated yet crucial for nurturing ideas to their full potential. Rushing through the creation of music can diminish the depth and authenticity of a track, while allowing time for ideas to mature adds richness to the final piece. Creativity is not always a smooth or fast-paced journey, and it's in these slower moments that true inspiration can arise.

Creativity isn't always loud or fast. Sometimes, the most profound ideas emerge in stillness.

The Challenge of Impatience

Impatience often arises from the frustration of not seeing immediate progress. This feeling is common when a track isn't coming together as quickly as expected or when inspiration seems absent. The temptation to force results can lead to compromises that strip away authenticity. Allowing yourself to pause, breathe, and let the music evolve naturally often leads to discoveries you hadn't anticipated. This is the essence of patience: letting the music unfold in its own time.

Personal Lessons in Patience

In my own work, patience has been an invaluable tool. For example, when creating the synth solo in "Focus" from my album *Hope*, I envisioned exactly how it should sound. But reaching that point took countless attempts—between 40 and 50 versions in total. Each iteration refined the details until it finally aligned with my vision. The process was slow and at times frustrating, but in the end, the result carried a depth and authenticity that only patience made possible.

Another example comes from my song "Drifting Through the Milky Way" on *Dreamscapes*. After accidentally deleting the entire Cubase project without a backup, I was devastated. The only thing left was an earlier demo mix. Initially, it felt like failure, but with fresh ears, I heard something unique in it. By reworking it into a lo-fi bonus track, the piece gained a new identity. Patience and perspective transformed a mistake into something emotionally resonant.

These experiences taught me that patience is not just waiting; it's about trusting the process, embracing setbacks, and understanding that every delay or detour can add richness to the final result.

Patience in Collaboration

Patience also plays a crucial role in collaboration. I've worked with artists who prioritize speed—finishing quickly and fixing details later. While I respect the energy this brings, my approach values intention and detail. True magic often emerges in the extra time spent refining a transition, sculpting a texture, or capturing the right emotion. Patience in collaboration ensures the shared vision is realized fully.

The Power of Stepping Away

One of the most valuable aspects of patience is the willingness to step back. When a track feels "done," the urge to release it immediately can be strong.

But taking a break—even just a few days—provides clarity. Returning with fresh ears reveals subtleties you couldn't hear before: a detail to enhance, an element to soften, or a section needing more space. Waiting, in this sense, turns a finished track into a compelling one.

Patience is not just waiting—it's listening more deeply to what the music wants to become.

Emotional Depth through Patience

Giving your music time allows you to connect to it more deeply. As your emotional state shifts, so does your perception of the track. What felt perfect on day one may not resonate later. This reflective space isn't wasted—it sharpens intuition and deepens artistry. Patience enables you to create music that matures alongside you, carrying authenticity and emotional weight.

Patience vs. Instant Gratification

In a culture of constant output, patience can feel almost unfashionable. But in my own catalog, some of the pieces that matter most to me are the ones that took the longest to settle into themselves. Their slower evolution felt truer to the music than rushing would have.

This doesn't mean every track must be endlessly refined. Momentum and instinct are important, too. The art lies in recognizing when to push forward quickly and when to slow down. Knowing the difference is a hallmark of creative maturity.

Sometimes, the soul of a song only reveals itself when you're willing to wait for it.

Patience as a Strategic Advantage

Beyond emotion, patience is a practical strength. It allows for clearer decisions, sharper quality control, and space to explore new ideas. Whether mixing an ambient track, writing lyrics, or layering harmonies, time opens doors to creative possibilities often hidden in the rush to finish.

In music, patience is not procrastination—it's precision guided by intuition.

Practical Ways to Cultivate Patience

Here are some practical strategies to weave patience into your creative process:

- **Set realistic timelines**:
  Plan with more time than you think you need. Larger projects often require months, not days. This buffer reduces stress and improves focus.
- **Take intentional breaks**:
  Step away and revisit with fresh ears. Many creative solutions reveal themselves during rest, not effort.
- **Work in layers**:
  Break the process into stages—rhythm, harmony, textures—rather than tackling everything at once. This reduces overwhelm and sharpens focus.
- **Embrace mistakes**:
  Instead of rejecting errors, experiment with them. What looks like failure may become the defining feature of a track.
- **Practice mindfulness**:
  Journaling, meditation, or simple breathing exercises help reduce frustration and build mental resilience.
- **Celebrate small wins**:
  Recognize progress in increments. Perfecting a sound or finishing a section builds confidence and sustains momentum.

Depth through Patience

Patience is not simply taking longer; it's about creating space for music to breathe, evolve, and fully express itself. In a culture that prizes speed, patience is a quiet yet transformative force. Those who master it create work with depth, resonance, and honesty—qualities only time can reveal.

True musical depth comes from patience; it's about allowing each note to find its place and resonate fully, shaping a richer sound experience.

Action Items

- **Slow down your creative timeline intentionally.**
  Allow ideas to mature over multiple sessions instead of forcing immediate results or premature decisions.
- **Practice stepping away before declaring a track finished.**
  Build in distance—hours or days—so you can return with fresh ears and deeper emotional clarity.
- **Notice impatience as a signal, not a failure.**
  When frustration arises, pause and ask whether the music needs more time rather than more effort.
- **Work in focused layers instead of solving everything at once.**
  Separate composition, sound design, arrangement, and refinement to reduce pressure and deepen attention.
- **Trust repetition as refinement, not wasted time.**
  Revisit ideas multiple times, knowing that subtle improvements accumulate into emotional depth.
- **Balance momentum with restraint.**
  Learn to sense when a track needs decisive forward motion—and when it needs patience to reveal its true character.

A Lifelong Journey: The Never-Ending Learning Process

The First Step: Just Do It

Music is a vast, endless field of discovery, filled with countless genres, sounds, and emotions. I began my artistic journey in my teenage years, around the age of 16, when I approached my piano teacher with a burning question: How do I write a song?

I was expecting some profound wisdom or a set of rules, but his response was simple: "*Just do it.*" At the time, I was taken aback. I thought, *What do you mean, just do it?* I was hoping for guidance, some concrete steps to follow, but instead, I was given freedom—the freedom to explore and create without boundaries.

Today, I realize that was the best advice I could have received. In music, much like in life, the process is as important as the result. As a young musician, I just had to start somewhere, no matter how uncertain it felt. Like a child playing with LEGO bricks, I began putting together chords, shaping melodies, and slowly building something, with no clear end in mind. It was pure creativity, unburdened by expectations or limitations.

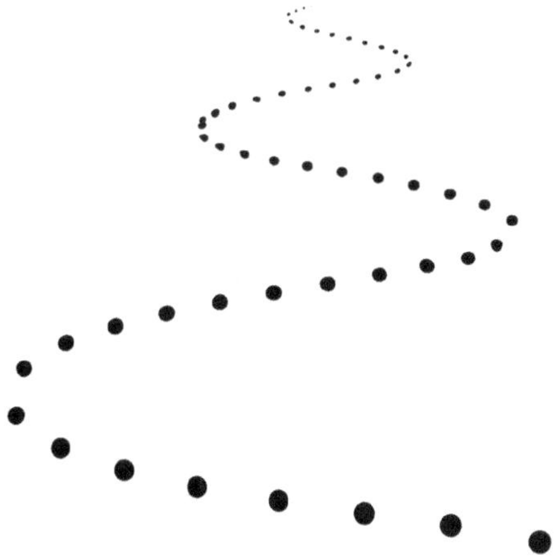

Every finished track is also a beginning. The next song always demands something new from you.

Learning By Doing

What inspires me about children's play is the freedom of it: the willingness to try, combine, and explore without over-policing the result. I often think artists can borrow something from that spirit when we sit down to write or produce.

The moment you believe you've learned it all is the moment your creativity stops evolving.

I've written and produced hundreds of songs, released a large body of work, and explored music through multiple genres and aliases—but the most valuable lessons I've learned have come from the journey itself, not the destination. Every project offers a chance to discover new sounds, ideas, and directions. That is what keeps my art alive, fresh, and evolving.

The journey of music has no final destination—only infinite discoveries along the way.

Intentional Learning and Growth

Over the years, I've developed a habit of intentional learning. When I wanted to learn mastering, I didn't just watch one video. I committed myself fully—I attended mastering courses, earned a certification as a mastering engineer, read books, listened to podcasts, and absorbed countless tutorials. These small learning moments, repeated over months, compounded into professional confidence. But beyond technical knowledge, it was the repetition and reflection that truly made the learning stick.

I apply the same mindset to all areas of music production. Whether I'm diving into a new plugin, exploring surround mixing techniques, or working with analog gear, I treat each encounter as a mini-lesson. Sometimes I'll dedicate a day to just learning one new feature in my DAW or experimenting with one new sound design method. Even small discoveries fuel bigger creative leaps later.

Every finished track is also a beginning. The next song always demands something new from you.

Collaboration as a Learning Tool

I've come to embrace the idea that not every learning experience has to lead to a finished product. Sometimes, what you learn in one project doesn't click until months—or years—later in a different context. That's okay. Knowledge builds slowly, and the key is to stay in motion.

I also find that collaboration is one of the most powerful forms of learning. Every time I work with another artist, I'm exposed to new workflows, mindsets, and musical instincts. These shared moments not only expand my skills but also challenge me to grow beyond my comfort zone. It's through this diversity of experience that my own voice has continued to evolve.

I also have producer friends that I regularly contact—or they contact me—if one of us has a question. We explore these things together. For instance, you hear something your producer friend created and you're curious: "*How did you do that?*" Whether it's how they created a specific sound, achieved the pressure in their drums, or mastered a track with such clarity and loudness—just asking opens doors. By sharing knowledge and being willing to ask for help, we all grow. One of my producer friends even contacts artists he admires and books one-on-one sessions with them just to ask questions. He learns a lot this way—and it shows in his work.

Curiosity is the fuel. Openness is the vehicle. Time is the teacher.

Staying Open to Growth

I encourage you to adopt the same mindset: don't be afraid to make mistakes or to fail. Every challenge or setback is a chance to grow, and those who are open to learning will always find new ways to innovate and push boundaries.

Success feels good, but failure teaches. That's where the real growth happens.

Ultimately, the true essence of creativity is to stay open-minded. Keep a curious heart, and continue to explore the endless possibilities that music has to offer. Your journey as an artist will be much richer for it.

Growth in music doesn't come from knowing everything—it comes from staying open to everything.

Practical Tips for Lifelong Learning in Music

- **Adopt a beginner's mindset**:
  Approach every project as if you're starting fresh.
- **Dedicate time to intentional practice**:
  Pick one skill, plugin, or concept and focus on it deeply.
- **Learn from others**:
  Collaborate, ask questions, and exchange ideas with peers.
- **Reflect and review**:
  Revisit old projects to notice how your skills and perspective have evolved.
- **Embrace failure**:
  Treat mistakes as stepping stones rather than setbacks.
- **Stay curious**:
  Let your curiosity guide your explorations—it's the spark for growth.
- **Keep learning outside of music**:
  Insights from other art forms, books, or life experiences often translate into richer musical expression.

Closing Reflection

Looking back on my own path, I see that the most important lesson has been to never stop learning. Every album, every collaboration, every experiment has shaped me—not because I arrived at a final answer, but because I stayed open to the process. If you carry that same openness with you, your own journey in music will not only endure but continue to surprise and inspire you.

When you stop being curious, your music stops evolving.

Action Items

- **Adopt a beginner's mindset in every project.**
  Approach new songs as opportunities to explore rather than to prove what you already know.
- **Commit to learning through action, not theory alone.**
  Let writing, producing, and experimenting be your primary teachers instead of waiting to feel fully prepared.
- **Dedicate focused time to one learning goal at a time.**
  Choose a single tool, technique, or concept and explore it deeply rather than skimming many at once.

- **Use collaboration as an active learning practice.**
  Ask questions, observe other workflows, and remain open to approaches that differ from your own.
- **Reflect on past work to recognize growth.**
  Revisit older projects to understand how your skills, taste, and perspective have evolved.
- **Stay curious beyond music itself.**
  Draw inspiration from other art forms, conversations, and life experiences to keep your creative thinking flexible and alive.

Finding Inspiration: How to Stay Creative in the Everyday

The Elusiveness of Inspiration

Inspiration is often seen as something magical—a bolt of lightning that strikes in moments of divine timing. But for most artists, it's rarely that dramatic. It's more like a gentle whisper, a fleeting thought, or a sense of curiosity that emerges when you're least expecting it.

The truth is, inspiration isn't always a sudden revelation. Sometimes it's the product of discipline, of creating the right conditions. If you show up consistently, you begin to notice more. You become more receptive. You train your creative muscle to notice, interpret, and shape ideas that might otherwise float away.

In this chapter, I want to share how I cultivate inspiration—not by waiting for it, but by creating habits and routines that encourage it to visit often.

Inspiration doesn't respond to longing; it responds to motion.

Everyday Curiosity: Staying Open to the World Around You

Inspiration is everywhere, but only if you're paying attention.

Sometimes, a simple walk through nature can trigger an idea. The rhythm of footsteps, the sound of wind through trees, or the texture of rain on a window can suggest a beat, a melody, or even the mood of an entire track. I've often found myself humming into my phone or recording a voice memo just to catch the emotion of the moment.

Sound itself is a big inspiration to me—maybe the biggest. I often improvise on synths or the piano and let the sound guide me. Sometimes a texture, a patch, or a harmonic surprise opens a creative door. I always make sure to record ideas quickly, even if rough, so I don't lose them.

The key is to stay open. Look at life like a collector of fragments—of colors, moods, sounds, and words. Don't judge what you find. Store it. Let it simmer. You never know which little moment will become the seed of your next piece.

Inspiration is everywhere—collect the fragments, store them, and let them float until they form something greater.

Rituals that Invite Inspiration

I've developed rituals that help me connect with inspiration more reliably:

- **Free improvisation sessions**:
  At random times, I sit down to play the piano or synthesizers with no agenda—just exploration. Sometimes this turns into a new song; other times, it just loosens my mind.
- **Listening walks**:
  I take walks with the sole purpose of listening. Not to music, but to the environment around me—birds, traffic, distant voices. It reawakens my sense of sonic detail.
- **Journaling ideas**:
  I keep a notebook of interesting phrases, titles, emotions, and random thoughts. These often become starting points for lyrics, track names, or musical moods.

The point isn't to be productive—it's to stay in touch with the creative self even when you're not "working."

Finding New Sources of Input

Sometimes, inspiration fades because the input is stale. If you only listen to one genre, work in one space, or follow the same routines, it's natural to feel stuck.

Try reading outside your comfort zone. Watch a documentary about something you know nothing about. Explore music from another culture. These changes don't need to be directly related to your work—they just need to shake up your perception.

I occasionally listen to music I normally wouldn't enjoy—just to hear how others approach structure, sound design, or emotional tension. It helps me grow, even if I don't imitate what I hear.

Create First, Evaluate Later

One of the fastest ways to kill inspiration is by being too critical too early. If you start editing before the idea is even born, you never give it a chance to live.

I've learned to create first and judge later. This means:

- Don't stop the flow to tweak the EQ.
- Don't rewrite the first line of lyrics ten times before moving on.
- Don't worry if the chord progression is too simple—yet.

When you're in a generative phase, let the idea come through as clearly and freely as possible. You can always edit, refine, and reshape later. But first, give the idea space to be born.

Don't interrupt the muse while she's speaking.

Trust the Downtime

There will be moments when you don't feel inspired—and that's okay. The creative mind needs rest, just like the body. Sometimes a period of stillness or even boredom is necessary for the next wave of inspiration to arrive.

Don't force it. Take a break. Absorb life. Let yourself miss the act of creating. That longing will often bring fresh ideas with it.

Silence is not the absence of sound—it's a space where ideas can incubate and grow. Embracing quiet moments, walks without headphones, or just sitting in stillness has often brought me breakthroughs I couldn't force through effort alone.

Final Thoughts

Inspiration isn't something you wait for—it's something you nurture. It lives in your habits, your environment, your mindset, and your willingness to show up even when you don't feel "ready."

Everyday life is full of textures, contrasts, and subtle patterns that can spark new ideas. You just need to stay receptive and courageous enough to follow where they lead.

Creativity thrives not on command, but on curiosity.

Action Items

- **Create conditions instead of waiting for inspiration.**
  Show up regularly and trust that inspiration follows motion, not longing.
- **Practice everyday curiosity.**
  Pay attention to small details in sound, movement, mood, and environment, and collect them without judgment.
- **Capture ideas immediately.**
  Record voice memos, sketches, or notes as soon as something sparks, even if it feels incomplete or rough.
- **Establish simple inspiration rituals.**
  Use habits like free improvisation, listening walks, or journaling to stay connected to your creative self.
- **Separate creation from evaluation.**
  Allow ideas to emerge freely first, and postpone critical judgment until the generative phase is complete.
- **Respect downtime as part of creativity.**
  Embrace silence, rest, and boredom as fertile spaces where new ideas can quietly take shape.

Openness as a Path to Growth: Staying Receptive in Music

Music is an ever-evolving art, and staying open to new ideas is vital for growth. Often, success can create the illusion that a particular method is the only way forward, but the truth is, there are countless roads to any goal. Sticking to one approach may limit creativity and potential. The journey itself, with its twists and turns, can be as rewarding as the destination. By keeping an open mind, we leave room for surprises, breakthroughs, and discoveries that we could never have planned.

The Power of Experimentation

Openness invites experimentation, and experimentation fuels innovation. While some experiments may not succeed, each one teaches something valuable. Exploring unfamiliar genres, tools, or techniques can spark unexpected ideas that enrich your sound. The willingness to explore, even when the outcome is uncertain, is what allows art to evolve.

I've experienced this throughout my own career. It's easy to fall into patterns when something works, but stepping outside of them often leads to the most significant breakthroughs. For example, when I was first introduced to

Dolby Atmos, I didn't immediately recognize its potential. But by embracing it and experimenting with it, I opened up a whole new dimension in my music that forever changed the way I think about sound. This was only possible because I allowed myself to be receptive to something unfamiliar.

How New Influences Shape Your Voice

Many artists find their strongest voice not by repeating what is familiar, but by remaining open to change. New influences, new technologies, and unfamiliar creative approaches can all become part of a deeper artistic evolution. Openness is not simply a matter of adding new tools; it is a willingness to let growth reshape the work itself.

This idea reaches across musical styles. Again and again, creative development emerges when musicians move beyond habit and allow the unfamiliar to challenge them. Every risk taken and every boundary crossed can open the door to a more personal and original form of expression.

Growth Through Discovery and Risk-Taking

Openness leads to discovery, and discovery leads to growth. By welcoming new ideas and taking risks, you open the door to artistic evolution. Not every experiment results in a finished track, and that's fine—sometimes knowledge surfaces months or years later in a different project. Growth in music is less about speed and more about depth. Staying receptive ensures that creativity never stagnates but instead reinvents itself with every project. Over time, this mindset creates a body of work that reflects evolution rather than repetition.

Practical Ways to Stay Open in Music

- **Challenge your routines**:
  If you always start tracks the same way, try beginning with an unfamiliar instrument, rhythm, or sound source. Shifting your process helps uncover fresh creative pathways.
- **Listen outside your comfort zone**:
  Explore genres you rarely touch. Even if they don't inspire you directly, they can introduce new textures, moods, or production techniques.
- **Experiment without the goal of finishing**:
  Dedicate sessions purely to exploration—test effects, twist sounds beyond recognition, or improvise freely. These sessions often plant seeds for future tracks.
- **Collaborate and learn from others**:
  Working with other artists exposes you to different workflows, mindsets, and creative instincts. Even one small idea can completely shift your approach.

- **Stay curious about new tools**:
  New plugins, instruments, or workflows aren't just trends—they can spark new directions. Approach them critically but with curiosity, and see if they expand your possibilities.
- **Embrace feedback**:
  Sharing unfinished tracks with trusted peers or mentors can reveal perspectives you might never consider on your own. Openness to critique accelerates growth.

A Closing Reflection

For me, openness has always been at the heart of artistic growth. It's not about discarding what you already know, but about staying curious enough to keep exploring. Each time I embraced something new—whether it was mastering new techniques, collaborating with diverse artists, or venturing into immersive formats like Dolby Atmos—I felt my creative world expand. That expansion keeps me inspired, and it ensures that my music remains alive, evolving, and deeply personal.

And now I invite you to reflect: In what areas could you be more open? Is there a genre you've never tried, a tool you've avoided, or a collaboration you've been hesitant to pursue? Ask yourself what your next step in openness could look like. Often, it is the smallest shift that sparks the biggest transformation. Staying receptive isn't just about keeping your music fresh—it's about keeping yourself in motion, constantly discovering what more you can become.

Staying open to new ideas and experiences is essential for growth; it enriches our music and expands our creative horizons.

Action Items

- **Disrupt one familiar habit in your next session.**
  Start a track from a place you usually avoid: a different instrument, a non-preferred tempo, or an unusual sound source. Notice how quickly new ideas appear when routine loosens its grip.
- **Listen intentionally outside your comfort zone.**
  Choose one genre or artist you normally wouldn't select and listen without judgment. Focus on textures, structure, or emotion—not whether you "like" it.
- **Schedule an exploration-only session.**
  Set aside time where finishing is not allowed. Experiment freely with sounds, effects, or techniques and let curiosity lead without outcome pressure.
- **Invite another perspective into your process.**
  Share an unfinished idea with a trusted collaborator or peer and listen openly to their response. Treat feedback as information, not instruction.
- **Approach a new tool with curiosity, not expectation.**
  Try one unfamiliar plugin, instrument, or workflow and ask only one question: does this open a door for me creatively?
- **Reflect on where resistance shows up.**
  Write down one area in your creative life where you feel hesitant or defensive. That resistance often points directly to your next opportunity for growth.

Navigating Feedback: How to Stay Open without Losing Yourself

The Art of Listening Without Losing Your Voice

Feedback is an inevitable and essential part of any creative journey. Once your vision has taken shape—once you've made something that feels true to you—it's natural to want to refine it, improve it, and maybe even share it. But how do you remain open to feedback without letting it override your artistic direction?

There's a delicate balance between protecting your creative voice and allowing yourself to grow through input. Some advice can elevate your work. Some can dilute it. The key is learning to listen intentionally, without surrendering your sense of self.

This chapter builds on the ideas in *Trusting Your Vision*, where I explored how early and misaligned advice can disrupt the creative process. Here, the focus shifts to what happens after your vision is clearer—how to grow without losing what makes your work yours.

The Role of Feedback in Creative Growth

Feedback can help you spot blind spots, uncover technical issues, and highlight emotional inconsistencies. But it's also personal. As artists, we pour ourselves into our work, so when someone critiques it—even constructively—it can feel like they're critiquing us.

This is why separating your**self** from your **output** is a powerful skill. Your song, design, or album is a product of your current level of understanding and emotion—it is not you. Seeing it this way creates space between the feedback and your identity, making it easier to hear the message without feeling wounded.

At the same time, not all feedback is created equal. Learning to evaluate **who** is giving the feedback, and **why**, is crucial.

In the end, you have to listen to everyone—and then make your own decision. That's how you learn to trust your gut.

Filtering Feedback: Who, How, and When

Before you take advice to heart, ask yourself:

- Does this person understand my artistic goals?
- Do they have relevant experience or insight?
- Are they critiquing the execution—or imposing their taste?

For example, when I receive feedback from someone who understands mixing or mastering, I pay close attention. Their technical suggestions often lead to real improvements. But when I share a nearly finished piece with someone unfamiliar with my genre, I remind myself that their reaction might reflect their taste more than any flaw in the work.

Some of the best advice I've received came from trusted engineers or fellow artists who know what I'm trying to achieve. Their suggestions didn't just sound good—they made sense in the context of my music. That's the kind of feedback that helps you grow.

Emotion vs. Insight

It's normal to feel defensive about feedback—especially when the project is fresh. When someone points out something they don't like, it's easy to shut down or feel disheartened.

That's why I let feedback sit. I give myself space. Then I return to it later with a cooler head. Does the suggestion still resonate? Is it still bothering me? If so, I explore it. If not, I let it go.

It's also okay to ask for clarification. "Can you tell me what didn't work for you?" or "Was it the sound, or the emotion behind it?" A follow-up question can transform vague criticism into useful input.

And if someone's feedback stings more than it helps, don't internalize it. Their comments might say more about their preferences—or their mood—than your work.

A mix is never finished—it just stops improving when you lose perspective.

Building a Trusted Circle

Over time, I've built a circle of people whose feedback I trust deeply. These are not just technically skilled individuals—they are people who understand me as an artist. They know the intention behind my work. They know what I'm trying to evoke.

When I share something with them, I listen carefully. I don't take everything at face value, but I do reflect. Sometimes their input leads me to change something significant. Other times, it confirms my choice to leave it as it is. But I always listen.

Having this trusted circle is one of the most powerful assets you can develop. You'll know whose feedback you can trust to sharpen your vision—not steer you away from it.

Knowing When to Say No

Not all suggestions are right for you. That doesn't make them wrong—it just means they don't align with your direction.

In my own career, there were moments when someone suggested a change that would have made a track more mainstream or accessible. But deep down, I knew it didn't fit. It might have made the song more "marketable," but it would have made it less *mine.*

Saying no to feedback isn't about arrogance. It's about alignment. If a piece of advice feels like a detour away from your message, it's okay to thank the person—and keep going your way.

When you follow advice that doesn't resonate, you end up sounding like someone else.

Final Thoughts

Feedback is a gift—but only if you know how to unwrap it.

Staying open doesn't mean bending to every opinion. It means staying curious, receptive, and reflective. It means understanding the difference between helpful critique and distracting commentary. And it means learning to say yes to the feedback that resonates—and no to the rest.

The more you develop your voice, the more confident you'll become in navigating this dance. You'll stop fearing feedback, and start using it as a mirror—not a map.

Let your ears be open, but let your heart hold the final word.

Action Items

- **Separate your identity from your work before asking for feedback.** Remind yourself that what you're sharing is a snapshot of where you are now—not a verdict on who you are as an artist.
- **Choose your feedback sources intentionally.** Ask yourself who understands your artistic goal, not just who has an opinion. Context matters more than volume.
- **Let feedback rest before reacting.** Give yourself time between receiving input and acting on it. Distance often reveals which suggestions carry real insight.
- **Translate vague criticism into clarity.** When feedback feels unclear or emotional, ask follow-up questions to uncover whether it's about taste, execution, or intention.

- **Notice where resistance appears—and why.**
  Strong emotional reactions can point either to a blind spot worth exploring or to advice that conflicts with your core vision.
- **Practice saying no without justification.**
  Thank the person for their perspective and trust yourself to keep what aligns—and release what doesn't—without guilt.

Section 4

Tools and Technology

Serving Creativity

Not just about gear—these chapters highlight the role of tools, evolving workflows, and how to use technology in support of art.

The Evolution of Sound: Staying Current Without Losing Your Essence

Balancing Growth and Identity

Evolving as an artist is essential to staying relevant in the ever-changing music industry, yet maintaining your core sound and identity is equally important. Your unique sonic fingerprint is what your listeners connect with on an emotional level. However, repeating yourself without change can lead to creative stagnation.

I've found that striking the right balance between exploration and consistency is key. For example, on my album *Dreamscapes*, I experimented with immersive Dolby Atmos mixes and expansive ambient textures while holding onto the melodic and harmonic DNA that defines my music. On earlier projects, I've set creative boundaries, such as producing an album entirely without drums, focusing instead on deeply relaxing soundscapes. These changes removed familiar rhythmic elements but kept my hallmark piano lines and signature chord structures—anchors that still made the music unmistakably mine.

Evolving Your Sound with Purpose

A powerful way to ensure evolution without losing identity is to set intentional boundaries for each project. Decide in advance which elements will remain consistent and which you'll push into new territory. Reflect on the core aspects

DOI: 10.4324/9781003710622-4

of your music—tone, instrumentation, harmonic language, or production style—and determine what's ripe for growth. This keeps your experimentation focused while preserving your recognizable sound.

Collaborations are another catalyst for growth. Working with Oine on *One Vision*, I felt his electronic sensibility meeting my atmospheric downtempo approach in a way that, to me, opened a richer and more layered sonic space. I still remember the moment he sent me a synth sequence that immediately shifted the direction of the track for me; it felt like something I would not have arrived at alone, yet it still belonged naturally inside the piece. Working with Andreas Bach brought a similar sense of discovery, because his guitar-led perspective introduced textures and harmonic turns that, to my ears, took the music somewhere new. For me, partnerships like these do not replace an existing sound but expand it, adding new color and depth while allowing its core identity to remain intact.

The Power of Remixes and Cross-Genre Connections

Many of my singles and albums have included remixes or alternate versions. With *One Vision (Remixed)*, I enjoyed hearing different artists pull the material toward moods that, to me, felt closer to deep house, ambient techno, or a more cinematic atmosphere. I had a similar experience with my EP *Berlin*, created with Oine and Electrix, where I became aware of how much a different treatment can change the way a piece is felt without losing its identity. To my ears, the alternative "Piano Version" revealed a different emotional center than the original and reminded me how powerfully a reinterpretation can reshape the way a piece connects.

I've also remixed other artists' music, such as my version of *Caught in Time* by SINE. To me, that remix felt like a genuine exchange: it moved into a deeper house direction while still keeping an atmospheric core, and it seemed to create a fresh point of connection between our musical worlds. Experiences like this have made me see remix culture as more than a secondary format. At its best, it becomes a conversation that lets a piece live differently and invites listeners to enter through a new door.

Practical Ways to Stay Current without Losing Your Essence

- **Identify your core elements**
  Know which parts of your sound must remain consistent to keep your identity intact. *For me, it's my piano tone and harmonic style.*
- **Experiment with one variable at a time**
  Change instrumentation, production style, or arrangement approach, but not all at once. *This keeps listeners anchored while still surprising them.*

- **Collaborate strategically**
  Choose partners whose strengths complement yours and open new creative directions. *They can introduce textures or rhythms you'd never have imagined.*
- **Use remixes to explore genres**
  Invite artists from different scenes to reinterpret your work. *It's a way to step into new worlds without leaving your own.*
- **Adopt new technology mindfully**
  Integrate tools like spatial audio or new synths while staying true to your emotional message.
- **Revisit your past work**
  Identify patterns that define you and use them as a foundation for new ideas.

Embracing Change Without Losing Your Core

Musical growth doesn't mean abandoning your roots—it means allowing them to branch out in new directions. When change is intentional, it strengthens your identity rather than diluting it. Whether by experimenting with new instrumentation, adopting emerging production techniques, inviting collaborators from different genres, or commissioning remixes that reimagine your work, you can evolve in ways that keep your art fresh and exciting without losing the thread that makes it yours.

As sounds evolve, so does your musical essence—transform but remain true.

Action Items

- **Define your non-negotiable sonic elements.**
  Identify the sounds, harmonic language, or emotional qualities that make your music recognizably yours, and consciously protect them as you evolve.
- **Experiment with one creative variable at a time.**
  Change a single element—such as instrumentation, production approach, or format—while keeping the rest familiar to maintain continuity for both you and your listeners.
- **Set clear boundaries before starting a new project.**
  Decide in advance what will stay constant and what is allowed to change, so exploration remains focused rather than overwhelming.
- **Use collaboration as expansion, not replacement.**
  Work with artists who bring complementary strengths, allowing their input to add color and perspective without diluting your core identity.
- **Explore remixes and alternate versions intentionally.**
  Use reinterpretations as a safe space to test new genres, tempos, or moods while keeping the original emotional DNA intact.
- **Regularly reflect on your creative trajectory.**
  Revisit older work to understand what has remained consistent over time, and let those patterns guide where and how you evolve next.

The Digital Renaissance: How Technology Is Shaping the Future of Music

Historical Shifts through Technology

Music technology has always shaped the musical landscape in the way I hear and experience it. From the earliest drums and flutes to the piano and organ, each innovation seems to open a new creative space. To me, instruments and tools such as the electric guitar, the TR-808, the TR-909, the Mellotron, Auto-Tune, and Ableton Live each carry a distinct musical world with them. I hear them not simply as equipment, but as creative turning points that expanded what artists could express and how listeners could experience music.

The Role of AI in Creativity

Today's scene is shaped by DAWs, samplers, real-time collaboration, and, increasingly, AI. Used imaginatively, I sometimes find that AI can suggest unexpected combinations, offer harmonic or textural prompts, or point toward directions I might not have reached on my own. At the same time, I do not hear it as the source of genuine artistic intent, because for me that still comes from the human choices behind the work. It can be a valuable reference or creative catalyst, but its real strength lies in how the artist applies, reshapes, and filters what it offers.

Maintaining the Human Touch

True artistic expression is personal. While AI and tech can inspire, the emotional truth, individuality, and intention come from the artist. A machine might produce something flawless on paper, but it's the human connection that makes it resonate.

Machines can play the notes, but only you can write the story.

My Experience: Breaking the Loop

In one project, I was stuck in a repetitive chord cycle. I used AI to suggest a new progression, keeping all decisions mine. It wasn't groundbreaking, but it shifted my perspective and let me finish the track. I remain critical of this approach—the AI was a spark, not the author.

Another time, a sample library reignited my creativity. Exploring unfamiliar textures set me on a path to a track I wouldn't have made otherwise. Like AI, the library didn't compose for me—it provided inspiration I shaped into my own.

Technology in Service of Expression

When I think of artists such as Brian Eno, Aphex Twin, or Bonobo, I hear technology being used in ways that still feel deeply connected to human expression rather than detached from it. To me, their music does not feel driven by tools alone, but by taste, sensitivity, and artistic intention. Even when the sounds are processed, layered, or electronically shaped, there is still a sense of emotion, atmosphere, and personality at the center.

From my perspective, examples like these show that innovation becomes most compelling when technology amplifies the artist's voice instead of replacing or overshadowing it. The tools may evolve, but what stays with the listener is not the machinery behind the music—it is the feeling, character, and sense of presence within it.

Looking Ahead: The Next Wave of Innovation

Spatial audio formats like Dolby Atmos have changed the way I think about listening and production. I began that journey with my album *Hope*, followed by *One Vision* with Oine, and those experiences made me feel that immersive formats could play an increasingly important role in music's future. To me, the most exciting part is the creative potential: the sense that sound can become more spacious, more dimensional, and more narrative.

Blockchain-based rights management may seem technical, but to me its appeal lies in the possibility of reducing administrative friction for artists. Any system that helps creators feel clearer about ownership and less consumed by logistics can create more mental space for the work itself. That is where I see its creative value.

Guidelines for Using Technology Wisely

- **Start with the idea**:
  Let creativity lead the choice of tools.
- **Use tech as an assistant**:
  Keep control of artistic direction.
- **Balance approaches**:
  Switch between tech-heavy and organic methods.
- **Assess the result**:
  Ensure the technology amplifies your unique voice.

In the digital age, technology should expand possibilities while preserving your individuality. It must remain the servant of creativity—not its replacement.

Embrace technology as a tool, but never replace the human touch with digital beats.

Action Items

- **Let the idea lead the technology**.
  Choose tools only after you understand the emotional or musical intention of the piece, not the other way around.
- **Use AI and advanced tools as creative assistants, not authors**.
  Allow technology to suggest, inspire, or unblock—but keep all artistic decisions firmly in your hands.

- **Balance digital and human workflows intentionally.**
  Alternate between highly technical processes and more organic, performance-based approaches to maintain emotional depth.
- **Question whether technology serves your voice.**
  Regularly ask if a tool is amplifying your artistic identity or merely adding complexity without meaning.
- **Explore new technologies through small experiments.**
  Test emerging formats or tools in limited contexts before committing them to full projects.
- **Protect the human core of your music.**
  Ensure that emotion, intention, and personal perspective remain the foundation—technology should enhance the story, not replace it.

Balancing Tools with Vision: Harnessing Technology without Losing Your Creative Soul

In today's music production landscape, the intersection of technology and creativity feels unavoidable to me. Digital audio workstations, synthesizers, and plugins can dramatically expand the sonic palette, offering an abundance of tools that, from my perspective, make experimentation with sounds and styles feel far more accessible than they once did; yet the real challenge lies not simply in having access to those technologies, but in integrating them in a way that complements and enhances your artistic vision without overshadowing it.

Technology as an Extension of Creativity

Technology, when used wisely, can tremendously enhance creativity. Algorithmic composition, AI-assisted tools, and advanced sound design possibilities open up avenues that might not have been explored otherwise. But it's crucial to remember that these tools are just that—helpers, not leaders of the creative process. They can spark ideas, but they should never dictate the final outcome. The heart of music lies in human intention, not in presets.

Learning from Artists Who Balance Both Worlds

To me, Brian Eno's work offers a compelling example of how technology can serve, rather than dominate, an artistic vision. When I think of his more generative and system based approach, I do not hear technology being used for its own sake, but as a way of creating music that remains spacious, thoughtful, and emotionally resonant.

In a different way, Jon Hopkins also feels like an example of this balance. His music sounds precise, immersive, and technologically sophisticated, yet still deeply emotional and human. What stays with me in both cases is not the technology itself, but the artistic intention behind it. That, to me, is when technology becomes truly meaningful: when it expands expression without overshadowing it.

The Creative Power of Limitations

I've often found that setting limitations frees creativity. When I have too many options, I can feel scattered; when I have fewer, my focus tends to sharpen. On my EP *In Silence*, I chose to work primarily with the piano and minimal instrumentation. That choice was not about restricting possibility, but about channeling energy into depth rather than breadth. By limiting the tools, I found a clearer form of expression and felt more closely connected to the emotional intent of the music.

Avoiding the Trap of Endless Options

Modern technology provides infinite choices, from virtual instruments to endless plugin chains. While tempting, chasing every new tool can fragment your focus and obscure your artistic voice. Before adding another plugin or piece of hardware, ask: *Does this serve my vision, or is it just adding noise?* Often, the answer reveals that less is more.

Practical Strategies for Staying Balanced

- **Define your vision first**:
  Know what you want to express before reaching for tools. Let intention guide technology.
- **Impose creative limits**:
  Restrict yourself to a set number of tracks, plugins, or instruments for a project. Constraints inspire innovation.
- **Master your existing tools**:
  Deep knowledge of a few instruments or plugins is more powerful than shallow familiarity with hundreds.
- **Use technology to enhance, not replace**:
  Tools should highlight emotion, not hide it. Focus on feeling, not perfection.
- **Revisit the basics**:
  Sometimes a single melody or raw performance can be more impactful than layers of polished effects.

A Closing Reflection

Ultimately, the balance between tools and vision comes down to intention. Technology is not the enemy of creativity—but without awareness, it can easily become a distraction. By consciously choosing when and how to use your tools, you give space for your true artistic identity to shine through.

Your sound is more than the sum of your gear. It's the stories you want to tell, the emotions you wish to share, and the vision only you can bring to life. Technology should be a collaborator in your creative journey—not the driver.

Technology can spark ideas, but it's your vision that gives them light.

Action Items

- **Clarify your vision before opening your tools.**
  Take a moment to define the emotion, message, or atmosphere you want to express before reaching for plugins or gear.
- **Treat technology as an extension, not the source, of creativity.**
  Use tools to support ideas that already exist rather than letting presets or algorithms dictate direction.
- **Limit your options deliberately.**
  Reduce the number of instruments, plugins, or tracks in a project to sharpen focus and avoid decision fatigue.
- **Go deeper instead of wider with your setup.**
  Master a small selection of tools until they feel like instruments, not utilities.
- **Question every addition to your workflow.**
  Ask whether a new tool truly serves your artistic intent or merely adds complexity without meaning.
- **Return to the emotional core regularly.**
  Step back and listen for feeling rather than detail—if the emotion translates, the technology is doing its job.

The Role of Intention in Sound Design: Crafting Emotion Through Every Sonic Choice

Sound design is often seen as a technical pursuit—an exercise in oscillators, filters, envelopes, and effects. But beneath the surface of synthesis and sampling lies something much more vital: **intention**. Without it, sound design is just noise sculpted into prettier noise. With it, each sonic decision becomes a brushstroke in your emotional canvas.

But intentional sound design isn't limited to synthesizers. It includes the selection of instruments, the use of mixing techniques, the placement of reverb and delay, and the sculpting of space with EQ and dynamics. Choosing an upright piano over a grand, recording a vocal with a specific microphone, using analog gear for warmth, or deciding to saturate a drum bus—these are all sound design decisions that shape the emotional identity of a track. Every one of them matters when intention is your guide.

Why Intention Matters

When you're intentional with sound design, you shift from random tweaking to purposeful expression. A simple pad isn't just a layer anymore—it's a feeling. A distorted bass isn't just texture—it's tension. The reverb tail on a vocal isn't just an effect—it's space, memory, or vulnerability.

Too often, producers stack plugins or flip through presets without asking: *What am I trying to say with this sound?* Intention means knowing why a sound is there, what role it plays, and how it serves the emotional or narrative arc of your track.

Recently, I was working on a cover version of a famous song from the 80s that I'm currently planning to release as part of a collaboration with another artist. While discussing how we wanted to reinterpret the song, we began exploring sound design ideas that didn't exist yet—we simply imagined how it might sound in the dreamy, textured aesthetic of a dream-pop track. Days later, I returned to the project and crafted the sounds we had envisioned. Each element, from the reverbs to the synth layers, was chosen with deliberate care. I used tape saturation, subtle noise layers, and created my own synth sounds for the intro. The result is a far more touching and emotionally resonant piece—because it was built on intention. Every detail mattered, and that love and focus made the final production truly come alive.

Every sound has a reason. If it doesn't, it doesn't belong.

Designing with Feeling

I often start with a mood, not a melody. I ask myself: *What do I want the listener to feel?* That feeling becomes a compass. A shimmering synth might evoke nostalgia. A filtered texture might signal distance. A warm low-end might invite grounding.

Sound design is emotional storytelling. It's the atmosphere that surrounds your composition, the character that whispers beneath the surface. When you approach it with that awareness, even subtle choices become powerful tools.

I remember designing the opening soundscape for one of my ambient pieces. Instead of choosing the cleanest or most pristine texture, I deliberately used tape saturation, subtle noise layers, and created my own synth sounds for the intro. The goal wasn't fidelity—it was intimacy. I wanted the listener to feel like they were stepping into a memory, guided by the warmth and imperfection of those intentionally crafted sounds.

For instance, in my own productions, I deliberately chose to use the same piano sound throughout an entire album. Even though each track was unique, this single choice created a subtle sense of continuity—listeners felt at home, even when entering a completely new piece. That familiarity builds trust and connection, anchoring the listener within the sound world you're shaping.

The Trap of Technical Perfection

When sound design becomes about perfection, you risk flattening its emotional impact. Not everything needs to be hi-fi, perfectly tuned, or surgically EQ'd. Sometimes, the flaws *are* the emotion. A click in a vocal. A slightly detuned pad. The wobble of a badly looped sample. These can all carry meaning—if used intentionally.

I often find that leaving a bit of unpredictability or "dirt" in a sound makes it feel more alive. It invites the ear to lean in, to wonder, to feel.

Listening as a Sound Designer

Intentional sound design begins with intentional listening. Pay attention to:

- What each sound evokes emotionally.
- How it interacts with space, silence, and other textures.
- Where it sits in the sonic story of the track.

Don't just listen to how a sound works. Listen to what it feels like.

A big shift in my process came when I stopped asking, "*Does this sound good?*" and started asking, "*Does this sound say what I want to say?*"

Sound Design as a Defining Element of Genre and Identity

In certain genres—like ambient, experimental electronic, cinematic, or soundscape-based music—sound design isn't just important; it *is* the music. The texture, tone, and atmosphere are the message. In my own ambient work, sound design carries the emotional weight just as much as harmony or melody.

To my ears, genres such as ambient or future garage depend heavily on intricate and expressive sound design for the way they communicate identity. In that kind of music, spaciousness, decay, warmth, or noise do not feel like decorative colors to me; they feel closer to the canvas on which the whole emotional experience is built.

Sound design also helps define the voice of an artist. When I listen to Coldplay, I hear not only the songwriting, but also a particular shaping of sonic texture—from reverb-drenched guitars and intimate piano tones to atmospheric pads swelling behind the vocals. To my ears, these do not feel like arbitrary details, but like part of the larger atmosphere the music creates. They are, from my perspective, one of the reasons the emotional character of the band's work feels so immediately identifiable.

Great bands and producers shape their identity through repetition and refinement of their sonic palette. Over time, the audience learns to recognize not just a melody, but a *sound world*. That world is crafted intentionally.

Intentional sound design shapes the **cohesion of an album**. It makes tracks feel like chapters of a greater narrative rather than disconnected singles. A shared atmosphere, tonal range, or texture palette can bind an entire record emotionally and aesthetically. This unity is rarely an accident. It's the result of repeated, conscious decisions about what a record *should feel like* from start to finish.

Collaborative Sound Design: Speaking Someone Else's Sound Language

When collaborating with another artist, sound design takes on a new dynamic. You're not just expressing your own voice—you're learning to respect and complement another's. That can mean adapting to someone else's palette or co-creating a new one together. I've often found that collaboration pushes my sound design in directions I wouldn't have explored alone. It becomes a shared language.

Organic Sources and Field Recordings

Field recordings—rainfall, footsteps on gravel, distant voices, the hum of a city—often carry strong emotional associations for me. When I use them intentionally, I hear them as a way of bringing a more human, lived-in quality to digital productions. From my perspective, they can suggest memory, atmosphere, and mood in a way that feels immediate.

One of my ambient tracks began with the sound of a train ride. The rhythmic clatter of the rails and the soft ambient murmur in the background became the pulse of the track "A I" from my album *Ambitronic*. It wasn't perfectly recorded or surgically cleaned—but it was emotionally resonant. That rawness brought honesty. And honesty connects.

Context and Purpose: Sound Design Beyond Music

Intentional sound design isn't only for albums or singles. It plays a crucial role in film, installations, games, and branding. A well-designed sonic identity can tell a story, evoke a brand's ethos, or deepen the emotional arc of a scene. In these contexts, sound design becomes narrative architecture.

Think of the startup chime on a computer, the deep boom in a sci-fi trailer, or the ambient textures in a gallery installation. These sounds stay with us. They're designed to.

Layering and Sonic Hierarchies

Not every sound needs to be front and center. Intentional sound design includes knowing which sounds support and which lead. Just like in visual art, depth is created through contrast. A background texture might barely be audible—but if you mute it, the track suddenly feels flat.

Hierarchy in your sonic elements builds clarity. The decision of what to highlight and what to let drift in the background is as creative as choosing the sound itself.

The Power of Constraints

Some of my best sound design has come not from having every plugin and synth imaginable, but from setting limits. Designing only with a single synth. Using field recordings from one day. Processing one sound in multiple ways until it becomes a whole track.

Constraints sharpen intention. They force you to focus not on variety, but on meaning. When you have fewer tools, each choice matters more. That's where creativity thrives.

My Own Experience

I've always felt that sound is not just heard—it's felt. And when you design with intention, you create music that people don't just listen to. They experience it.

Someone once described my music to me in a way that stayed with me for a long time. It reminded me that, no matter how far technology advances, I still experience the emotional core of a sound as the thing that creates the deepest connection. You can build a track with countless plugin chains and endless layers of technical refinement, but that alone does not guarantee that it will move anyone. For me, if the feeling is missing, the music may remain impressive on the surface while failing to reach something deeper.

Design every sound like it's carrying a message. Because it is.

Final Thoughts

Sound design is not about impressing other producers. It's about communicating what words can't. That's why intention matters.

Don't settle for "cool" sounds. Aim for *true* ones. Sounds that fit the feeling. Sounds that move the story forward. Sounds that mean something.

Because when you design with intention, you stop producing sounds—and start producing experiences.

Intention turns noise into music, and music into meaning.

Action Items

- **Define your artistic intention before opening any tools.**
  Pause before you start a session and articulate—mentally or in writing—what you want the music to *express*. Let this intention guide every technical decision, so tools serve the idea instead of distracting from it.
- **Limit your available tools for each project.**
  Choose a fixed set of instruments, plugins, or hardware at the start and commit to them. Constraints reduce decision fatigue and help you go deeper emotionally instead of wider technically.
- **Deepen mastery of what you already own.**
  Pick one instrument, synth, or plugin and explore it thoroughly over time. True creative freedom comes not from having many tools, but from knowing a few so well that they become extensions of your intuition.
- **Regularly question whether technology is adding meaning or noise.**
  When adding layers, effects, or processing, ask whether they strengthen the emotional message or simply increase complexity. If a sound doesn't support the feeling, remove it—even if it's technically impressive.

- **Alternate between technology-heavy and stripped-back sessions.** Balance sessions focused on sound design or experimentation with sessions that emphasize raw performance, melody, or silence. This contrast keeps your creative instincts sharp and prevents over-reliance on tools.
- **Revisit the emotional core of your work before finalizing.** Before committing to a mix or arrangement, listen once without thinking technically. Ask yourself what the track *feels* like—and whether the technology helps that feeling come through clearly and honestly.

The Heart of Creation: Reclaiming Personal Input in a World of Automation

We live in a time where automation, convenience, and limitless access to tools are reshaping the way many of us create music. It can feel as though increasingly complete musical sketches can appear almost instantly, and sample packs or templates can make the process faster and more polished from the outset. While I find these tools potentially inspiring, I'm also aware of how easily they can create distance from the thing that gives music its life: our own voice.

The challenge is learning how to embrace these possibilities without letting them drown out the human essence that makes music personal and meaningful.

The Temptation of Automation

As artists and producers, we often find ourselves caught between efficiency and expression. It's tempting to offload parts of the process to AI tools or rely on pre-designed sounds—after all, the results can be shockingly good and save countless hours. But here's the truth: the more we automate, the more we risk diluting the personal fingerprint that makes our work unique. If you're not careful, the music can begin to sound like it could have been made by anyone, rather than carrying your unmistakable voice.

The Double-Edged Sword of Samples

Sample libraries and sound packs can open up vast creative potential. To me, sampling represents one of the clearest examples of how reusing and transforming sound can become a creative language of its own. Used intentionally, these materials can spark inspiration and breathe life into a project. The important thing, for me, is that they remain a starting point for expression rather than a substitute for it.

But there's a shadow side to that convenience. I've found that browsing endlessly in search of the "perfect" sound can become exhausting and can pull me away from the state where meaningful music tends to emerge. From my perspective, some of the most valuable breakthroughs come not from endless options but from working creatively within limitations.

Crafting Your Own Sonic Identity

There's magic in recording your own sounds, sculpting them from scratch, and embracing imperfections. I once worked with a lo-fi producer who was originally a drummer. His drum sound stood out for its raw, organic character. His secret? He recorded his own kit and processed it meticulously for the lo-fi aesthetic. That effort created a sonic signature—recognizable, characterful, and authentic. By committing to such a personal approach, he not only built a unique sound but also developed a deeper connection to his music. That's the kind of identity technology can't replicate and the kind that builds long-term recognition among listeners.

Collaboration as an Alternative

This philosophy extends to collaboration. Instead of reaching for a string library, why not work with a violinist or small ensemble if possible? Sometimes it's less about money and more about relationships. A fellow musician might be eager to exchange skills or collaborate simply out of shared passion. Collaborating with musicians adds unpredictability, emotion, and humanity that no algorithm can deliver. These interactions also often lead to fresh ideas you wouldn't have conceived on your own, reminding you that music is as much about community as it is about individuality.

When Mastering Meets Intention

AI mastering tools can produce polished results quickly, but to my ears they often sound flatter, more generic, and less emotionally specific than I want a finished release to be. I experience mastering as a matter of nuance, where the final polish is shaped not only by technical adjustment but also by communication, intention, and sensitivity to the music itself. Whether I work with a mastering engineer on my own music or master a song for another artist, I value the sense of dialogue and emotional judgment that comes with careful listening. What matters most to me is that the final version reflects who I am artistically rather than sounding merely efficient or technically polished.

The exchange of feedback—explaining why you want a section to breathe differently or why a chorus should lift higher—is a deeply creative act in itself and one that strengthens the emotional bond with your work.

The Question of Authorship

There's a deeper question worth reflecting on: how connected are you with your art if most of it is generated by AI? Pride comes from being able to say, "*I made this.*" Using AI consciously can support you, but when it begins replacing your creative decisions, your authorship fades. Authorship is more than technical execution; it's about your values, your emotions, and your life experiences woven into the music. If those are missing, no matter how technically polished the track is, it will struggle to connect on a human level.

Returning to the Core

AI can still be a helpful collaborator—especially in early stages. It's useful for demos, quick gloss, or testing tonal balance. But when preparing a final release, always ask: *Is this version truly mine? Does it carry my message, my emotion, my identity?* Once your music is released, it represents you forever, and listeners often connect most strongly to what feels deeply personal. Reintroducing yourself into the process ensures that, beyond the tools, the result is a piece of art that speaks with your own voice.

Reclaiming personal input doesn't mean rejecting technology. It means using it intentionally—always returning to the core of who you are as a creator. Technology can provide shortcuts, but it should never substitute the heart you bring to your work. As you finish this chapter, consider how you personally engage with automation: are you using it to enhance your ideas, or allowing it to replace them? Taking time to reflect on that balance will help ensure that your music remains truly your own.

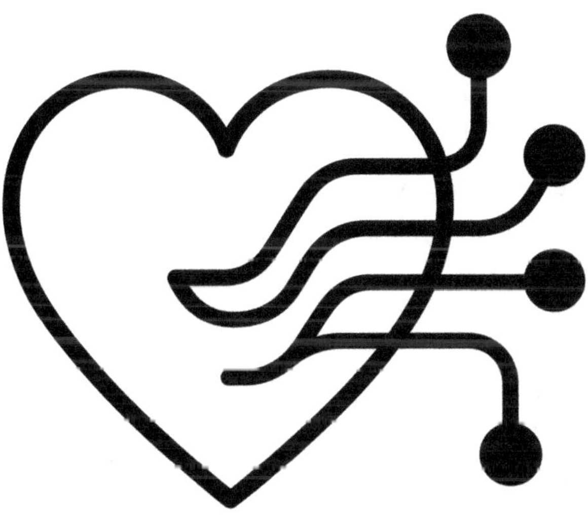

Technology can finish your song, but only you can give it a soul. Use every tool available—but let your heart leave the fingerprints.

Action Items

- **Decide consciously where automation belongs in your workflow.**
  Before starting a project, define which parts may benefit from automation and which must remain personal. This awareness prevents tools from quietly taking over decisions that should carry your emotional signature.
- **Create something from scratch in every project.**
  Whether it's a sound, rhythm, texture, or recording, include at least one element that only exists because you made it yourself. This anchors the track in authorship and strengthens your connection to the result.
- **Limit sample use by transforming rather than selecting.**
  Instead of searching endlessly for the perfect sound, choose one imperfect sample and shape it until it becomes yours. The process of transformation often leads to more identity than perfect selection ever could.
- **Regularly ask yourself where pride comes from in the process.**
  Notice which moments make you feel ownership and satisfaction. Those moments usually involve decision-making, risk, or emotional investment—and they point directly toward your creative core.
- **Prioritize human interaction when possible.**
  Whenever you can, collaborate with musicians, engineers, or artists instead of relying solely on automated solutions. Human exchange introduces unpredictability, emotion, and depth that no algorithm can replicate.
- **Review finished work through the lens of authorship.**
  Before releasing a track, ask yourself whether it truly feels like something you *made*, not just assembled. If the answer feels uncertain, revisit the process and reintroduce yourself where it matters most.

The Journey of Sound: Evolving Your Music with New Tools and Techniques

The Ever-Changing Landscape

The evolution of sound in music production is a journey of constant growth, adaptation, and curiosity. As producers, we can never remain static—the landscape of technology is always shifting. With each new piece of equipment or software, from modular synths to groundbreaking DAWs, new possibilities emerge, inviting us to push our sonic boundaries further than before. This constant change can feel overwhelming, but it also keeps the creative process vibrant and alive, ensuring that no two eras of your music ever sound the same. By acknowledging this constant flux, we can see evolution not as pressure but as opportunity.

Your sound is a living tree: rooted in identity, branching through discovery.

Expanding the Palette

One of the most exciting aspects of modern production, to me, is accessibility. Many tools that once felt distant or specialized now seem available to far more creators, and that changes the energy of what becomes possible. Modular synths, granular processing, and AI can all open surprising layers of texture and direction. When I work with granular ideas, for example, I hear a sound being broken into tiny pieces and reimagined as something fluid, evolving, and unexpectedly rich. What excites me most is that wider access invites more voices into the creative conversation and broadens the range of sounds we hear around us.

AI as a Creative Partner

AI has become an increasingly present part of the wider creative conversation. I can understand why some artists use it for melodic prompts, arrangement ideas, or sound-design directions, and why it may speed up certain stages of a workflow while opening unexpected paths.

Used intentionally, it may expand possibilities; used carelessly, it may begin to flatten the distinct identity of the music. What matters to me is that the artist remains the decision-maker, treating AI, at most, as a prompt rather than a replacement. I think of it less as a creator and more as a kind of external mirror, reflecting back combinations or directions that still require human judgment, taste, and intention to become meaningful music.

The Importance of Integration

Buying new gear or downloading a plugin is only the beginning. Mastery comes through experimentation and learning how each element fits into your process. Seamless integration ensures that new tools enhance your voice instead of overwhelming it. In my own ambient and downtempo projects, adopting granular synthesis was challenging but ultimately gave my tracks a new depth and dimension I couldn't achieve before. By spending time with these tools, testing them in different contexts, and learning their limitations as well as their strengths, I was able to bring them into my workflow without losing the identity of my sound. Integration is less about the novelty of a tool and more about how it strengthens the backbone of your creative process, allowing new techniques to feel like an extension of your identity rather than a distraction from it.

Beyond Tools: Techniques That Shape Sound

Sound evolution is not only about tools but also about methods, at least in the way I experience it. Alternative recording techniques, unconventional mic placements, or immersive formats like Dolby Atmos mixing can open up a listening experience that feels very different from stereo. I often hear these approaches as creating more layered, dimensional soundscapes, where music begins to feel less like a flat presentation and more like an environment. Experimenting with space, perspective, and layering can lead to surprising results, and even subtle shifts in technique can completely change the emotional character of a piece to my ears. This kind of exploration reminds me that breakthroughs are not always about new gear, but often about reimagining the act of recording itself. To me, techniques are often the invisible framework that allows tools to come fully to life.

Learning from Innovators

When I think of artists such as Ólafur Arnalds, I hear a spirit of experimentation that still feels emotionally grounded. In his work, I hear acoustic warmth and electronic manipulation meeting in a way that, to me, broadens the emotional range of the music without losing its sense of intimacy.

What I take from examples like this is the feeling that new tools do not have to erase tradition in order to matter. They can instead become a way of extending, reframing, and reanimating older musical languages for the present.

Looking outward at these examples can inspire us to ask: what combination of tools and techniques could similarly expand our own creative possibilities? By observing the journeys of innovators, we gain permission to shape our own paths without fear of breaking convention.

Balancing Innovation with Authenticity

Embracing innovation must go hand in hand with remembering what makes your sound unique. I experienced this while reimagining "The Power of Love." Beginning with only piano and vocals, I focused on intimacy before gradually layering spatial audio techniques to enrich the production. The final track carried both raw emotion and expansive depth—a balance between old and new. This process taught me that the most effective use of new techniques often comes from knowing exactly what emotion you want to preserve and then choosing tools to enhance it rather than redefine it. Holding onto the emotional thread ensures that no matter how much technology is involved, the core essence of the song remains intact, safeguarding its soul.

Field recordings can also ground music emotionally in ways no plugin can. The sound of ocean waves or wind through trees adds authenticity and texture, telling a story rooted in real places. These organic details remind us that evolution doesn't always mean more technology—it can also mean deeper connection. Each recording becomes a kind of sonic diary entry, capturing the essence of a moment and embedding it into the music in a way that listeners instinctively recognize as real. By blending technology with nature's unpredictability, you create an interplay that keeps the music alive and personal, grounding futuristic tools in timeless human experience.

Rediscovering the Old with New Ears

Growth sometimes comes not from adding, but from returning. Revisiting a synth you once set aside or rediscovering forgotten gear can reveal new creative avenues. With fresh perspective, tools that once felt limiting can inspire breakthroughs. Evolution is not only about chasing the future—it's about seeing the familiar in new ways. This practice can also serve as a reminder of how far you've come, since revisiting old tools with new skills often highlights your growth as both a musician and a producer. In these rediscoveries, you may find the roots of your sound freshly illuminated, offering continuity in the midst of change.

Choosing with Intention

Ask yourself: *Why am I adopting this tool?* Is it to solve a real creative need, or out of fear of missing out? Intentional choices keep your sound aligned with your vision instead of bending to passing trends. This discipline ensures your evolution serves artistry, not distraction. Taking a step back before investing in a new tool can also prevent creative overwhelm, keeping your focus on growth rather than accumulation. In the end, choosing with clarity preserves both your artistic integrity and your creative energy, allowing your music to grow in ways that feel purposeful rather than pressured.

Closing Reflection

Your journey as a producer is shaped by exploration, experimentation, and a willingness to grow while staying rooted in what makes your voice unique. Tools should amplify your vision, not dictate it. Each step you take, whether through new gear, fresh techniques, or rediscovered instruments, brings you closer to unlocking the full potential of your sound. Take a moment to reflect: which tools have truly deepened your music, and which have distracted you from your core? How might you use your next discovery not just as an addition, but as a way to sharpen your vision? By inviting these reflections, you align your evolution with intention. The process may be complex, but the reward—pushing the boundaries of your sound—makes it all worthwhile.

Embrace each new tool and technique with curiosity; they are the keys to evolving your sound and keeping your music alive.

Action Items

- **Audit your current tools with fresh awareness.**
  Take time to review which tools genuinely contribute to your sound and which ones you rarely use or rely on out of habit. This clarity helps you evolve intentionally rather than accumulate distractions.
- **Introduce new tools slowly and deliberately.**
  When adopting something new, focus on learning one feature or technique at a time. Deep integration builds long-term value and prevents your sound from fragmenting under too much novelty.
- **Use AI and advanced tools as idea catalysts, not decision-makers.**
  Allow technology to suggest possibilities, then consciously choose what stays and what goes. Your role is not to accept outcomes, but to shape them.
- **Experiment with techniques before chasing new gear.**
  Explore alternative recording methods, sound placement, or spatial approaches using what you already have. Often, evolution comes from perspective shifts rather than new purchases.

- **Balance innovation with emotional continuity.**
  When you add something new to your process, ask how it supports the emotional core of your music. Growth is strongest when it expands feeling rather than replaces it.
- **Regularly reflect on why you evolve your sound.**
  Check whether your changes are driven by curiosity and expression, or by pressure and comparison. Evolution rooted in intention will always feel more authentic and sustainable.

From Concept to Final Master: The Full Lifecycle of a Track

The Spark of Inspiration

Creating a track is an exhilarating journey—a beautiful dance between inspiration and craftsmanship. It all begins with that elusive spark of creativity, where an idea flits through your mind like a whisper. This initial moment is vital—it's where your vision takes shape, setting the course for everything that follows.

Inspiration can strike anywhere: while walking, listening to music, in dreams, or during moments of silence. I often carry a voice recorder or use my phone to hum a melody or jot down a phrase before it vanishes. These fragments often become seeds for full songs later.

Inspiration visits more often when my hands are already on the keys and I'm willing to begin.

In my own sessions, I've found this to be true again and again. Most of my ideas don't appear out of thin air—they emerge while I'm actively creating. I improvise at the piano, experiment with sounds, and let things happen. Through that flow, something usually awakens. Not every session bears fruit, but showing up consistently creates the conditions for inspiration to appear.

Over time, I've come to feel that creativity often meets us when we are already working rather than waiting passively. The artists who inspire me most seem to show up, explore, and trust the process, even knowing that much of what they make may never be used. That willingness to generate freely in order to discover the few ideas that truly matter has become an important lesson in my own practice.

So start—even if it's just a few notes. Trust that inspiration will meet you once you're in motion.

Composition: Shaping the Core

Once inspired, the next step is shaping that idea into a coherent musical structure. This is the composition phase, where melodies, harmonies, chords, and lyrics take form. I believe this is one of the most crucial stages—and one that deserves time and attention.

I often compose away from the computer—on a piano or even with pen and paper. Removing production distractions allows me to focus purely on the musical message. When the composition works in its rawest form, I know I have something strong.

Take your time here. Ask yourself: if you stripped away all the production, would the core idea still move someone? Could another artist take this composition and bring it to life in a different way? These questions help me focus on the emotional strength of the song.

I've spent hours refining a single chord progression or melody, knowing that once it's right, the rest of the song flows naturally. This is the foundation of your track—the part that touches people, that they hum later or play on repeat. Treat it with the respect it deserves.

Production: Giving the Song a Voice

With the composition in place, production becomes your canvas. This is where you bring the musical idea to life using instruments, sounds, effects, and textures. Depending on the genre, production may even be intertwined with composition. In ambient music, for example, sound design *is* the composition.

This phase is all about creative exploration. Try new synths. Layer unexpected textures. Process a vocal in a strange way. Push boundaries. Trust your ears and your emotions. I often make production decisions based on feeling—not just aesthetics.

One important aspect of production is arrangement—deciding how the song unfolds over time. This includes knowing when to introduce new elements, when to strip things back, and how to keep the listener engaged. Ask yourself: does this moment create surprise? Does it build tension? Does it offer relief?

Keep the listener in mind. Avoid monotony. Make space for dynamics and movement.

Mixing: Crafting Clarity and Balance

Mixing is where all your elements are balanced, refined, and shaped to work together. It's part technical, part emotional. This is where decisions about volume, EQ, space, and dynamics are made.

I often close my eyes during mixing and focus purely on how it *feels.* Numbers and meters are helpful, but what matters is emotional impact. Is the vocal intimate or distant? Do the drums hit hard enough? Is the reverb helping or muddying the mix?

Mixing is a discipline in itself. If you're not experienced or satisfied with your results, don't hesitate to reach out to someone who is. A poor mix can bury a great song. A strong mix can elevate it. If mixing isn't your strength, it's okay to delegate.

There are countless resources available—books, tutorials, and online courses. If you choose to learn mixing, treat it as a long-term skill worth investing in.

Mastering: The Final Polish

Mastering is often misunderstood. It's not just about loudness—it's about cohesion, clarity, and ensuring the track sounds great across all playback systems. Mastering is also the final chance to correct mix issues and unify tracks in an album.

I recommend working with a mastering engineer you *trust.* They bring a fresh, objective ear, and often catch things you've grown blind to after weeks of work. Their tools, environment, and experience make them ideal for this final stage.

Personally, I've taken several mastering courses over the years, and after years of experience, I sometimes master my own tracks. But it took me a long time to get there. If you're just starting out or want to ensure top quality, don't hesitate to hand this step off to a pro.

A great master can lift your song to professional standards. That final polish matters more than most people realize.

Collaboration and Outsourcing

Each step in the journey offers opportunities to collaborate. Whether it's co-writing, additional production, or hiring a mixing or mastering engineer, outside input can elevate your work.

Know your strengths—and know when to bring in others. I've had collaborations where one element—like a new bassline or drum groove—shifted the entire mood of a song for the better.

Teamwork doesn't dilute your voice. It enhances it.

Embracing the Full Journey

From the first spark to the final polish, music production is a deeply fulfilling process. It teaches you to listen, to trust your instincts, and to continually improve.

Not every step will come naturally to everyone. That's okay. Grow at your own pace, ask for help when needed, and remember that the goal isn't perfection—it's connection.

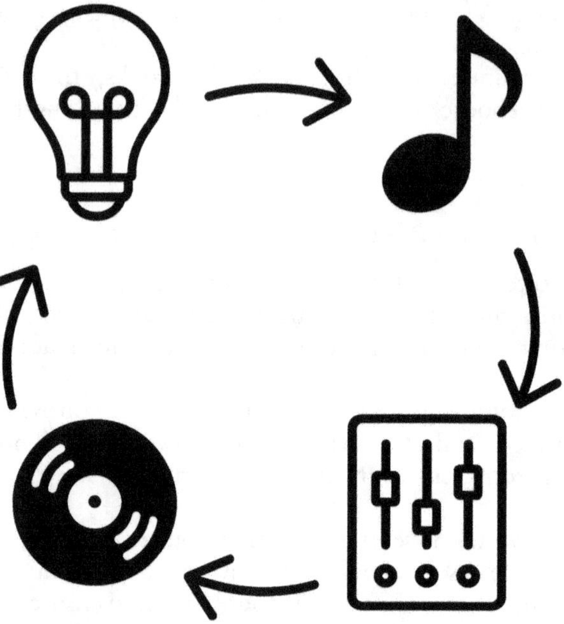

Inspiration sparks, Composition shapes, Production gives voice, and Mastering completes—together, they form a cycle of creation that reflects life's own rhythm.

Action Items

- **Capture ideas immediately, without judgment.**
  Keep a simple system ready at all times—a phone recorder, a notebook, or a DAW template—so ideas don't disappear before they can grow. Don't evaluate quality in this moment; your only task is to preserve the spark. Many strong tracks begin as fragile fragments that only reveal their value later.
- **Strengthen the composition before touching production details.**
  Spend focused time ensuring that the melody, harmony, and structure work on their own. Try playing the piece on a single instrument or singing it without accompaniment. If the song holds emotional weight in this stripped-down form, production will enhance it rather than compensate for weaknesses.
- **Treat production as emotional translation, not decoration.**
  Choose sounds, textures, and effects based on what the music should *feel like*, not what is currently fashionable or impressive. Ask yourself what each element contributes emotionally. If a sound doesn't deepen the message, remove it—even if it sounds "cool."
- **Mix with your ears, not your eyes.**
  During mixing, shift your attention away from meters and plugins and toward sensation. Listen for balance, depth, intimacy, and movement.

Take breaks, change listening environments, and return with fresh perspective to avoid overworking the track and losing its emotional core.

- **Decide consciously whether to master yourself or collaborate.** Be honest about your skills and objectivity at this stage. If you master your own work, approach it as a separate phase with distance and restraint. If you work with a mastering engineer, communicate your artistic intention clearly—mastering is a dialogue, not a technical service.
- **Honor the entire lifecycle instead of rushing the finish line.** See each phase—idea, composition, production, mixing, mastering—as part of a coherent journey rather than hurdles to clear. Respecting this arc not only improves the final result, but also deepens your relationship with your own creative process. A track finished with care carries that care into the listener's experience.

The Evolution of the Music Producer: From Studio Wizard to Multi-Disciplinary Artist

In today's music landscape, the role of a producer feels far broader to me than it once did. I often experience producers not only as studio-based technicians or arrangers, but also as artists, entrepreneurs, sound designers, engineers, brand builders, and sometimes even marketers or content creators. To me, that widening of the role opens new creative possibilities while also bringing with it an entirely new set of demands.

From the Console to the Creative Frontier

To me, the role of the producer has shifted dramatically over time. When I think of figures such as George Martin, I picture a model of production that feels more centered on shaping a project from behind the scenes, whereas today I often experience the producer as someone who may carry a project from the first idea to the final release in a much more visible and encompassing way. That change feels, from my perspective, closely connected to the wider availability of production and release tools, and I experience it as both liberating and demanding because greater independence also brings greater responsibility.

My Own Journey: From Tapes to Digital Mastery

My journey began long before DAWs and virtual instruments were mainstream. My very first experiments were made using a hi-fi stereo tape deck. I would record an instrument, then play it back and perform over it, recording the new layer onto another tape deck. It was primitive—but it was how I first discovered the magic of multi-tracking.

Recognizing my passion, my father eventually bought me a Tascam Portastudio 488—a huge leap forward at the time. That 8-track tape recorder became my new home base for years. I later began syncing it via MIDI to a PC-based sequencer, which was another milestone. I was learning recording from the ground up, step by step.

Eventually, I upgraded to the Roland VS-1680, which offered a huge step in sound quality, workflow, and editing flexibility. That move taught me more about digital recording, effects processing, and mixing techniques than I had ever imagined. Later on, I transitioned to Cubase VST32—my first true DAW—and the rest, as they say, is history.

I had no idea where the technology would be today. But I'm deeply grateful for this analog-to-digital path, because it taught me the fundamentals. It made me who I am as a producer. I didn't just learn how to use tools—I learned *why* each step matters, how to troubleshoot, how to listen deeply, and how to build something from scratch.

Today, I not only write and produce my own music—I also record, mix, and master it. I design my own artwork, plan marketing campaigns with my label, manage social media, engage with my fans, and handle countless technical and creative tasks. All of this has become part of what it means to be a music producer now.

The music production landscape has changed enormously over the past couple of decades, as I have experienced it. I've grown alongside those changes, and each phase of that process has helped shape the multi-disciplinary artist I have become today.

The Rise of the Multi-Disciplinary Creator

Being a producer today is more than being a "music maker." You are expected to wear many hats:

- Composer and arranger
- Sound designer and engineer
- Project manager and label
- Marketer, social media strategist, and sometimes videographer
- Visual curator of your brand and artwork
- Distribution coordinator and metadata expert

It's both liberating and overwhelming.

At one point, I found myself spending more time organizing than composing. The thrill of total control gave way to the weight of total responsibility. It was a turning point: I had to learn to prioritize, streamline, and decide what I could—and should—delegate.

A modern producer is not just a music maker, but a multi-disciplinary artist shaping sound, vision, and connection.

Navigating the Label vs. DIY Landscape

While self-releasing music gives you complete creative control, working with a label has its merits. A trustworthy label can offer:

- Professional mastering
- Access to promotional networks and playlists
- Press coverage and blog features
- A team handling artwork, release planning, and platform strategy

I've worked with labels that took all the weight off my shoulders and allowed me to focus purely on the music. But I've also worked with others that failed to deliver on their promises. Over time, I've learned how valuable it is to partner with labels that not only respect your vision but enhance it—without trying to own or control it.

Your experience matters. The more you've released independently, the better you'll recognize whether a label is right for you—or if you're better off steering the ship yourself.

Responsibility Requires Professionalism

One lesson stands out across both independent and label releases: professionalism matters.

I've seen incredibly talented artists lose opportunities—not because of the music, but because they were unreliable, unorganized, or difficult to work with. In an industry driven by collaboration, your reputation travels faster than your latest release.

Being respectful of timelines, responsive in communication, and clear about your intentions can make or break how people perceive you—not just as an artist, but as a person they want to work with again.

Embracing the Expanding Role

The goal isn't to become everything—but to understand everything enough that you can shape your artistic identity with intention and coherence.

In my case, I've grown into this role gradually. Each step of the way, I learned how to edit videos, run a website, write newsletters, manage a release schedule, and much more. And while I do seek help when needed, I've found that a broader understanding of all moving parts helps me keep my artistic voice consistent across everything I do.

The modern music producer is no longer confined to the studio. You're an architect of experience—building music that moves people and curating the context in which they discover it.

And as technology continues to evolve, so does this role. I increasingly see tools that can support areas once treated as completely separate—audio finishing, writing assistance, visual development, and more. Even so, I still believe the decisive element has to come from us. The human spark remains the thing that gives music its soul.

Final Thoughts

Whether you're flying solo or working with a trusted team, success in today's world comes down to balance: knowing when to DIY and when to delegate, when to learn and when to ask for help, when to follow your instincts and when to collaborate.

What hasn't changed is this: at the heart of it all, it's still about making music that connects. That's our constant—no matter how the tools or titles shift.

In the symphony of production, wear many hats—but always conduct with your heart.

Action Items

- **Map your current roles honestly.**
  Take time to write down every role you currently occupy as a music producer—composer, engineer, marketer, visual curator, administrator, communicator.

Seeing this list clearly helps you understand where your energy actually goes and where overload may be silently draining your creativity.

- **Decide which roles fuel you—and which deplete you.**
Not every task deserves equal emotional investment. Reflect on which activities genuinely support your artistic identity and which feel like obligations. This clarity allows you to protect your creative core while still operating professionally in a complex ecosystem.
- **Strengthen fundamentals instead of chasing shortcuts.**
Resist the temptation to rely solely on modern convenience. Deepen your understanding of recording, arrangement, mixing, and sound design fundamentals. A strong foundation makes you adaptable across technologies and prevents dependency on trends that may fade.
- **Build systems before adding more output.**
If your creative life feels scattered, pause production briefly and design simple systems—file organization, release timelines, communication routines, and task prioritization. Structure is not the enemy of creativity; it is what allows creativity to sustain itself long-term.
- **Learn when to delegate without losing authorship.**
Identify tasks that can be handled by others without compromising your artistic voice—such as distribution, artwork execution, or promotion—while retaining final creative oversight. Delegation is not surrender; it is a strategic choice that preserves focus.
- **Define success on your own terms.**
Clarify what a "successful" career means to you beyond numbers, algorithms, or external validation. Whether it's artistic freedom, longevity, balance, or deep listener connection, this definition becomes your compass in an industry full of shifting expectations.

Breaking Free from the Algorithm: Making Music for Art, Not Streams

The Lure of Metrics

In today's music landscape, it's easy to get caught up in the numbers—streams, likes, playlist placements. The temptation to create music for the algorithm can feel immense, especially in a streaming environment where certain trends or patterns may appear to be rewarded more visibly than others. But I keep returning to a different question: is chasing the algorithm really what makes us artists? To me, pressure from metrics can distort the creative process and pull us away from the deeper reasons we started making music in the first place.

The Checklist Mentality

For many, the goal becomes checking off certain boxes in hopes of landing on an editorial playlist. You might study the BPM, the song length, the genre, or even the specific production techniques that dominate certain successful tracks. But is that truly the path to long-term fulfillment? Reducing music-making to a formula strips it of the spontaneity and depth that make it meaningful. Instead of chasing numbers, we must ask: what do these boxes really achieve for our art?

When music is written for boxes and formulas, it risks becoming a prisoner of the algorithm—captured, but never truly free.

Music as Personal Expression

When you're writing music, the first and foremost goal, at least from my perspective, should be to create something that resonates with you. I experience music as an art form—a reflection of personal experiences, emotions, and a way of responding to the world. Crafting songs to meet algorithmic standards might bring temporary visibility, but to me it risks pulling the work away from who you are as an artist. I believe listeners often respond most strongly when the music feels authentic.

Authenticity Over Conformity

Serving the algorithm is not inherently bad. Sometimes, the kind of music you want to create aligns naturally with trends or playlist aesthetics. That's perfectly fine, as long as it remains authentic. The issue arises when you start molding your music purely to fit what you believe the algorithm demands, losing touch with your artistic vision. Algorithms shift constantly, but the uniqueness of your voice can remain timeless.

A Personal Example

I have a close friend who went through this process. A talented producer, he was constantly attempting to craft the perfect track to hit all the right algorithmic cues—hoping for that one editorial playlist placement that would launch him into the stratosphere. He thought that if he ticked off all the necessary boxes, it would be a sure path to success. But each release left him more and more disillusioned. No matter how closely his music seemed to fit the streaming platform's standards, success never came. His story is a reminder that chasing formulas is no guarantee of fulfillment.

The Trap of Expectation

It was a frustrating cycle: making a track, being sure it would get the placement, releasing it, and then waiting—only for nothing to happen. He was doing everything "right," yet his creativity felt boxed in, and his expectations consistently went unmet. This is the risk when you rely too much on chasing trends dictated by algorithms. There's no guarantee that following the formula will lead to success, and worse, the process can drain the joy from creating.

The Beauty of Artistic Freedom

The beauty of music is that it is deeply personal and expressive. Creating solely for streams or playlists risks diluting that personal connection. It's easy to feel like a cog in a machine rather than an artist with something unique to say. Moreover, even the most rigid algorithms can't predict the emotional depth or creative spark that comes from genuine artistry. That spark is what makes your music irreplaceable.

Learning from Risk-Takers

Some of the most meaningful artistic breakthroughs seem to happen when creators resist the pressure to repeat what already works. Moving away from an established formula can feel risky, but it can also open the door to more honest and lasting work. For me, the deeper lesson is that difference often begins with the courage to disappoint expectation.

Flipping the Narrative

Rather than letting the algorithm dictate the kind of music you create, flip the narrative. Create the music that feels right to you, then find the playlists or communities where that music belongs. The internet, despite all its complexities, offers nearly endless possibilities for niche genres and unique sounds to find their audience. There's likely a place for the music you make—whether it's ambient, downtempo, or something completely uncategorizable—without needing to conform to trends.

Finding the Right Fit

Streaming platforms offer playlists for virtually every genre. Instead of molding yourself to fit a playlist that's popular now, think about which playlists are a natural fit for your music. Find the ones where your songs, even if unconventional, will resonate with listeners who appreciate your style. Building a genuine connection with smaller, dedicated communities often leads to more lasting satisfaction than chasing mass exposure.

Staying True to Your Vision

Creating music that reflects who you are as an artist is infinitely more satisfying than trying to game the system. You want to look back on your work and feel proud that it was an honest representation of your journey, not just a series of tracks designed for the algorithm. True art will always find its way to an audience, even if it takes a little longer than chasing trends. The patience to stay true to your voice is what builds a legacy. Take a moment to ask yourself: are you writing music for numbers, or for meaning?

Create music that moves souls, not just metrics. Let your art lead, not algorithms.

Action Items

- **Audit your motivation before starting a new track.**
  Before opening your DAW, pause and ask yourself why you are creating this piece. Is it driven by curiosity, emotion, or something you genuinely want to express—or by an imagined requirement of the algorithm? Naming this intention upfront helps you stay anchored throughout the process.
- **Create at least one piece with zero algorithmic considerations.**
  Deliberately write a track without thinking about duration, BPM, playlist friendliness, or genre conventions. Allow yourself to follow structure, pacing, and emotion freely. This practice reconnects you with intrinsic motivation and reminds you what unfiltered creativity feels like.
- **Separate artistic creation from distribution strategy.**
  Make it a rule that creative decisions happen first, and marketing decisions come later. Once a piece is finished, you can decide how and where to release it—but never let distribution logic shape the music at its core. This separation protects the integrity of your work.
- **Identify communities, not metrics, that resonate with your sound.**
  Instead of chasing large playlists, look for smaller scenes, curators, or listener groups that genuinely connect with your style. Engagement from the

right audience—even if it's smaller—often leads to deeper, longer-lasting relationships than fleeting exposure.

- **Limit how often you check performance statistics**.
  Constantly monitoring streams and likes conditions your nervous system to associate self-worth with numbers. Choose a fixed interval—weekly or monthly—to review metrics objectively, without emotional attachment. This creates distance between your identity and external validation.
- **Define success in terms that outlive trends**.
  Write down what artistic success means to you five or ten years from now. Is it a body of work you're proud of? Emotional impact? Longevity? Growth? Let this long-term vision guide your decisions instead of short-term algorithmic rewards.

Section 5

Collaboration and Connection

Creating with Others

Explores the relational side of music-making—collaboration, listening, trust, and mutual growth.

The Power of Collaboration: Learning and Growing Together

Collaboration in music and art has the power to create something far greater than the sum of its parts. When two or more creative minds come together, the synergy often leads to unexpected results, surpassing what each individual might have achieved alone. Working with others naturally pushes you to give your best, and the immediate feedback from collaborators opens doors to ideas and paths you may not have considered on your own.

Overcoming the Fear of Letting Go

In the beginning, I found it difficult to relinquish control. I was used to working alone, perfecting every detail, and holding tightly to my vision. Allowing someone else to influence the process felt daunting. Over time, however, I learned that trust is essential. When I gave my collaborators space to shine, the music took on new life and grew in ways I hadn't anticipated. The process became less about control and more about discovery—less about defending my ideas and more about embracing the unexpected.

The Magic of Shared Creation

One of the most magical aspects of collaboration is that once the music is complete, it often feels as if it has always existed. It's as though the collaboration unearthed something timeless. The music carries the DNA of each person involved, resulting in something that none of us could have created alone. These moments remind me that collaboration is not just about blending talents—it's about revealing something larger than ourselves and connecting with listeners in new, powerful ways.

DOI: 10.4324/9781003710622-5

Collaboration is where two voices intertwine, creating a song neither could sing alone.

Learning from Each Other

Collaboration is also an invaluable learning opportunity. Every time you work with someone new, you have the chance to absorb new techniques, perspectives, and approaches. Be curious: ask your collaborators why they chose a certain chord, how they shaped a sound, or what inspired their rhythm. By being open, you expand your artistic vocabulary and grow in ways you never could alone. Collaboration is both a mirror and a window—a mirror that shows you your own strengths and weaknesses more clearly, and a window that opens onto entirely new creative landscapes.

Legendary Examples of Collaboration

Artists such as The Beatles and Queen feel like vivid reminders of what collaboration can sound like at its best. When I listen to songs like “A Day in the Life, Come Together,” “Bohemian Rhapsody,” or “We Are the Champions,” I hear contrasting personalities meeting inside a shared musical identity. I am not using these songs here as historical proof, but as listening references that, to my ears, reflect how individual strengths can merge into something larger.

Daft Punk’s *Get Lucky (feat. Pharrell Williams and Nile Rodgers)* feels like a compelling example of how different musical sensibilities can meet in a way that sounds seamless and alive. In a different way, the music Billie Eilish has made with Finneas reminds me how closely connected collaboration can shape a highly distinctive atmosphere. I hear these examples not as proof of universal rules, but as personal listening references for how trust and contrast can deepen a shared sound.

My Personal Experience

In my own journey, collaborating with Adrián Márquez (Oine) on *One Vision* was transformative. To me, we combined distinct musical perspectives into a sound that felt uniquely ours something I do not think either of us would have reached in the same way alone. From my perspective, trusting each other’s instincts and allowing space for creative freedom were central to how the album found its shape.

Beyond Oine, I've co-written and produced albums with Christoph Sebastian Pabst, whose atmospheric and fresh composing style continually inspires me. Together, we created *Meerblick* and *Bergblick*, both of which blended our strengths into expansive, melodic ambient journeys.

With Andreas Bach—an outstanding guitarist and composer—I produced the albums *Night Travellers* and *Pulse*. His guitar work and harmonic sensibility brought a lyrical, human edge to my soundscapes, and our collaborations seamlessly combined guitar-driven expressiveness with atmospheric electronic textures.

Working with Lukas Midub opened another creative door. His strong dub influence—deep bass, spacious rhythms, and hypnotic delays—shaped our joint album *Perspectives*. The result was a warm, groove-oriented sound that expanded my palette and added a new dimension to my music.

Across many other projects, I've collaborated with singers as well, shaping keys and sound design around their timbre and phrasing, letting lyric and voice lead the arrangement. These are just a few of the artists I've worked with—there are so many more. Each collaboration has been completely different, and each one has expanded my palette while reinforcing the joy of letting go and building something together. Just as importantly, I have learned something valuable from every single partnership. These experiences have shaped me not only as a producer but also as a person, and I deeply value the growth and inspiration that each collaboration has brought into my journey.

The Spirit of Collaboration

Collaboration requires patience, trust, and humility. It's not about ego or being right; it's about serving the music and allowing each voice to matter equally. When everyone works with a shared sense of purpose and love for the art, something remarkable happens—the music finds its own course. By embracing different perspectives, we not only create better art but also forge deeper human connections. And perhaps most importantly, I've learned and grown with each collaboration, carrying those lessons forward into every new project.

Collaboration is the harmony of different minds, creating a masterpiece greater than the sum of its parts.

Action Items

- **Identify where control is limiting your creative growth.**
  Reflect honestly on which parts of your process you guard too tightly. Is it arrangement, sound design, mixing, or decision-making speed?

Recognizing where fear of letting go lives is the first step toward meaningful collaboration.

- **Choose collaborators for perspective, not similarity**.
  Seek out artists whose strengths differ from yours—different genres, workflows, instruments, or cultural backgrounds. Growth happens when your habits are gently challenged, not when they are mirrored.
- **Create space for your collaborator's instincts to lead**.
  During at least one project, consciously resist the urge to steer every decision. Allow your collaborator to take creative ownership in areas that feel unfamiliar to you. This surrender often reveals ideas you would never have reached alone.
- **Ask questions instead of giving directions**.
  When something surprises you in a collaboration, respond with curiosity rather than correction. Ask why a choice was made, what emotion it serves, or what inspired it. These conversations are often where the deepest learning occurs.
- **Reflect after each collaboration on what changed you**.
  Once a project is complete, take time to note what you learned—not just musically, but personally. Did your patience grow? Did your listening deepen? Did your palette expand? These insights are as valuable as the finished track.
- **Carry collaborative lessons back into your solo work**.
  Apply what you've learned from others to your independent projects. New harmonic ideas, arrangement approaches, or ways of trusting intuition often continue to shape your music long after the collaboration ends.

Fostering Creative Synergy: The Art of Collaborative Music Production

Collaboration in music is not just about sharing ideas. It's about creating something greater than the sum of its parts. When artists come together—whether musicians, producers, or visual artists—their unique perspectives synergize to inspire fresh ideas and breathe new life into their work. Beyond the music itself, collaboration enriches professional growth, expands fan bases, and deepens creative processes. It becomes a vital force in an artist's journey.

The Mutual Benefits of Collaboration

From my experience, collaboration has been a cornerstone of both creativity and visibility in my work. Working with artists like Oine, Sinatic, Andreas Bach, Christoph Sebastian Pabst, Lukas Midub, and various singers has broadened my musical horizons and brought my music into contact with listeners I might not have reached otherwise. I have experienced collaboration not only as a creative exchange, but also as a way for different artistic worlds to meet.

Different Forms of Collaboration

Collaborative efforts in music can take many forms. Featuring another artist on a track can bring a fresh dimension and expand its appeal. Songwriting partnerships merge different writing styles, often producing lyrics and melodies that resonate more deeply with listeners. Inviting musicians to add live instrumentals or working with a co-producer can transform the texture and depth of a track, enriching its emotional and sonic layers.

Collaboration can also happen in different settings: remotely over the internet, directly in the studio, or in hybrid formats that combine both. From my perspective, remote collaboration offers flexibility and makes it easier to work across distance and schedule differences. To me, in-person studio sessions often create a more immediate energy and a faster feedback loop. Hybrid approaches, such as live-streamed writing sessions or sending stems back and forth while occasionally meeting in person, can combine elements of both. In my experience, each approach has its own strengths and trade-offs depending on the people involved and the kind of project.

The Key to Successful Collaboration

A significant aspect of collaboration is openness—the willingness to embrace others' ideas and leave room for each voice to contribute meaningfully. The focus must remain on serving the song and artistic vision rather than individual egos. When trust and humility guide the process, creative magic emerges naturally. Everyone feels empowered to bring their best to the table.

Collaboration begins with trust—and from trust, harmony is born.

Personal Examples of Creative Synergy

Collaboration has profoundly shaped my music. Andreas Bach, an outstanding guitarist and composer, contributed to albums such as *Night Travellers* and *Pulse*. His expressive guitar work added a lyrical edge that I could never have achieved alone. It steered my compositions into new creative directions and highlighted how instrumental dialogue can transform a track.

With Christoph Sebastian Pabst, I created *Meerblick* and *Bergblick*. His atmospheric and fresh composing style inspired me deeply. Together, we crafted expansive, melodic ambient journeys that reflected both of our artistic voices, showing how complementary aesthetics can form a cohesive whole.

Working with Lukas Midub brought a dub-influenced dimension to my music. Our joint album *Perspectives* blended deep bass, spacious rhythms, and hypnotic textures. It enriched my palette with warmth and groove, demonstrating how genre fusion creates new sound worlds.

Collaborating with Adrián Márquez (Oine) on *One Vision* was equally transformative. Our contrasting perspectives merged into a unified sound, creating something uniquely ours and unattainable individually.

Across many other projects, I've also worked with singers. I shaped arrangements and sound design around their timbre and phrasing, letting lyric and voice lead the journey of a track. These are just a few examples—there are so many more artists I've had the privilege of working with. Each collaboration has been different, and from each I have learned invaluable lessons. These partnerships have helped me grow both as a producer and as a person. They remind me how much I value and cherish the process of working together.

Beyond the Music

Collaboration extends beyond the act of creating songs. Sharing production techniques, co-developing marketing strategies, partnering with visual artists on cover design or videos, or engaging in cross-promotional activities all strengthen the bonds between creatives. Each partnership becomes a learning experience, offering insights not only into artistry but also into navigating the wider creative industry side by side.

Building a Creative Community

Embracing collaboration means fostering a creative ecosystem where artists support, challenge, and enhance each other's strengths. It's about building a community where innovation thrives and where the collective goal of creating impactful music becomes the true winner. Through collaboration, we learn, grow, and ultimately discover that music is not just a solitary pursuit but a shared journey—one that deepens both art and human connection. In the end, collaboration is not only about sound but about the humanity we bring into it together.

In the orchestra of collaboration, every note contributes, creating a symphony of collective creativity.

Action Items

- **Clarify what you want to gain from collaboration before you begin.** Before starting a joint project, take time to reflect on your intention. Are you looking to expand your sonic palette, learn a new workflow, reach a new audience, or simply rediscover joy in the process? Clear intention prevents misalignment and helps collaborations feel purposeful rather than accidental.
- **Choose the form of collaboration that fits the project—not your comfort zone.** Decide consciously whether a project benefits most from remote exchange, in-person sessions, or a hybrid approach. Each format shapes the creative outcome differently. Selecting the structure intentionally helps the collaboration serve the music rather than forcing the music to adapt to convenience.
- **Practice shared ownership by letting the song lead the decisions.** Actively shift your mindset from "my idea" to "our song." When disagreements arise, ask what best serves the emotional core of the track rather than defending personal preferences. This perspective dissolves ego and allows genuine synergy to emerge.
- **Create psychological safety so ideas can surface freely.** Encourage experimentation without immediate judgment. Make it clear—through words and behavior—that unfinished ideas, rough sketches, and unconventional thoughts are welcome. Creative synergy thrives when collaborators feel safe enough to take risks.
- **Use collaboration as an active learning space.** Pay close attention to how your collaborators work. Observe their decision-making, sound choices, communication style, and problem-solving approaches. Ask questions, not to challenge, but to understand. Treat every collaboration as a masterclass rather than just a production task.
- **Extend collaboration beyond music into shared growth.** Explore how collaboration can include visual concepts, release strategies, or cross-promotion. Supporting each other beyond the studio deepens trust and builds long-term creative relationships rather than one-off projects.

Collaboration vs. Isolation: Finding the Balance in Creativity

Collaboration and solitude are two fundamental creative modes, each offering unique benefits and challenges. Finding harmony between them is essential for artistic growth and authentic expression.

The Power of Collaboration

Collaborations can be deeply enriching, where combined efforts lead to results far beyond what any one artist could achieve alone. The synergy created can inspire new directions, push boundaries, and elevate the work. When collaboration works well, the final outcome exceeds all expectations. Yet, collaboration also requires compromise. At times, this balance may tip unequally, causing frustration or diluting the original vision.

The Freedom of Solitude

In contrast, working alone offers total creative freedom. Every decision reflects your personal artistry, allowing for deep introspection and the pursuit of a singular vision. However, solitude has its drawbacks. Without external input, you may fall into creative loops, unable to break patterns or see blind spots that collaboration might reveal.

Hybrid Approaches

During the pandemic, I experienced a hybrid form of collaboration: working remotely while exchanging ideas with other artists at different stages. This process allowed me the solitude to shape my own ideas while still benefiting from the diversity and freshness of external input. Hybrid approaches can combine the best of both worlds—freedom and collective inspiration. Today, these hybrid models remain powerful, whether through remote file sharing, virtual meetings, or combining studio sessions with online exchanges.

Learning from Artists and Experience

Kiasmos, the duo of Ólafur Arnalds and Janus Rasmussen, feels like a strong example of how collaboration can open new musical directions. I hear the meeting of different musical backgrounds in their sound, and that contrast gives the music a distinct identity. By contrast, Bonobo's work reminds me that solo work can also lead to deeply immersive results. I mention both here not as proof, but as personal listening references for how different creative paths can shape the final music.

In my own collaboration with Andreas Bach, a guitarist with different musical ideas, we pushed beyond our contrasting perspectives to create something neither of us could have achieved alone. The diversity of approach made the collaboration expansive and opened new horizons in sound design. These experiences reminded me how stepping into both solitude and collaboration fuels artistic evolution.

Striking the Balance

Balancing collaboration and isolation is key to refining artistry. Collaboration forces you out of your comfort zone, while solitude fosters deep self-reflection. Sometimes, balance requires putting ego aside and embracing differences that enhance the work. Trusting both processes—collective and individual—leads to richer, more authentic art.

Balance solitude and collaboration like notes in a melody—each has its place, its time, its magic.

Action Items

- **Identify which creative mode you need before starting a project.** Before beginning a new piece, pause and ask whether the idea calls for solitude or collaboration. Early emotional exploration often benefits from isolation, while expansion, refinement, or perspective shifts may benefit from others. Choosing intentionally prevents frustration later.
- **Use collaboration as a catalyst—not a default.** Collaborate when you want to be challenged, inspired, or pulled out of habitual patterns. Avoid collaborating simply out of fear of being alone with your ideas. The strongest collaborations emerge when they are chosen with purpose rather than avoidance.
- **Protect solo time as a non-negotiable creative resource.** Even highly collaborative artists need periods of uninterrupted solitude to reconnect with their inner voice. Schedule solo sessions where no feedback is allowed. This preserves clarity, strengthens identity, and ensures you don't lose yourself in collective decision-making.
- **Experiment with hybrid workflows to combine depth and perspective.** Try shaping ideas alone first, then inviting collaborators at specific stages. Alternatively, collaborate early and retreat later for refinement. Hybrid models allow you to retain authorship while benefiting from external input.

- **Observe how each mode affects your energy and output.** Notice whether collaboration energizes or drains you—and when. Likewise, observe whether solitude leads to flow or stagnation. Understanding your personal rhythm helps you design a creative process that sustains rather than exhausts you.
- **Accept that balance shifts over time—and that's healthy.** There will be seasons where you need isolation to rediscover your voice, and others where collaboration fuels growth. Don't force a permanent formula. Let balance remain flexible, responsive, and aligned with where you are creatively and emotionally.

Becoming the Collaborator Everyone Wants: How to Attract Artists and Build Creative Partnerships

Being the kind of artist that others want to collaborate with isn't just about raw talent or technical skill. It's about creating relationships and an atmosphere where creativity can thrive. In the world of electronic music—and in any creative industry—reputation and attitude are everything. People talk, and when you're known for being respectful, open-minded, and easy to work with, others will naturally be drawn to collaborate with you. Talent might open the door, but your approach, professionalism, and the way you treat people will determine whether they want to stay. Often, your energy, presence, and reliability become just as important as the music itself.

The Role of Humility

Collaboration requires humility. You need to set aside your ego and allow someone else's ideas to shine. It's about realizing that the music isn't just about you, but about what can be created together. This spirit of openness and willingness to nurture creativity makes collaborations strong and long-lasting. Humility also creates space for experimentation, ensuring the process stays focused on growth rather than competition, and allows everyone involved to feel respected and acknowledged.

The Power of Listening

Listening is one of the most underrated collaboration skills. This is not just about hearing notes or beats, but about trying to understand what your collaborator is reaching for creatively. Deep listening builds confidence, and mutual respect can become the foundation of a strong partnership. When I think of Brian Eno, I think of a collaborator whose work often seems to create space for other ideas to unfold. That openness is one of the qualities I hear in his collaborations with artists such as David Bowie and U2. When you really listen, you notice details and nuances that might otherwise slip by, often opening fresh directions or unexpected creative breakthroughs.

Adding Contribution without Overshadowing

To be a valuable collaborator, you need to bring something unique to the table. This might be expertise in a genre, technical skills, or the ability to guide a project. The key is to make a meaningful contribution while leaving space for your partner's ideas. Striking this balance ensures that your individuality is heard while still respecting the shared artistic goal. Great collaborations feel like a conversation, not a competition, and the result becomes greater than the sum of its parts.

Managing Ego and Conflict

Leaving ego behind is essential. Disagreements are inevitable, but compromise is part of the creative process. What matters most is serving the music—not your personal agenda. The most successful collaborations often emerge when both artists surrender control, allowing something greater to take shape than either could achieve alone. Conflict, when handled respectfully, can even be constructive, helping refine ideas and encouraging growth. By viewing challenges as opportunities rather than obstacles, you can transform potential tension into deeper creative synergy.

Passion as a Driving Force

Passion and dedication are contagious. When you are genuinely enthusiastic about a project, that energy often encourages your collaborators to bring more of themselves into the process as well. When I think of Jon Hopkins, I think of an artist whose passion for sound design feels inseparable from the music itself, and that kind of commitment can shape the atmosphere of a collaboration. Passion communicates seriousness and involvement, showing others that you are fully invested in the process and willing to go the extra mile for the project. When your excitement is authentic, it inspires confidence and fuels momentum.

Adaptability and Flexibility

Every artist has a different workflow. Some thrive in face-to-face studio sessions, while others prefer remote exchanges. Some work in structured ways, while others prefer to let ideas evolve freely. Being adaptable to these differences makes you easier to collaborate with and increases the chances of being invited back for future projects. Flexibility also demonstrates respect for your collaborator's creative process, which fosters goodwill and strengthens long-term partnerships. Adaptability means you can flow with change and still deliver your best, no matter the environment.

The Bigger Picture

Ultimately, becoming the collaborator everyone wants to work with is about far more than musical talent. It's about humility, contribution, passion, adaptability, and the ability to build mutual respect. When you focus on creating a positive and inspiring environment, your collaborators will want to return again and again. Collaboration becomes not just about making music, but about building meaningful relationships and shared experiences that last well beyond a single project. These bonds often lead to new opportunities, both personal and professional, enriching your journey as an artist and deepening your connection with others. At its core, collaboration is as much about human connection as it is about artistic achievement, reminding us that the best music often grows out of shared respect, joy, and trust in one another.

Be the artist that adds value, not ego, to every collaboration—be the note that resonates harmony.

Action Items

- **Practice humility as an active creative skill.**
  Approach every collaboration with the mindset that the music matters more than personal validation. Make space for others' ideas to exist fully before shaping them. Humility builds trust, and trust is what turns one-off sessions into long-term partnerships.

- **Listen beyond sound—listen for intention.**
  Don't just hear what your collaborator is playing or suggesting; try to understand what they are trying to express emotionally. Ask clarifying questions and reflect ideas back in your own words. Feeling understood is often what makes artists want to work with you again.
- **Contribute clearly without dominating the process.**
  Bring your strengths forward confidently, but avoid flooding the project with ideas simply to prove value. The best collaborators know when to add—and when to step back. Meaningful contribution is about precision, not volume.
- **Handle conflict with curiosity instead of defensiveness.**
  When disagreement arises, treat it as a signal that something important is trying to emerge. Ask why a suggestion matters to the other person instead of immediately rejecting it. Respectful conflict often sharpens the final result rather than weakening it.
- **Let your passion show through commitment, not pressure.**
  Demonstrate enthusiasm by being prepared, responsive, and reliable—not by pushing others to move faster than they're ready to. Consistent energy and follow-through communicate seriousness far more effectively than verbal excitement alone.
- **Adapt to different workflows without losing yourself.**
  Be flexible with formats, tools, and pacing while staying anchored in your values. Whether collaborating remotely or in person, structured or free-flowing, adaptability makes you easier to work with—and more likely to be invited into diverse creative spaces.

The Art of Listening: Finding Inspiration in the Work of Others

Finding fresh musical ideas can often feel elusive. Trust me, I've had my share of frustration staring at a blank page, waiting for the right chord or melody to emerge. The truth is, every time we sit down to compose, we begin again from zero. No matter how experienced we are, the challenge of starting remains.

Creativity is like a muscle—it needs regular exercise to remain active. I've found that when I'm in a creative flow, especially during the production of an album, ideas seem to come naturally. But once that flow is interrupted, restarting the process can feel daunting. This is why it's important to make a habit of constant composition, to keep that muscle engaged and ready.

Learning through Listening

One of the most valuable lessons I've learned is that, when inspiration runs dry, it's the perfect time to immerse yourself in the music of others. You don't have to restrict yourself to your own genre either. Different sounds, textures, and approaches can spark ideas in unexpected ways. The key here is not imitation, but inspiration. Minimalist classical compositions, cinematic film scores, or electronic soundscapes infused with world music can all expand your perspective and ignite new directions in your own work.

Active listening strengthens this process. By noticing production details, instrumentation choices, or the emotional pacing of a piece, you sharpen your own craft and learn techniques that can subtly inform your music without directly copying it.

Turning Influence into Inspiration

Personally, I maintain a playlist titled *Inspirations.* Whenever a song resonates with me—whether for its rhythm, mood, or chord progression—I add it to this list. When I'm stuck, I revisit these tracks. More often than not, something in them rekindles the creative spark. Whether it's a chord progression, a melody, or even a sound texture, these songs serve as jumping-off points.

However, it's crucial to make whatever you take in your own. The goal is not replication but transformation. Absorb the influence, then reinterpret it through your unique voice. Let those external ideas fuel your creativity, but always stay true to what defines your sound.

In the end, listening is not only a technical practice but also a way of connecting emotionally with music and with the artists who create it. It reminds us that creativity is part of a larger conversation.

Listen deeply, for every piece of music has a story that could inspire your next symphony.

Action Items

- **Practice intentional listening instead of passive consumption.** Choose moments to listen without distraction—no multitasking, no scrolling. Focus on how a piece unfolds emotionally, how tension is built and released, and how silence is used. This kind of listening trains your intuition and deepens your understanding of musical storytelling.
- **Listen outside your genre to expand your creative vocabulary.** Deliberately explore styles you wouldn't normally work in—classical, jazz, film music, world music, or experimental electronic genres. You're not looking for sounds to copy, but for structures, moods, and approaches that can subtly inform your own work in unexpected ways.
- **Analyze what moves you, not just what impresses you.** Instead of focusing solely on technical brilliance, ask yourself why a piece resonates emotionally. Is it harmony, pacing, texture, or restraint? Understanding emotional impact is far more valuable than memorizing production tricks.
- **Create a personal inspiration archive.** Maintain a dedicated playlist, notebook, or folder for music that sparks something in you. Revisit it intentionally when you feel blocked. Over time, patterns will emerge that reveal what truly inspires you—and those patterns can guide your artistic direction.
- **Transform influence through your own creative filter.** When an idea arises from something you've heard, don't recreate it directly. Change the tempo, the harmony, the instrumentation, or the emotional context. Let influence pass through your personality until it becomes something unmistakably yours.
- **Use listening as a dialogue, not a comparison.** Approach other artists' work as part of a creative conversation rather than a benchmark you must compete with. Let their music remind you that you are part of a larger artistic ecosystem—one where inspiration flows freely and originality is strengthened through connection, not isolation.

Trust and Compassion: Working Harmoniously with Others

Collaboration as a Foundation

Collaboration in music requires trust, compassion, and sometimes pushing back the ego. It's not just about merging ideas but about truly listening and being open to different approaches.

Embracing Differences in Collaboration

While producing *One Vision* with Oine, we embraced our contrasting styles. His perspective as a composer introduced ideas I wouldn't have considered on my own. Trusting each other's instincts, we let the process flow naturally. There were moments when I might have pushed in one direction, but I had to trust his vision as well. Splitting those choices between us allowed the album to grow beyond anything I had initially imagined.

Working with Andreas Bach, a guitarist from a more traditional, melodic background, required me to adapt my usual approach to production. Our artistic visions sometimes diverged, and that opened new creative directions for me. His guitar brought an organic texture into my ambient soundscapes, and I experienced that exchange as something that pushed the music beyond what either of us might have reached by holding too tightly to our own preferences. At times, I held back my initial ideas and gave more space to his, trusting that the result would grow stronger through that openness.

Growth through Letting Go

This dynamic collaboration also taught me that sometimes, to achieve something great, you have to put the ego aside and embrace the other person's perspective wholeheartedly. It's not just about allowing them to take the lead but trusting that their vision can enrich your own. These contrasts aren't obstacles; they're opportunities for growth, helping to push boundaries and develop as an artist.

Trust and compassion are the invisible bridges that transform collaboration into harmony.

Trust in the Wider Music World

In the ambient and downtempo music world, these principles are often mirrored. By listening deeply and staying open, you unlock new sonic possibilities. Confidence and compassion in collaboration are what allow us to move beyond our individual limitations and create music that speaks to something greater than ourselves. They also nurture meaningful human connection, extending the impact beyond music itself.

Building our music careers on a foundation of trust and compassion not only enriches our collaborations but also deepens our connections to our music and audience.

Action Items

- **Practice trust as an active creative choice.**
  Instead of holding tightly to your own ideas, consciously decide to trust your collaborator's instincts at key moments in the process. This doesn't mean agreeing with everything, but allowing space for ideas to unfold before judging them. Trust often reveals strengths you couldn't access alone.
- **Listen with the intention to understand, not to respond.**
  In collaborative situations, pause before reacting to suggestions. Ask yourself what your collaborator is trying to express emotionally or artistically. Deep listening builds respect and prevents ego-driven conflict, creating an environment where ideas can evolve organically.
- **Embrace differences as creative opportunities.**
  When contrasting styles or perspectives arise, resist the urge to smooth them out too quickly. Differences often point toward unexplored territory. Lean into those tensions and explore how they might enrich the music instead of seeing them as obstacles to overcome.
- **Practice letting go of ownership when it serves the music.**
  Notice moments where your attachment to an idea is driven more by pride than by artistic necessity. Consciously stepping back can strengthen the final result and deepen mutual respect. Collaboration thrives when the music—not individual control—leads the process.
- **Build compassion into creative feedback.**
  When offering critique, frame your thoughts with care and clarity. Focus on the shared goal rather than personal preference. Compassionate feedback encourages openness and keeps collaborators emotionally invested instead of defensive.
- **Extend trust and respect beyond the studio.**
  Carry the same principles of reliability, honesty, and empathy into communication, deadlines, and decision-making. Long-lasting collaborations are built not only on creative chemistry but on human integrity and mutual support over time.

Section 6

Professional Practice

Balancing Art and Career

Practical, career-facing chapters that explore business, sustainability, and maintaining creative integrity.

Navigating Legal Soundscapes: Understanding Music Rights, Identifiers and Creative Protection

In the music industry, navigating the legal landscape is often viewed as a mundane yet crucial aspect of a musician's career. But the truth is: legal literacy is creative freedom. Understanding how rights work, how royalties are tracked, and what your responsibilities and protections are as an artist doesn't hinder creativity—it empowers it. It allows you to make informed decisions that support both your artistic goals and your long-term sustainability.

Whether you're an independent artist or working with a label or publisher, legal clarity allows you to take ownership of your music—not just creatively, but financially and professionally. If you've poured your heart into a song, you owe it to yourself to protect it.

Understanding Music Rights

Understanding music rights involves four core types:

- **Composition rights**
  The rights tied to the underlying musical work and lyrics.
- **Master rights**
  The rights tied to the actual sound recording.
- **Performance rights**
  Rights and royalties connected to the public performance of music.
- **Synchronization licensing**
  Licensing music for use with visual media such as film, television, or advertising.

Each of these areas serves a different function in the music business and affects how a work is protected, used, and monetized.[1]

DOI: 10.4324/9781003710622-6

To me, examples like radio play, visual use, and streaming make clear that different uses of music involve different rights and payment paths. I treat these as distinct parts of the professional landscape, which is why I believe artists benefit from understanding them early.

These rights are managed and tracked through various systems involving codes and identifiers, such as the *ISRC*, *ISWC*, and *IPI* codes.

Understanding Music Identifiers: ISRC, ISWC, and IPI

To ensure correct attribution and royalty distribution, each song and contributor is assigned specific identifiers:

- **ISRC (International Standard Recording Code)**
  Identifies a specific sound recording (the master). Used for tracking plays on digital platforms. Assigned during distribution by your label or digital distributor.
- **ISWC (International Standard Musical Work Code)**
  Identifies the musical composition (melody, lyrics, etc.). Assigned by collecting societies like GEMA, ASCAP, or PRS.
- **IPI (Interested Party Information)**
  Identifies the interested parties connected to the work, such as songwriters, composers, and publishers.

Together, these identifiers help link creators to their works and recordings across professional music systems.[2]

Example – ABBA's "Dancing Queen"

A useful historical example is ABBA's "Dancing Queen," which received the first ISWC, **T-000.000.001-0**. This illustrates how a musical work can be identified separately from its recordings and linked to contributor data in professional rights systems.

In practice, identifiers such as ISWC, IPI, and ISRC help connect the composition, the interested parties, and specific recordings across registration, distribution, and rights-management workflows.

A Simple Flow of Music Rights and Identifiers

1 A composition is registered through the relevant professional rights-management or registration-agency process.
2 Once the necessary creator information is in place, the work may be allocated an ISWC.
3 The contributors connected to the work are identified in the relevant interested-party system.
4 When a specific recording is prepared for release, that recording is assigned its own ISRC.

Together, these identifiers help support attribution, data matching, and royalty processing across different professional systems.[3]

Registering with a Collecting Society

To me, registering work with a collecting society is one of the clearest ways to take authorship seriously, even without a publishing deal. I see it as a practical step that helps keep the connection between the music, the creator, and any future use of the work from becoming vague or fragile.

If you have a publishing deal, a publisher may register your works on your behalf and collect your share of publishing income. But I would still double-check that all works are properly registered.

For me, staying independent does not remove the need to think seriously about the publishing side of your work. That can include:

- Registering your songs in a way that clearly connects them to you
- Paying attention to how your work is tracked and managed over time
- Making thoughtful decisions about where and how your songs are used

If you sign a deal with a publisher, they may help to:

- Register your work for you
- Handle royalty collection more broadly
- Pursue sync placements and other monetization avenues

But I would never assume they have registered your songs. I would always ask and confirm.

Record Labels and Master Rights

A label relationship can, in my experience, offer things such as:

- Financial support
- Access to studio or production resources
- Help with marketing, release planning, or distribution

At the same time, I see it as important to look closely at what kind of control, ownership, or participation you may be giving up in return.

Before signing:

- Ask how long they retain the rights
- Confirm your royalty percentage
- Check if you retain creative control

An independent release path can offer more direct control, but it can also shift more practical responsibility onto the artist. Whether that balance feels worthwhile depends on the person, the project, and the support around it.

Real-World Scenarios to Learn from

Scenario 1: The Unwritten Collaboration

A beat-maker and vocalist write a track together but never sign a split sheet. Later, the track goes viral, and now they're in a legal battle over ownership.

Lesson:
Always document your splits, even with friends. It saves you from heartbreak later.

Scenario 2: The Beat License Trap

An artist leases a beat under a non-exclusive license, assuming they can release it freely. Later, another artist buys exclusive rights—and the first artist must take their track down.

Lesson:
Know what rights you're purchasing. If it's exclusive, ensure no one else can use it. If it's non-exclusive, understand the limits.

Scenario 3: The "AI Said It's Fine" Contract

An artist once reached out to me saying an AI tool had reviewed their music contract and claimed everything looked fine. But when I double-checked, I found several serious legal issues. That AI hallucinated facts—and the artist almost signed away full ownership of their masters for life.

Lesson:
AI is helpful, but not reliable for legal decisions. Always verify.

Scenario 4: The Misunderstood Split Sheet

A group writes a song together but doesn't agree on the contribution split. Months later, arguments break out when royalties arrive. Avoid this with a signed **split sheet** stating each contributor's percentage. It's a simple but powerful tool.

Best Practices to Stay Legally Safe and Creative

- Educate yourself regularly on music law and industry standards.
- Register your works with your local PRO (Performance Rights Organization) or collecting society.

- Understand what you're licensing—especially when buying beats, loops, or using samples.
- Always use split sheets in collaborations.
- Keep contracts for everything: session work, co-writes, remixes, sync deals, and producer agreements.
- Be clear on what "exclusive" and "non-exclusive" rights mean—and only grant them if you fully understand the implications.
- Never sign anything under pressure. Ask for time to review, and don't hesitate to get legal advice.
- Ask experienced artists in your circle for guidance. Their practical advice can help you avoid common pitfalls.
- Don't just use AI tools or templates to check contracts—while they can be helpful for a first-pass review or to flag areas of concern, they are not a substitute for human judgment or legal expertise. Always review them yourself or consult a professional. You're responsible for what you sign.
- Document everything. Email confirmations, session agreements, and even chat logs can support your case if issues arise later.
- Organize your metadata and keep a spreadsheet of your ISRCs, ISWCs, and IPIs. It may seem tedious now, but it will protect you in the long run.

Protecting your music is protecting your voice—it ensures your art is heard, credited, and safeguarded for the future.

Why It Matters

The legal side of music may not feel creative, but it protects your creativity. Without legal knowledge and proper rights management, artists risk losing credit, missing out on royalties, or even facing disputes over ownership.

I do not see registration as a minor administrative detail; it is part of how I protect the path between the work and the recognition or income it may generate. That groundwork feels to me like part of taking the music seriously over the long term.

Your songs are your intellectual property—your voice, your ideas, your livelihood. Understanding how to protect and manage them is an essential part of being a professional artist. The more you learn about these processes, the more empowered you'll be in every negotiation, collaboration, or release.

Final Thoughts

Don't be intimidated by music law—just be informed. The more you understand your rights and responsibilities, the more confidently you can move through the industry and keep the focus where it belongs: on making meaningful music.

Know your rights, protect your music, and let your creativity flourish within the chords of the law.

Action Items

- **Learn the four core music rights and how they interact.**
  Make sure you clearly understand composition, master, performance, and synchronization rights, and how each one generates income in different scenarios. Knowing who controls which right allows you to negotiate deals confidently and avoid unintentionally giving away ownership or revenue.
- **Register every work properly and early.**
  Register your compositions with your local collecting society as soon as they are finished, even if you don't have a publisher. Early registration ensures accurate tracking, protects your authorship, and prevents royalty loss when your music is performed, streamed, or broadcast.
- **Treat identifiers as essential creative infrastructure.**
  Keep organized records of your ISRCs, ISWCs, and IPIs in a dedicated spreadsheet or database. These identifiers silently power global royalty tracking, and losing control of them can result in missing income or misattribution that is difficult to correct later.
- **Document every collaboration with written agreements.**
  Always use split sheets and written agreements, even when working with friends or long-time collaborators. Clear documentation prevents misunderstandings,

preserves relationships, and ensures everyone is credited and paid fairly once the music is released or licensed.

- **Read every contract slowly and critically.**
  Never sign agreements under time pressure or based solely on trust, templates, or AI-generated summaries. Take time to understand royalty splits, term lengths, exclusivity clauses, and ownership transfers. If something feels unclear, seek clarification or professional advice before committing.
- **See legal literacy as long-term creative protection.**
  Shift your mindset from viewing legal tasks as boring obligations to seeing them as safeguards for your artistic future. Proper rights management protects your income, your reputation, and your creative freedom—allowing you to focus on making music without fear of losing control over your work.

The Producer as Co-Creator: Navigating Roles, Credit, and Ownership

The Blurred Lines of Modern Music Production

In today's collaborative music-making landscape, the role of a producer can extend far beyond technical execution. To me, producers are often not just engineers or beat-makers, but also co-writers, sound architects, and creative partners who help shape the emotional and structural DNA of a song.

This shift raises an important question: **What share of the song should a producer receive?** When a producer plays a significant role in building the harmonic, melodic, or emotional foundation of a track, the line between producer and co-writer becomes increasingly hard to define.

Creative Roles in Flux

I often think of the traditional producer role as overseeing the recording process, coaching artists in the studio, and polishing the final product for release. But in genres like pop, electronic, hip-hop, and ambient music, the producer can also initiate or co-create the core musical ideas. They may write chord progressions, shape toplines, edit arrangements, guide the vocal performance, or even contribute lyrics.

In such cases, I would see the producer as part of the songwriting process, even if that was not the original intention. Their contribution can alter the emotional direction or catchiness of the track so strongly that the final version would feel different without them. In that situation, co-writing credit can feel not just fair, but necessary.

Great collaborations thrive not only on creativity, but on clarity.

Why Clarity and Communication Matter

Because the creative process is fluid and collaborative, it's easy to delay or avoid discussing ownership and credit. But postponing these conversations can lead to misunderstandings and even legal conflict.

Clear communication upfront saves time, strengthens trust, and prevents future disputes. It also ensures everyone feels respected and acknowledged for their work. These conversations don't have to be awkward—they just need to be honest. And the earlier they happen, the better.

When Is a Producer a Co-Writer?

There's no single rule that defines when a producer becomes a co-writer, but here are a few guiding questions:

- Did the producer contribute to the melody, chord progression, or lyrics?
- Did they help shape the topline or hook?
- Would the song exist in its current form without their creative input?
- Did they direct or influence the vocal delivery in an emotionally meaningful way?

If the answer is yes to any of these, co-writing credit is worth discussing.

Holding the note together ensures the song belongs to everyone.

Setting Expectations: Percentages and Agreements

Whenever possible, use a split sheet to document the songwriting and production shares. This one-page agreement can outline each contributor's role, the agreed percentages for publishing and royalties, and who owns the master recording.

In my experience, equal splits can feel natural when both parties have shaped the composition in a meaningful way. In other collaborations, different percentages may better reflect how the creative work actually unfolded.

Here are some core elements to clarify:

- Ownership of the **composition** (songwriting credit)
- Ownership of the **master recording**
- Publishing splits and collection rights
- Backend royalties via PROs

If a beat was licensed, understand whether it's **exclusive** or **non-exclusive**. The terms of usage, monetization, and credit must be clearly defined.

My Own Experience

I usually discuss the share in advance with everyone involved. There are always various options, but with most people, I opted for an equal share. I believe that when everyone has an equal stake, they're naturally more invested in achieving the best possible result. A sense of shared ownership often brings out the best in each collaborator.

That said, not every situation is the same. There were cases where, over the course of a project, I ended up investing significantly more time or effort. When that happened, I brought it up for discussion. We talked openly about it, and in most cases, we adjusted the shares fairly. I always left the final decision open, prioritizing a respectful and honest dialogue.

What I've learned is this: these conversations—while sometimes delicate—are essential. Discussing roles and shares upfront, or at least during the process, helps set expectations and prevents misunderstandings or disappointments later. Fairness and transparency are key to preserving both the collaboration and the relationship.

The Role of Professional Registration

After determining splits and credits, register the work with a performance rights organization (like GEMA, PRS, ASCAP, or BMI). Include:

- IPI numbers of all songwriters
- ISWC for the composition
- ISRC for the master recording
- Percentages of each contributor's share

I see accurate metadata as essential to professional release practice. When those details are unclear, the connection between the work and the people behind it becomes more fragile.

Final Thoughts

The producer's role has evolved—and that evolution deserves recognition. As producers become true co-creators, the need for open, honest conversations about credit, ownership, and roles has never been greater.

Set expectations early. Put agreements in writing. Respect the creative input of everyone involved. And most of all, don't be afraid to have the conversation.

Fairness isn't just about percentages. It's about building a culture where every voice feels heard, and every contribution is valued.

Collaboration without clarity is chaos. But with clear roles and shared respect, it becomes magic.

Action Items

- **Define creative roles before the session begins.**
  Before starting a collaboration, openly discuss who is contributing what: songwriting, production, sound design, arrangement, or artistic direction. Even if roles evolve later, an initial shared understanding sets a healthy foundation and avoids unspoken assumptions that can lead to conflict.
- **Acknowledge when production becomes authorship.**
  Pay close attention to moments where production crosses into composition — writing chord progressions, shaping toplines, guiding vocal melodies, or defining the emotional arc of a track. When this happens, recognize that the producer is no longer just supporting the song, but actively co-creating it. This awareness is key to fair credit.
- **Have the credit conversation early — and revisit it if needed.**
  Don't wait until release day to discuss ownership. Address songwriting and production shares early in the process, and revisit the conversation if the creative balance shifts. Transparency during the journey is far easier than damage control at the end.
- **Use split sheets as a creative safety net, not a legal threat.**
  Treat split sheets as tools that protect relationships, not as cold legal documents. Writing things down ensures clarity, preserves trust, and allows everyone to focus fully on creativity instead of worrying about future misunderstandings.
- **Separate emotion from fairness when discussing percentages.**
  Creative contribution is rarely equal in effort, time, or responsibility. When discussing shares, focus on contribution rather than sentiment. Fairness doesn't always mean equal — it means consciously agreed upon. Respectful dialogue keeps these discussions constructive rather than personal.

- **Understand and clarify master vs. composition ownership.**
  Always distinguish between who owns the composition (publishing) and who owns the master recording. Many conflicts arise because these two are blurred or misunderstood. Clear separation protects both creative and financial interests long-term.
- **Register works correctly and collaboratively.**
  Once splits are agreed upon, ensure all contributors are properly registered with PROs and distributors, including correct IPIs, ISWCs, ISRCs, and percentages. Incomplete or incorrect metadata can silently erase someone's contribution from royalty flows.
- **View clarity as a creative enabler, not a constraint.**
  Clear agreements don't limit creativity — they free it. When everyone knows where they stand, trust deepens, collaboration becomes more open, and the focus returns to making the best possible music together.

DIY vs. Outsourcing: Knowing When to Seek Professional Help

The All-In-One Artist Era

In today's music landscape, it can feel easier than ever to do everything yourself. With powerful software, endless tutorials, and affordable gear, independent artists may find themselves writing, producing, mixing, mastering, designing their own artwork, and promoting their music from a home studio. But while the tools may feel accessible, the expectations can still be overwhelming. To me, it often feels as if we live in an age where being multi-skilled is not just encouraged, but quietly assumed.

Yet a vital question remains: just because you *can* do it all, does that mean you *should*?

This chapter explores the value of knowing when to take the reins and when to hand them over. Understanding the difference between independence and overload is key to protecting both your creative energy and the quality of your work.

Let's be honest: we're not experts in every field—and we're not meant to be. Some artists do develop multi-specialty proficiency and enjoy the process of mastering multiple disciplines, which can lead to incredible independence and skill depth. However, for most of us, trying to handle everything alone can be creatively and mentally exhausting. While learning new skills is empowering, it's easy to fall into the trap of trying to master everything at once. And in doing so, we risk losing sight of the very reason we started making music in the first place.

Our primary goal as artists should be to create and express ourselves through sound. That's where the magic happens. So it's worth asking: what's essential for *you* to handle personally, and what might be better left in the hands of someone who lives and breathes that specific craft?

Outsourcing isn't defeat—it's a strategy for sustainability, clarity, and creative excellence.

The Pros and Cons of Doing It All Yourself

Pros

- **Creative control**:
  You shape every detail according to your vision.
- **Cost-effective**:
  You save money by not hiring external professionals.
- **Speed and flexibility**:
  No need to wait on others to move forward.
- **Learning and growth**:
  You gain skills that make you more self-sufficient.

Cons

- **Time-consuming**:
  Doing everything takes significant effort.
- **Creative fatigue**:
  Spreading yourself too thin can lead to burnout. For example, trying to design a cover late at night after mixing all day can drain your energy and joy.
- **Blind spots**:
  You may miss technical or emotional flaws in your own work.
- **Quality risks**:
  Tasks outside your strengths might not meet professional standards.

Before I attended multiple mastering courses because I was fascinated by the art of mastering music, I outsourced this highly important task to my label or organized a trusted mastering engineer myself. In doing so, I ensured that my music sounded as professional as it could be. I don't regret spending the money on it because I'm still proud of the result. If I had done it myself at the time when I wasn't yet skilled in mastering, I would probably regret not having sought professional help. The same applies for Dolby Atmos mixes. I outsource these mixes to a professional, since I currently don't have the time or equipment to mix in Dolby Atmos myself on a professional level. Of course, I could try and learn this—and I would love to—but I decided to save time and resources here and focus on composing and producing instead.

When to Consider Outsourcing

There's a fine line between self-sufficiency and self-sabotage. If you find yourself stuck tweaking endlessly, missing deadlines, or consistently unhappy with your results, it might be time to bring in support.

Common tasks to consider outsourcing:

- **Mixing**:
  An objective mix engineer can balance your track with fresh ears.
- **Mastering**:
  Final polishing by a dedicated specialist ensures consistency and quality.
- **Dolby Atmos**:
  Some projects benefit from specialist support at technically demanding stages, especially when a format introduces its own workflow, translation, and presentation challenges.
- **Session musicians/vocalists**:
  Bring nuance and emotion you can't create alone.
- **Artwork and design**:
  A strong visual identity is part of a professional release.
- **Promotion and PR**:
  Professionals can get your music in front of the right ears.
- **Music videos/visualizers**:
  Outsourcing visuals can make your release stand out.

I, for instance, outsource music videos, promotion, and PR to my label. I don't enjoy creating music videos myself, and PR is something that's better handled by the label. It frees up time for me so I can focus more on the music itself.

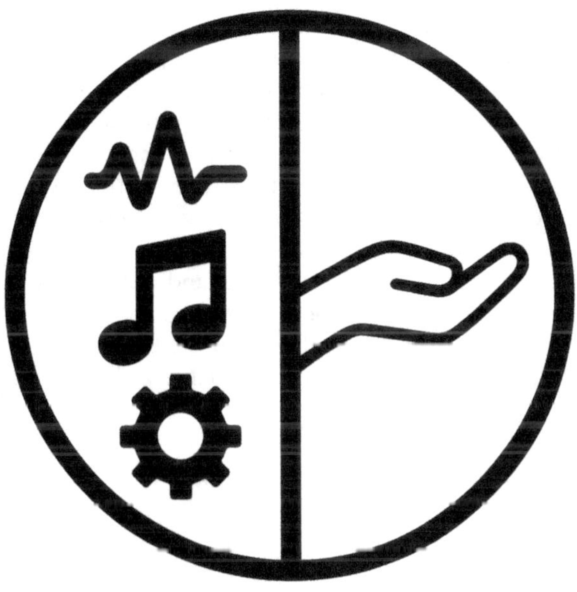

Independence fuels creativity, but trust sustains it—master both.

Collaboration Is not a Compromise

Outsourcing doesn't mean you're giving up control. On the contrary, it's often the most powerful form of collaboration. Many of the producers I most associate with lasting influence—Rick Rubin, Max Martin, Brian Eno—do not suggest a model of doing everything alone. To me, their work points to the value of knowing when to bring in others.

The best music is rarely made in isolation. Choosing the right collaborators can enrich your vision rather than dilute it.

For example, I collaborated several times and even produced several albums with different artists like Oine, Andreas Bach, Christoph Sebastian Pabst, and others. I did this not only because I absolutely love their music, but also to enrich my own sound, grow through them, and through the collaboration itself. I learned and discovered so many new things through these wonderful people and musicians that I see this as a great enrichment—and ultimately, a source of wonderful new music we've put out into the world.

The Financial Equation

Budget is a real concern. But think of outsourcing not as an expense, but as an **investment**.

If a properly mixed and mastered song gets editorial playlist placement or sync licensing, the return can outweigh the upfront cost.

I tend to think about budget less in rigid numbers and more in terms of matching limited resources to the stage of the project. At the leanest end, I would keep more in-house; with a bit more room, I would usually prioritize one specialist step, such as mastering, design, or mixing.

Prioritize based on what's holding your music back the most. For instance, I once had a track where I felt very confident about the production and mix. But I knew that the mastering step would make or break how the track was perceived by others. I decided to hand it over to a trusted mastering engineer, who brought a new level of depth, loudness, and polish to the track. It was a great decision—I received much more positive feedback after the final version, and the track performed better than expected on streaming platforms. Sometimes, trusting someone else with the final step allows your work to shine as it truly should.

Hybrid Approaches: The Best of Both Worlds

You don't have to go all in on one side. A hybrid workflow is often ideal:

- **Produce and mix yourself**, but outsource mastering.
- **Record a full demo**, then bring in a session player to re-record key parts.
- **Create rough artwork**, then hire a designer to refine it.

For example, for my collaboration album *One Vision* that I did with my friend Oine (Adrián Márquez Salas), we collected some outstanding photography from the Antelope Canyon but handed the full cover design and artwork over to a professional designer. She did an amazing job. So we laid the foundation and saved time by giving a clear direction, but the designer refined it to perfection.

This approach saves time and money while elevating the overall quality.

Trust, Communication, and Choosing the Right People

Hiring someone to work on your art is an act of trust. Beyond reviewing their portfolio, it's also important to evaluate their professionalism through communication style, responsiveness, and reliability. Do they respond to emails promptly? Are they clear and respectful in their interactions? These qualities often make a big difference in collaborative experiences and outcomes. Here's how to protect your vision:

- **Communicate clearly**:
  Provide references, goals, and examples.
- **Start small**:
  Test the waters with a single task before committing to a full project.
- **Ask for revisions**:
  Most professionals offer at least one revision round.
- **Listen to your gut**:
  If something doesn't feel right, it probably isn't.
- **Review their portfolio**:
  Look at past work to ensure alignment with your style.

Final Thoughts

Being a music producer today often means being a multi-disciplinary artist. But that doesn't mean you have to go it alone.

Professionalism includes knowing your limits and building a creative team when needed. Whether you handle everything yourself, outsource a few steps, or assemble a full team, what matters most is that your music shines—and that you enjoy the journey of bringing it to life.

Your job isn't to do everything alone. It's to bring your vision to life—however that needs to happen.

Action Items

- **Clarify what *must* stay personal.**
  Identify the parts of your creative process that define your artistic identity—composition, sound design, lyrical work, or emotional direction—and commit to keeping these in your own hands, even when outsourcing other tasks.

- **Audit your current bottlenecks honestly.**
  Look at where projects tend to stall, drain your energy, or fall short in quality. These friction points often reveal the exact areas where professional help would elevate both the result and your creative well-being.
- **Separate learning goals from release goals.**
  Decide whether a project is meant for skill development or for public release. It's valid to mix and master your own tracks when learning—but for key releases, consider outsourcing to protect the artistic impact.
- **Define a sustainable hybrid workflow.**
  Design a repeatable process that combines independence with support—such as producing yourself while outsourcing mastering or visuals—so each release benefits from both personal vision and professional polish.
- **Set a realistic creative budget in advance.**
  Determine how much you can invest per project and decide *where* that investment will make the biggest difference. Treat outsourcing as a creative amplifier, not a financial loss.
- **Choose collaborators with intention, not urgency.**
  Work only with people whose communication style, values, and aesthetic align with yours. A good collaborator doesn't just deliver quality—they protect your vision and your peace of mind.

Finding Balance: Navigating the Creative and Business Sides of Music

The Dual Role of the Modern Musician

Every artist dreams of living purely for their art, free from the constraints of business and financial obligations. Yet, the reality of being a musician today is much more complex than that. Once you release a track, whether as a side project or full-time career, you're not just an artist—you're also a business owner. Striking that delicate balance between creativity and commerce is no small feat, and learning to embrace both roles is essential for a sustainable career.

The Business Behind the Music

Most musicians would rather spend their time making music than dealing with contracts, taxes, and the minutiae of running a business. After all, isn't music supposed to be about expressing your soul, not crunching numbers? But the moment you upload a track to any platform or perform at a paid gig, you're stepping into the world of business. Whether it's paying session musicians, coordinating with mastering engineers, or signing contracts with labels and publishers, you have a responsibility to treat this as a professional endeavor. Recognizing this early can help prevent frustration and setbacks later on.

Building a Support System

Of course, it doesn't mean you have to do everything by yourself. In fact, it's often a smarter move to seek help where you lack expertise. This could mean working with a trusted tax advisor, a label to handle your releases, or a publisher to manage your rights. A good team can free you up to focus on what you do best: making music. The key is finding partners who share your vision and genuinely care about your success, so your support system feels like an extension of your creativity rather than a burden.

Why Knowledge Still Matters

It's crucial that you understand the basics of what you're getting into. In my experience, many musicians spend far less time on the business side than on the creative side, whether that means understanding the difference between a label contract and a publishing deal or grasping the implications of exclusive vs. non-exclusive agreements. Without at least some knowledge here, it can become easier to sign away more than intended or miss opportunities that were not obvious at first. To me, uncertainty in these areas can carry financial consequences, but also creative ones, because the wrong deal can narrow your artistic freedom. A foundation of knowledge empowers you to make informed decisions, even if others handle the details.

My Approach to Balance

In my own career under my artist name, Thomas Lemmer, I've found a way to strike that balance. I work with a label that handles my releases on an exclusive basis, meaning they take care of much of the business side for me. This allows me to pour my energy into the creative process without getting bogged down by administrative tasks. When it comes to performance rights, I have a company that registers my performances globally and ensures that those royalties make their way into my account. Meanwhile, my publisher manages the composition rights, saving me the hassle of registering them myself with a collecting society. It's a system that keeps the business side professional without stifling my creativity.

The Value of Delegation

Yes, they take a cut, but for me, it's a fair trade. I get more time to create, knowing that the business side is in capable hands. Even my performance rights, as both the composer and performer, are managed by a company that ensures those royalties end up where they should. Sharing a percentage of the revenue is worth it when it means your art remains at the center of your day-to-day focus. The relief of not having to oversee every detail opens space for deeper creative exploration.

Lessons from Doing It All Alone

Can you do all this on your own? Absolutely. For years, I did everything myself, from negotiating contracts to managing royalty collections. But I realized that the more I took on, the less time I had for the one thing I started all of this for—creating music. Running the business side started to feel like a full-time office job, and that's not what I signed up for. So, I began outsourcing, piece by piece, until I found a setup that allowed me to focus on my strengths while trusting others to handle the rest. That experience taught me the value of letting go where necessary and reminded me that independence sometimes comes from collaboration.

Finding Your Own Balance

There's no one-size-fits-all solution here. Everyone's situation is different, and the right balance for me might not be the right balance for you. But if you feel like the business side is swallowing up your creativity, take a step back and see which aspects can be outsourced or delegated. Sometimes, sharing a piece of the pie with the right people can lead to greater success, both creatively and financially. After all, when your partners have a vested interest in your success, they'll push your music as hard as you do. The important part is to stay intentional about where your time and energy go, regularly reassessing whether your setup still serves your goals.

The Sweet Spot Between Art and Business

In the end, it's all about balance. And when you find that sweet spot between art and business, you'll not only enjoy the creative process more—you might just find that your music reaches new heights. The harmony between creative passion and professional responsibility is what allows you to build a career that's both sustainable and fulfilling. Take a moment to reflect on where you currently stand in this balance—are you leaning too heavily toward one side? Adjusting even slightly can bring new clarity and renewed joy to both your music and your career.

True harmony comes when music and business flow together, not against each other.

Action Items

- **Define your creative and business boundaries clearly.**
  Take time to write down which parts of your music career energize you creatively and which drain your focus. Decide consciously which tasks you want to keep close to your art and which ones you are willing to delegate or outsource. This clarity prevents burnout and ensures your creative energy is protected.
- **Build a support system you trust.**
  Identify professionals or partners—such as labels, publishers, tax advisors, or distributors—who can handle business responsibilities reliably. A strong support system should feel like an extension of your creative vision, not an obstacle to it, allowing you to focus more fully on making music.
- **Learn the basics, even if you delegate.**
  You don't need to become a legal or financial expert, but you should understand the fundamentals of contracts, royalties, and rights. This knowledge empowers you to ask the right questions, recognize red flags, and make informed decisions without feeling dependent or exposed.

- **Regularly audit how you spend your time.**
  Look honestly at how much of your week is spent on creative work vs. administrative or business tasks. If business duties consistently overshadow music-making, it may be time to adjust your setup, outsource specific areas, or simplify your workflow.
- **Evaluate delegation as an investment, not a loss.**
  When you give up a percentage of income to collaborators or service providers, assess what you gain in return—time, focus, quality, and peace of mind. Often, the long-term creative and professional benefits outweigh the short-term cost.
- **Reassess your balance as your career evolves.**
  The right balance today may not serve you in five years. Make it a habit to revisit your creative–business setup regularly, especially after major releases or life changes, ensuring that your structure continues to support both your artistic growth and personal well-being.

Sustaining Longevity in the Music Industry: How to Adapt without Losing Yourself

Embracing Change While Staying True

Maintaining a long-lasting career in the music industry requires embracing change and innovation while staying true to your core sound and artistic values. The music industry is an ever-changing landscape, with new trends that come and go. Some genres evolve over time, while others fade into obscurity. As an artist, you're always surrounded by others producing similar music, many of whom strive to stand out by experimenting or gradually shifting their sound.

To sustain success in the long term, you must consistently create exceptional work while also evolving and adapting to the market. However, staying relevant doesn't mean abandoning your identity. The key lies in knowing which parts of your sound define you and holding onto those elements while incorporating fresh ideas. Whether it's production techniques, songwriting, or sound design, the aspects that make you unique should be embraced as part of your personal artistic voice. At the same time, remaining open to new influences and continually learning will keep your music innovative and exciting.

Learning from Industry Icons

Some of the artists I most associate with longevity seem to have mastered this balance. Björk, for example, strikes me as an artist who keeps evolving her sound through technology, visuals, and experimentation while remaining grounded in a strong artistic identity. Despite her movement into electronic, avant-garde, and multimedia territory, she still feels instantly recognizable to me, with core elements of her voice and atmosphere remaining intact.

Phil Collins is another example that comes to mind. To me, his work maintains a strong sense of continuity through distinctive songwriting, emotive vocal delivery, and a recognizable rhythmic voice, even while moving across a wide range of musical settings. I do not hear him as an artist defined by only one narrow frame, but as someone whose musical identity remains present even as the surrounding context shifts.

From Genesis to his solo work, I hear an artist whose voice, sensibility, and instinct for direct, heartfelt storytelling remain clearly intact. Even when the musical setting changes, there is still, to my ears, a familiar combination of melodic clarity, emotional directness, and rhythmic character that holds the work together. That continuity is what stands out to me more than any one style he moved through.

What I take from an example like this is that artistic identity does not have to depend on staying in one fixed musical space. To me, it can remain intact across very different settings when the underlying voice, perspective, and expressive instinct are strong enough to carry through.

My Journey in Longevity

In my own journey, producing music in the downtempo and ambient scenes for over 20 years, I've witnessed firsthand how these genres have evolved. I've always strived to push the boundaries, continuously learning and adapting. With each album, I set key elements or ideas I want to explore—whether in sound design or production techniques—while staying true to my signature style.

Collaborating with other artists who share this mindset has been essential. These partnerships allowed me to exchange ideas and gain fresh perspectives, enriching my work. For example, embracing Dolby Atmos has pushed my music into new dimensions, offering listeners a more immersive experience. I began this journey with my album *Hope*, followed by *One Vision* (with Oine), and since then, I have been convinced that this format will play a major role in future music production. Collaborating with engineers and producers skilled in this technology bridged gaps in my own expertise and inspired new creative directions.

Staying Innovative through Collaboration and Technology

Another key aspect of sustaining longevity is leveraging collaboration and remix culture. Over the years, I've had remix editions of my albums, inviting artists from different genres to reinterpret our work, as with *One Vision (Remixed)*—a project Oine and I created together. This not only brought new life to the music but also introduced it to entirely new audiences. Similarly, my remix of SINE's "Caught in Time" benefited both of us by reaching new listeners and offering a fresh take on the original. These exchanges keep the creative energy flowing and help music evolve beyond its original form.

Practical Strategies for Longevity

- **Define your core identity**
  Know the non-negotiable elements of your music that must remain.
- **Stay curious and learn**
  Explore new tools, genres, and workflows without losing your artistic voice.
- **Collaborate with intention**
  Work with artists and producers who expand your perspective.
- **Adopt technology mindfully**
  Integrate innovations like Dolby Atmos, where they enhance your storytelling.
- **Engage with remix culture**
  Invite reinterpretations of your work and remix others to keep your sound fresh.
- **Reflect and adapt**
  Periodically review your evolution to ensure growth aligns with your core.

Evolving without Losing Yourself

The roots anchor your identity, while the branches remind you to keep reaching outward.

The key to longevity as an artist and producer is to continually strive for growth without compromising your identity. Embrace who you are and what you stand for, but never shy away from new opportunities to push your artistry forward. Stay true to your voice, keep learning, and remain adaptable, and you'll find the keys to a long-term, fulfilling career in the music business.

Staying true to yourself while evolving with the industry is not just about adapting; it's about deepening your essence in a changing world.

Action Items

- **Define the elements that form your artistic core.**
  Take time to clearly identify which aspects of your music are non-negotiable—this might be your harmonic language, emotional tone, pacing, or production aesthetic. Writing these down helps you recognize which changes strengthen your identity and which risk diluting it.
- **Commit to continuous learning without chasing trends blindly.**
  Make learning a long-term habit rather than a reaction to hype. Explore new tools, formats, or genres with curiosity, but always ask how they serve your artistic goals instead of adopting them out of fear of falling behind.
- **Use collaboration as a source of renewal, not replacement.**
  Work with artists who challenge your perspective and introduce new ways of thinking, while still respecting your voice. Healthy collaborations expand your creative range without requiring you to abandon what defines you.
- **Adopt new technology with a clear artistic purpose.**
  Before integrating innovations such as immersive audio formats or new production workflows, ask what emotional or narrative value they add. Technology should deepen your expression, not distract from it.
- **Revisit and reinterpret your own catalog.**
  Reflect on past work to identify recurring patterns, strengths, and ideas worth evolving. Remix projects, alternate versions, or reinterpretations can refresh your music while reinforcing continuity across your body of work.
- **Schedule regular moments of reflection on your direction.**
  Periodically step back and evaluate whether your creative evolution still aligns with your personal values and long-term vision. Longevity is built not through constant acceleration, but through intentional, well-aligned growth.

The Artist's Journey: Beyond Milestones and Media

Rethinking Success in Music

In the realm of creative arts, particularly music, the traditional narrative often focuses on reaching specific milestones—achieving that hit single, that breakthrough album, or that signature sound that defines a career.

However, this viewpoint can obscure the true nature of artistic growth, which is far more about the journey than the destination. As artists, we can sometimes find ourselves ensnared by the notion that our worth is measured by singular successes. But it is essential to recognize that not every artist will enjoy meteoric rises or headline-grabbing triumphs. Success has many faces, and often the most enduring careers are built steadily, not suddenly.

Lessons from Iconic Journeys

When I think about artists such as The Beatles or Ed Sheeran, I do not think first of instant success. I tend to read those journeys as stories of gradual development, persistence, and a growing connection with listeners over time. What stands out to me is not the myth of sudden arrival, but the sense of an artistic path taking shape step by step.

To me, examples like these suggest that a lasting career often grows through continued effort, adjustment, and a willingness to keep refining both the work and the way it reaches people. I hear in those kinds of trajectories a reminder that momentum can build slowly, and that artistic progress does not always announce itself in a single dramatic moment.

That is why I see resilience, patience, and steady artistic growth as qualities that can matter just as much as talent. From my perspective, some of the most meaningful creative journeys are not defined by speed, but by the accumulation of experience, clarity, and connection over time.

Embracing Evolution and Innovation

In a parallel vein, someone like Björk illustrates, to me, a relentless pursuit of musical evolution. When I listen across the different phases of her work, I hear an artist who seems deeply committed to exploring new directions rather than settling into one fixed language. Even as the surrounding forms change, I still sense a strong internal logic holding the work together.

Across the path I associate with her name, I hear a willingness to move into electronic, pop, and avant-garde territory without losing a distinct artistic center. To me, that is part of what makes her work feel exploratory rather than restless. The changes do not come across as trend-chasing, but as the expression of an artist continuing to search, refine, and redefine her own vocabulary.

From my perspective, her longevity seems tied less to commercial calculation than to a deep commitment to the creative process itself. I hear her work as a reminder that artistic endurance can come from shaping one's own path, trusting reinvention, and allowing change to become part of identity rather than a departure from it.

My Own Path of Continuous Growth

Reflecting on my own journey, having produced numerous albums, I see each project as a step in a continuous progression. I am driven not by the prospect of 'finishing' but by the endless possibilities that the act of creating presents. Each album represents a chapter in an ongoing narrative, each with its own lessons and revelations. This approach keeps the artistic fires burning, ensuring that every day in the studio is an opportunity to explore new ideas, confront new challenges, and refine my craft. What motivates me most is not the finish line, but the discovery that comes with each new piece of music.

The Long View of an Artist's Career

Therefore, it's vital for artists to view their careers as an evolutionary process. Consider each phase of your career not as a sprint toward a finish line but as a segment of a much larger marathon—one that offers countless opportunities for growth, experimentation, and self-discovery. Embrace the slow burn of your career; appreciate the times of struggle just as much as the moments of triumph. Let your love for the creative process be the fuel that drives you, and let each project build upon the last, pushing your artistic boundaries and enriching your musical vocabulary. The artist's life is a long journey of learning, and every step forward is valuable in itself.

Remember, the journey of an artist isn't just about hitting milestones or gaining media attention, but about the continual pursuit of personal and creative growth.

Action Items

- **Redefine what success means for you personally.**
  Take time to consciously separate your own sense of fulfillment from external validation, such as streams, press coverage, or milestones. Write down what a "successful year" looks like for you in terms of growth, learning, and creative satisfaction rather than numbers alone.
- **Shift your focus from outcomes to process.**
  Practice valuing the daily act of creating—writing, experimenting, refining—regardless of immediate results. When the process itself becomes meaningful, motivation becomes more sustainable and less dependent on recognition.
- **Study long-term artistic careers instead of overnight success stories.**
  Look closely at artists whose careers span decades and identify the habits, mindset, and resilience that supported their longevity. Use these examples as reassurance that steady progress is not failure, but a proven path.
- **Document your creative evolution over time.**
  Keep notes, journals, or recordings that capture how your ideas, skills, and perspectives change from project to project. Revisiting earlier phases of your work helps you recognize growth that may be invisible in the moment.
- **Release projects as chapters, not final statements.**
  Approach each album, EP, or release as part of a larger narrative rather than a definitive peak. This mindset reduces pressure and allows experimentation without fear that one project must define your entire identity.
- **Anchor your motivation in curiosity rather than validation.**
  Regularly ask yourself what genuinely excites you to explore next—sonically, emotionally, or conceptually. Curiosity keeps the journey alive and ensures that your creative path remains deeply personal and sustainable.

Embracing the Journey: Fostering Creative Spirit in Music Production

Embarking on a journey in music production is about embracing each step, regardless of where you stand. It's about committing to your craft, not merely as a means to an end but as a pathway to personal fulfillment and artistic expression. My own journey through the world of music, with numerous projects and collaborative efforts, stands as a testament to what perseverance and dedication can achieve. This is not just about hitting milestones but about the enrichment that comes from continuously evolving and engaging deeply with your work.

Committing to Your Craft

Committing to music production involves more than just making music; it's about giving people something they value—something that enhances their lives. For me, this commitment has meant delivering compositions that not only resonate on a personal level but also connect universally. The dedication to refining each track, to ensuring that every piece I release meets a standard of emotional and technical quality, is what defines my artistry.

Staying Inspired with Others

Engaging with other artists in music production is more than just a shared creative journey—it's a profound learning experience and an invaluable networking opportunity. Each collaboration introduces you to new methods and ideas that can transform your musical approach, while also expanding your professional network. This can open doors to new audiences and experiences, enriching your musical career. Embrace the diversity of perspectives that collaborators bring; their insights can spark innovative ideas and inspire your own creative process.

Learning from Every Step

Every challenge and setback is an opportunity for growth. Throughout my career, I've viewed each obstacle as a stepping stone, essential for learning and improvement. This perspective is crucial not only in navigating the music industry but in all creative endeavors. Embrace every hurdle as a chance to enhance your skills and refine your approach to music production.

Sharing Your Journey

This book is an embodiment of my experiences, distilled into insights and strategies designed to support your growth as an artist. By sharing my journey, I hope to inspire you to pursue your own path in music production with enthusiasm and determination. Whether you're just starting out or looking to deepen your existing practice, remember that your unique voice and perspective are your greatest assets.

Music production is a celebration of creativity, a way to convey profound emotional narratives through sound. It's a gift to be shared, a means to connect with others across the globe. Embrace your musical journey with passion, and let your artistry shine, making a lasting impact on those who encounter your work.

Embrace each step of your musical journey, for each note played contributes to the symphony of your artistic life.

Action Items

- **Commit to your craft as a long-term practice, not a short-term goal.** Treat music production as a lifelong relationship rather than a project with a finish line. Show up regularly, even when motivation is low, and allow consistency to shape your skills, confidence, and creative identity over time.
- **Define the value you want your music to give to others.** Reflect on how you want your work to affect listeners emotionally, mentally, or atmospherically. Creating with intention—whether to calm, inspire, or connect—gives your process deeper meaning and direction beyond personal satisfaction.
- **Actively seek inspiration through connection with other artists.** Surround yourself with creatives who challenge and inspire you, whether through collaboration, conversation, or simply listening to their work. Shared perspectives often unlock ideas you would never reach alone.
- **Reframe challenges and setbacks as essential learning stages.** When something doesn't work—creatively, technically, or professionally—pause and extract the lesson instead of judging the outcome. Growth often hides inside moments that initially feel like failure.
- **Document your journey instead of only showcasing results.** Keep notes, sketches, unfinished ideas, or reflections that capture your evolution as an artist. Looking back on these traces helps you recognize progress that might otherwise go unnoticed.

- **Share your journey with honesty and generosity.**
  Whether through music, writing, or conversation, allow others to see the human process behind your work. Authentic sharing builds deeper connections and reminds you that your story is as valuable as your output.

Embracing Uniqueness: Daring to Differentiate in Music Production

In the vibrant world of music production, distinguishing oneself from the crowd is not just beneficial—it's essential. Each artist must constantly explore: *What makes me unique? What can I offer that sets me apart?* This quest for distinctiveness is crucial in defining your musical identity and ensuring your work resonates in a world saturated with sound.

The Challenge of Standing Out

With streaming platforms, release culture can feel far more open, and almost anyone with a computer can imagine reaching a global audience. While that creates real opportunities, it can also feel as if the sheer volume of new tracks is overwhelming. In that environment, standing out seems to require more than technical skill or polished production. To me, it also demands authenticity, creativity, and the courage to explore paths that others might avoid.

Beyond the Digital: The Value of Physical Formats

In today's digital-first environment, physical releases can feel rarer, which to me can make them powerful tools for differentiation. Whether it is CDs, DVDs, Blu-rays, vinyl, or even retro formats like cassettes, tangible products can create a sense of exclusivity and permanence. To me, they especially speak to listeners who value the tactile ritual of owning and interacting with music.

Throughout my career, embracing physical releases has not only broadened my reach but also attracted media attention. A CD, Blu-ray, or vinyl isn't just a medium—it becomes a piece of art, a collectible, and a statement that the music deserves to exist beyond the endless stream of digital playlists.

Pioneering New Formats: Dolby Atmos as a Gateway

Experimenting with cutting-edge technologies is another way to set yourself apart. For me, diving into **Dolby Atmos productions** has been transformative. Despite the higher production costs and steeper learning curve, Atmos has opened new dimensions in musical storytelling. It expanded my market presence and led to unexpected opportunities, including collaborations with Dolby Germany and invitations to present my work at the Genelec Experience Center in Berlin. These experiences not only strengthened my artistic profile but also positioned me as an innovator in my field.

This example highlights how taking risks in format and technology can propel an artist forward—not just musically, but also in terms of visibility and credibility.

Learning from Innovators

Many successful artists, to my eyes, build their careers by creating experiences that go beyond traditional listening:

- **Schiller**, for example, makes me think of immersive live shows where electronic music meets visual spectacle. Elaborate stage design, multimedia collaboration, and guest performances can turn the event into something strongly multisensory.
- **SINE**, to me, also integrates visual art with his music. One example that stands out is a photo book paired with a CD, where landscape photography becomes part of the release experience. To me, that kind of fusion can turn a standard release into something more collectible and emotionally resonant.

These examples suggest to me that uniqueness does not always come from reinventing the sound. It can also come from how you present and contextualize your music.

Building a Holistic Artistic Identity

Creating music today is not just about composing tracks; it's about building a brand and a story around them. Every choice—visuals, packaging, collaborations, performance style, even how you communicate online—contributes to your artistic identity. By daring to take unconventional paths, you can elevate your work into something memorable and inspiring.

Uniqueness is often found in the small details: a carefully chosen album artwork, a live performance in an unusual location, or a release strategy that challenges expectations. Collectively, these decisions communicate to your audience that you are intentional, thoughtful, and dedicated to offering something special.

Final Thoughts

Music thrives on experimentation and individuality. By embracing uniqueness, you don't just stand out—you invite your audience to embark on a journey that only you can guide them through. Whether it's through physical formats, immersive technologies, or creative collaborations, the key is to remain authentic while daring to innovate.

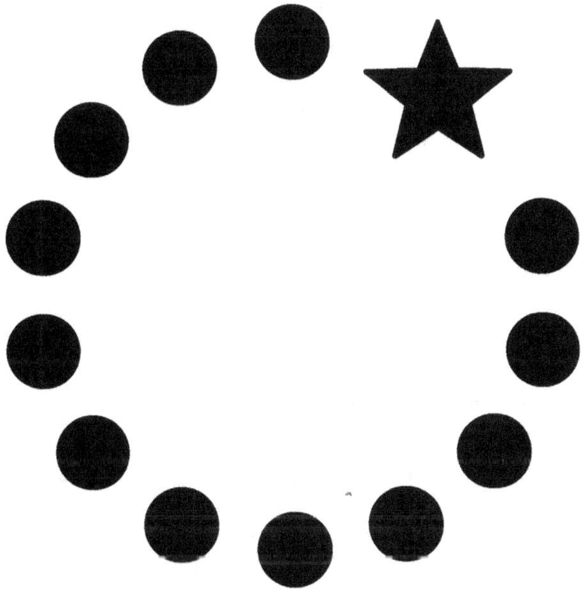

Dare to be different, for music thrives on the notes between conformity.

Action Items

- **Identify what genuinely makes your music different from others in your field.**
  Take time to reflect on your sound, your influences, your emotional focus, and your creative decisions. Uniqueness often lies in combinations—your background, your habits, your limitations—not in trying to invent something completely new.
- **Make intentional choices that reinforce your artistic identity.**
  Consider how your sound, artwork, formats, and presentation work together as a whole. Every decision—from instrumentation to packaging—should support the story you are telling as an artist.
- **Explore formats beyond standard digital releases when it serves your vision.**
  Physical formats, special editions, or immersive technologies like Dolby Atmos can deepen the listener's connection and differentiate your work, but only when they align authentically with your music and audience.
- **Be willing to take calculated creative risks.**
  Innovation always involves uncertainty. Whether experimenting with new formats, unconventional collaborations, or atypical release strategies, allow yourself to step outside safe expectations while staying grounded in your artistic values.

- **Study artists who create complete experiences, not just songs.** Observe how musicians integrate visuals, live performance concepts, storytelling, and cross-disciplinary elements. Use these observations not to copy, but to inspire new ways of framing your own work.
- **Trust that differentiation is a long-term strategy, not an instant reward.** Standing out may not always lead to immediate results, but over time, it builds recognition, credibility, and a deeper bond with your audience. Consistency and authenticity will amplify your uniqueness far more than trend-following ever could.

The Importance of Revisions and Iterations: Balancing Perfection and Completion

Creativity, like any craft, involves a continuous process of refining and reworking. The art of revision is where the essence of music is shaped and perfected. For me, the act of revisiting tracks opens up new layers of emotional depth and technical polish, but it can also be a double-edged sword.

The Subjectivity of Perfection

Perfection in art is subjective. As artists, we naturally strive to present our best work, but what defines "perfection" is fluid, shaped by personal tastes and interpretations. While one person may find a track incomplete, for the artist, it may represent the exact emotion or sound they set out to create. The fine line between true self-satisfaction and catering to external expectations can often cloud our judgment.

Lessons from Perfectionism

I tend to be a perfectionist. Early in my career, this habit sometimes kept me in endless cycles of tweaking and adjusting, driven by a need for external validation. I'd wonder: *Will listeners resonate with this? Will this track stand out?* Over time, I learned the power of trusting my instincts. Ultimately, as the creator, it is my perspective that matters most. After all, asking ten people for feedback will give you ten different answers, which may only serve to confuse your vision further.

Knowing When a Track Is Complete

Through years of producing, I've come to develop a technique that works for me. I listen to a track repeatedly until there's nothing left that I want to change. That's when I know it's complete. It's a personal checkpoint. It's a moment when I feel the music is true to my original vision, resonating with the emotion or story I want to convey. This doesn't mean it's flawless by every listener's standard, but it means I have imbued it with everything I can.

The Danger of Over-Polishing

However, there's a danger in over-polishing. The pursuit of perfection can sometimes lead to losing the raw, human qualities that make a track unique. When you try too hard to smooth every edge or align every beat, you risk polishing the soul out of the music. Music should reflect life's imperfections, its rough edges, and its unpredictability. It's these imperfections that breathe life into a track, making it relatable and emotionally resonant.

Consider the charm of a rough acoustic guitar or a slightly offbeat rhythm. These small quirks give music character, much like the unique flaws we cherish in the people we love. A song without soul, no matter how technically polished, can feel sterile and disconnected. To avoid falling into this trap, I remind myself to embrace the beauty of imperfection.

Learning to Let Go

The process of revising and iterating is not just about polishing the final product, but about learning when to let go. It's about recognizing when a piece of music has reached a state of emotional truth, rather than waiting for some unattainable standard of "perfection." In the end, music is a reflection of who we are—flawed, evolving, but always authentic. And sometimes, those imperfections make the music unforgettable.

Perfection is found in the process, not just the outcome. Revise, refine, and realize the art within the iterations.

Final Thoughts

Finding that balance between perfection and completion is a personal journey every artist must undertake. My advice is simple: trust your instincts, know when your track feels right to you, and be willing to let go of the need for external approval. The world will embrace your work, flaws and all, as long as it reflects your genuine self.

Action Items

- **Define what "perfect" means for *this* track before you touch a single knob.**
  Write down a short target description in plain language: *What emotion should it carry? What reference world does it live in? What is "done" supposed to feel like?* This prevents you from chasing random improvements and gives every revision a purpose.
- **Separate "taste notes" from "problem notes" while you revise.**
  When you listen back, capture two lists: (1) *objective issues* (timing, masking, harshness, imbalance, muddy low end), and (2) *personal preferences* (brighter vocal, drier reverb, more energy). Fix the true problems first—then decide which taste notes actually support the song's message.
- **Use distance as a tool, not a luxury.**
  If you feel stuck or obsessive, stop and create a reset: step away overnight, take a full day, or even a week if the schedule allows. Then return with fresh ears and do one "first-impression" playback where you only write notes—no editing—so you don't revise from fatigue.
- **Protect the soul by limiting your "final pass" to a defined scope.**
  Choose a revision boundary such as: *only balance + dynamics*, or *only transitions + arrangement*, or *only vocal tone + space*. Over-polishing usually happens when you keep expanding the scope. A narrow focus preserves the character that made the track special in the first place.
- **Create a clear completion checkpoint and treat it like a professional sign-off.**
  Decide what "complete" means in measurable terms: for example, *three consecutive listens with no urgent change notes*, *translation check passed on headphones + speakers + car*, and *one trusted listener confirms the emotional impact matches your intention*. When those conditions are met, you commit to stop.
- **End revisions by choosing forward momentum over infinite improvement.**
  Once the track expresses the emotion you intended, release it mentally—even if tiny imperfections remain. Remind yourself: the goal is not a flawless artifact, but an honest one. Finishing frees creative energy for the next work, and that continuity is what builds a career.

The Art of Letting Go: Knowing When a Track Is Finished

Knowing when a song is finished is one of the most delicate balances in music production. Sometimes, you feel it instantly—there's a sense of completeness, and you're eager to share it. Other times, self-doubt creeps in, and you get stuck in a loop of refining every detail, afraid to call it done.

Creating Distance to Gain Clarity

When you start feeling like you're going in circles, distance is your ally. Stepping back from a track, even for just a night, can work wonders. Sometimes, it helps to take several days—or even weeks—away from it. The next time you return, you'll have fresh ears, a clearer mind, and a more objective view of your work.

While on that break, jot down brief notes whenever ideas or impressions come to mind. Capture your gut reactions without overthinking—these quick observations can guide your final tweaks. Upon returning, listen in two ways: actively, with focused attention, and passively, while doing something unrelated. This combination reveals both technical details and emotional impact. Play it in different environments—studio monitors, headphones, car speakers—to hear how it lives in the real world.

Using Feedback and Deadlines

Some artists benefit from sharing their work with a trusted collaborator, mentor, or even a small group of listeners. Honest outside feedback can confirm your instincts or highlight areas you've overlooked. For instance, I've sent nearly finished tracks to a fellow producer who, with one sentence, reassured me the song was ready—saving me from weeks of unnecessary tweaks.

For others, deadlines—whether self-imposed or set by a label—are the catalyst that forces completion. Without them, perfectionism can spiral into endless revisions. Even a simple commitment, like premiering the track on a livestream or submitting it to a playlist by a certain date, can create a healthy sense of urgency.

The Danger of Over-Polishing

Over-refining can strip a track of its emotional core. Sometimes, the imperfections are what give it personality and authenticity. I've had moments where tracks that felt raw but honest connected far more deeply with listeners than those I labored over endlessly. Music is about connection, not sterile perfection.

Trusting Your Intuition

Ultimately, knowing when to stop is an act of self-trust. Ask yourself: does this track capture the emotion, story, and energy I set out to create? Would more changes elevate its essence or just alter it? If the answer leans toward the latter, it might be time to release it.

Letting Go to Move Forward

Finishing a track isn't just about completion—it's about making space for the next creative chapter. Holding on too long can stifle your momentum. Letting go allows you to apply lessons learned to new projects, connect more quickly with your audience, and evolve as an artist.

In the art of music, knowing when to let go is as important as knowing how to begin. Trust that pause.

Action Items

- **Define your personal definition of "done" before you start revising.** Decide what completion means for you emotionally and artistically before entering the revision phase. This gives you a clear internal reference point and prevents endless tweaking driven by doubt rather than intention.
- **Limit revision cycles to protect the emotional core of the track.** Set a conscious boundary for how many focused revision passes you allow yourself. Beyond that point, changes often become cosmetic rather than meaningful and can slowly erase the character that made the track special.

- **Create distance before making final decisions.**
  Step away from the track for a defined period—overnight, several days, or even longer. Returning with fresh ears helps you hear the music as a listener rather than as its creator, revealing what truly needs adjustment and what does not.
- **Use feedback selectively and intentionally.**
  Choose one or two trusted listeners whose taste and experience you respect. Ask specific questions instead of seeking general approval, and remember that feedback should inform your instincts, not override them.
- **Learn to recognize when refinement becomes avoidance.**
  Ask yourself honestly whether further changes improve the emotional message or simply delay the moment of release. Perfectionism often disguises fear, not quality control.
- **Practice letting go to maintain creative momentum.**
  Finishing and releasing work creates space for growth. Each completed track teaches you more than one endlessly revised piece ever could, allowing your artistic evolution to continue moving forward.

Creating Moments: The Profound Impact of Music and Art in People's Lives

As artists, we do not just create sounds or visuals. I believe we also craft experiences that others may invite into their lives. Music and art can accompany people in countless ways. They can serve as a quiet soundtrack to daily routines, a powerful emotional anchor during moments of joy or grief, or even a symbol of personal identity. A single piece of music can evoke vivid memories of significant life events and reconnect people with moments they may have thought were long forgotten. For some, a song from decades past can still feel alive, weaving itself into the present. That possibility is part of what makes music and art feel profoundly influential to me.

The Responsibility of Creation

This influence underscores the responsibility we bear as creators. It's not merely about producing work; it's about enriching lives and making moments memorable. What we release into the world can leave lasting impressions, shaping how people feel, remember, and even dream. Over the years, I've received heartfelt letters and messages from listeners. They've shared how my music carried them through difficult times, celebrated their happiest occasions, or became the soundtrack to their personal journeys. These stories are humbling reminders of the privilege that comes with creating art. Every chord, texture, or melody carries the potential to become part of someone's emotional landscape.

Examples of Music's Lasting Influence

The history of music is filled, to me, with examples of this enduring impact. When I think of John Lennon's "Imagine," I do not hear only a song. To my ears, it carries a reflective, open emotional space that many people, myself included, may read in very personal ways. When I turn to M83's "Midnight City," I hear something different but equally lasting: a sound world of nostalgia, distance, and longing that still feels vivid to me whenever I return to it. In both cases, what stays with me is not a fixed public meaning, but the sense that certain songs continue to live emotionally in the listener long after their first moment has passed.

Other examples come to mind. When I think of "Bohemian Rhapsody," "Blowin' in the Wind," "In the Air Tonight," or "Someone Like You," I do not hear them as interchangeable songs. To my ears, each one holds a distinct emotional character and a different kind of artistic presence. One feels theatrical and expansive, another reflective and searching, another dark and suspended in mood, and another intimate in the way it expresses heartbreak. What connects them for me is the sense that certain recordings remain emotionally available across changing times, generations, and listening situations.

Music often feels larger to me than entertainment alone. From my perspective, some songs become woven into the private way listeners may remember periods of their lives, recognize parts of themselves, and feel more deeply connected to the world around them.

Personal Lessons Learned

At the start of my career, I saw my music primarily as personal expression. I didn't fully grasp how deeply it could affect others. Over time, through messages and stories from listeners, I came to understand that my work often became much more: a form of companionship, solace, or inspiration. Knowing that my music might resonate so profoundly with someone has changed the way I approach creation. It compels me to strive for excellence—not out of perfectionism, but out of respect for the role art plays in people's lives. With every project, I remind myself that my work could become a permanent part of someone's memories—a song tied to love, growth, or transformation.

Balancing Responsibility and Joy

It's essential, however, to balance this responsibility with joy. Taking our role seriously doesn't mean burdening ourselves with pressure or overthinking every note. The best art often comes from moments of playfulness, spontaneity, and lightness. Recognizing the potential of our work to inspire should elevate the process, not weigh it down. By combining purpose with freedom, we can create with both heart and authenticity. This ensures the results are meaningful and filled with life and energy. In this way, the act of creation itself becomes as fulfilling as the impact it generates.

Each piece of music we create has the power to become a significant moment in someone's life; let's craft these moments with intention and heart.

Final Thoughts

Through our music and art, we hold the privilege of touching hearts and shaping memories. A listener once described my work to me as feeling deeply personal and emotionally direct, even without words. Moments like that remind me how privately and powerfully art can travel from one inner world to another. With intention and care, we can craft works that resonate far beyond ourselves, becoming part of the larger human story.

Action Items

- **Acknowledge the emotional responsibility behind every release.** Before finalizing a piece of music or art, take a moment to consider how it might be received in someone else's life. Your work may become a companion in moments of joy, loss, healing, or transformation—treat that potential with care and respect.
- **Create with intention, not just expression.** While personal expression is vital, ask yourself what emotional space your work inhabits. Is it meant to comfort, energize, inspire reflection, or

provide escape? Clarity of intention strengthens the emotional resonance of your art.

- **Listen to audience feedback as insight, not validation.**
  When listeners share how your work affected them, view these stories as windows into the real-world life of your music. Let them deepen your understanding of impact—without allowing them to dictate or dilute your artistic voice.
- **Strive for emotional honesty over technical perfection.**
  Technical excellence matters, but emotional truth is what embeds music into memory. Prioritize authenticity, atmosphere, and feeling over flawlessness, trusting that genuine emotion connects more deeply than polished precision.
- **Balance responsibility with creative freedom.**
  Recognize the influence of your work without allowing it to become a creative burden. Maintain playfulness, curiosity, and joy in the process—these qualities often produce the most alive and meaningful results.
- **Remember that your work becomes part of a larger human story.**
  Every release joins an ongoing cultural and emotional continuum. Create with humility and gratitude, knowing that even a quiet piece can leave a lasting imprint on someone's life.

Notes

1 U.S. Copyright Office, *How Songwriters, Composers, and Performers Get Paid*, Music Modernization Act educational materials, accessed March 8, 2026; U.S. Copyright Office, *Copyright and the Music Marketplace* (Washington, DC: U.S. Copyright Office, 2015).

2 International Federation of the Phonographic Industry (IFPI), "ISRC," accessed March 8, 2026; International Confederation of Societies of Authors and Composers (CISAC), "International Identifiers," accessed March 8, 2026; International Confederation of Societies of Authors and Composers (CISAC), "IPI," accessed March 8, 2026.

3 GEMA, "What is an ISWC and why works do not have one," accessed March 8, 2026; International Federation of the Phonographic Industry (IFPI), "ISRC," accessed March 8, 2026.

Epilogue

From Silence to Sound: Make Something Beautiful

As you close this book, I hope you don't feel like something has ended—but rather that something has begun.

You've walked through the thoughts, emotions, tools, challenges, and rituals that make up the path of a music creator. You've explored the inner landscapes where creativity is born—the doubts, the sparks, the routines, and the breakthroughs. You've seen that music production isn't just about hitting the right frequencies. It's about tuning into yourself. Listening. Feeling. Trusting.

I wrote this book not to tell you how to produce music, but to remind you why you do it. To help you reconnect with what matters most: your voice, your emotion, your curiosity, your humanity. In creative work, making has become more immediate, but it can also be easy to lose sight of the human being behind the sound.

That's why I believe creativity isn't something you master once. It's something you return to, again and again. From silence to sound—and back to silence. Each time, with more awareness. More authenticity. More heart.

So wherever you are in your journey—whether you're just starting out or decades in—I hope this book has helped you feel less alone and more inspired. I hope it has encouraged you to experiment boldly, rest when needed, and keep showing up for your art.

I also hope it gave you permission to work differently. To slow down. To challenge how things "should be done." To protect your energy. To value your story, your sound, and your process above the noise of trends and metrics.

Because what truly matters isn't the perfect mix. It's the emotion that moves someone. The story that lingers. The silence you dared to fill with something beautiful.

And most of all, I hope it reminded you that the person creating the music matters more than any tool.

Now, go make something beautiful.

— Thomas Lemmer

Your music is your story. No one else can tell it the way you can.

DOI: 10.4324/9781003710622-7

Index

Pages in *italics* refer to figures and pages in **bold** refer to tables.

For Product Safety Concerns and Information please contact our EU representative GPSR@taylorandfrancis.com
Taylor & Francis Verlag GmbH, Kaufingerstraße 24, 80331 München, Germany

www.ingramcontent.com/pod-product-compliance
Lightning Source LLC
LaVergne TN
LVHW020805080826
845179LV00035B/295
9781041192060